Developing
Learner-Centered Teaching

Developing Learner-Centered Teaching

A Practical Guide for Faculty

Phyllis Blumberg
Foreword by Maryellen Weimer

JOSSEY-BASS
A Wiley Imprint
www.josseybass.com

Published by Jossey-Bass

A Wiley Imprint

989 Market Street, San Francisco, CA 94103-1741—www.josseybass.com

Jossey-Bass books and products are available through most bookstores. To contact Jossey-Bass directly call our Customer Care Department within the U.S. at 800-956-7739, outside the U.S. at 317-572-3986, or fax 317-572-4002.

Jossey-Bass also publishes its books in a variety of electronic formats. Some content that appears in print may not be available in electronic books.

Library of Congress Cataloging-in-Publication Data

Blumberg, Phyllis, 1951-
  Developing learner-centered teaching : a practical guide for faculty /
Phyllis Blumberg, foreword by Maryellen Weimer.—1st ed.
      p. cm.
  Includes bibliographical references and index.
  ISBN 978-0-7879-9688-8 (pbk.)
  1. College teaching. 2. Student-centered learning. I. Title.
  LB2331.B55 2008
  378.1'25—dc22   2008027546

Printed in the United States of America

PB Printing

10   9   8   7   6   5   4   3   2   FIRST EDITION

The Jossey-Bass
Higher and Adult Education Series

Contents

Tables, Exhibits, Figures, and Boxes

Tables

Exhibits

Figures

Boxes

Dedicated in loving memory of my parents,
Morton and Dora Blumberg, who encouraged me
to learn and who were my first teachers

Foreword

AUTHOR PHYLLIS BLUMBERG is right. Faculty are increasingly open to the ideas of learner-centered teaching. Today's college students, particularly those in the eighteen-to-twenty-three-year-old cohort, are not easy to teach. They are best reached when teachers use a broad repertoire of instructional strategies, especially those that engage and involve them in learning tasks. However, many faculty do not know how to go about designing or implementing strategies that make students more responsible for learning. *Developing Learner-Centered Teaching: A Practical Guide for Faculty* addresses those needs. The kind of specifics and details offered herein do much to ensure that when faculty implement strategies focused on student learning, those strategies work successfully.

I couldn't agree more that faculty new to learner-centered approaches need to implement changes incrementally. I always worry when faculty have instructional conversion experiences. They read a book or attend a workshop and suddenly see the light. They head out to class the next day as changed instructors. Given the reality of teaching loads plus other academic responsibilities such as research and service, it is very difficult to implement and sustain extensive amounts of instructional change, regardless of how appropriate those changes are or how much they may be needed. Besides the difficulty of sustaining the change, the effects of trying something new and having it fail are not positive. After faculty have too many of those experiences, their motivation to change decreases significantly. So the gradual approach to change advocated in this book makes good sense.

Beyond advocating for a reasonable approach to change, this book identifies what those incremental steps might be and how they could be ordered. It does so for a wide range of learner-centered strategies using a comprehensive set of rubrics that make the process of implementing these approaches thoughtful and systematic.

I enthusiastically concur that examples are the best way to show what this way of engaging students looks like in the classroom. And this book is full of examples, including a case study that is carried through the book and multiple other illustrations drawn from the literature and Blumberg's extensive experience working with faculty who are interested in making their teaching more learner-centered. Moreover, these examples are ones busy teachers can apply without extraordinary effort. And the examples are applicable across a wide range of disciplines.

I couldn't agree more that all courses can have learner-centered components, but being completely learner-centered is not realistic for all courses. It is both sad and unnecessary when faculty dichotomously position learner-centered teaching and lecturing, assuming the use of one rules out inclusion of the other. There are times when students learn best through the teacher's telling. There are times when such telling rolls off students like water off a duck's back. Teachers need to be able to look at the content and the students in light of their learning goals and make sanguine decisions about methods. This book helps inform that decision-making process.

I couldn't agree more that learner-centered approaches are not about watering down course content and otherwise compromising academic standards. However, faculty with questions about the viability of these approaches are not likely to be persuaded by assertions. This book answers these objections by demonstrating how and why learner-centered approaches maintain content integrity while at the same time they help students achieve a deeper mastery of the material.

This book is not escapist reading with a few instructional nuggets to be gleaned here and there. It's not a book to be digested during that fifteen-minute lunch break. It's not a book that renews teacher dedication to a noble vocation. The book does highlight relevant theory, but it is not a theoretical tome. This book is a workbook—a self-help book in the best sense of the word. As Blumberg notes, "the more actively you engage with the book, the easier it will be for you to transform your teaching to more learner-centered approaches." Said even more directly, it is a book that will give back in full measure what is put into it. If used as it is designed, it will encourage faculty to look deeply and honestly at the instructional strategies they use. It will challenge them to consider other strategies—ones that might better accomplish their goals for learners. It will guide them through the process of designing and implementing new approaches to teaching. And it will help them determine how successful those endeavors were.

Regularly now in the presentations I give about my book, *Learner-Centered Teaching*, I note how much I wish my book offered more on implementation issues. Now there is a whole book to which faculty can be referred—a well-documented book that handles the implementation of learner-center approaches to teaching with integrity, robustness, and careful attention to detail. Thanks to Phyllis Blumberg for this much-needed contribution to the literature on teaching that promotes learning.

MARYELLEN WEIMER
Professor Emeritus, Penn State University

Preface

LEARNER-CENTERED TEACHING shifts the role of the instructors from givers of information to facilitators of student learning. There is still some confusion about how to achieve learner-centered teaching. For many educators, moving toward learner-centered teaching requires significant adjustments and takes a while. To make that shift successfully, instructors need further explanations about what learner-centered teaching is and how they can apply it in all kinds of college and university courses.

At my institution, I persistently tried to assist instructors to make their teaching more learner-centered (Blumberg, 2004). The more I tried to get instructors to make changes in their teaching, the clearer it became that some of them did not know how to make these changes. Therefore, I decided that I needed to develop a better way to help instructors transition to learner-centered teaching. This book is the product of my largely fruitful efforts.

Rationale for This Book

Many of us need further explanation about how to change our teaching to be more learner-centered. As instructors, we are still unsure about how to achieve learner-centered teaching. Some instructors believe that they can implement such practices only in small classes or advanced courses. Others feel that using learner-centered approaches would negatively affect the content and rigor of their courses because the time students spend on active learning activities would force a reduction in the amount or level of content covered (Blumberg & Everett, 2005). This book addresses these issues and concerns.

Another impediment is the fact that learner-centered approaches may appear difficult to achieve. Even those of us who see the need to make this change are unsure about how to proceed. Often our teaching is so unlike what the literature describes as "learner-centered" that we are overwhelmed by the apparent enormity of the task. To teach using learner-centered practices requires the development of new skills and attitudes (Sorcinelli, Austin, Eddy, & Beach, 2006). To show you how to teach using learner-centered approaches, this book advocates for making small, incremental changes that you can implement both immediately and over time. Although achieving a learner-centered course is the desired goal, it may not be practical to be completely learner-centered in all courses.

Scope of This Book

This book is a practical, self-instructional guide to transforming teaching incrementally. It includes explanations, guidelines, examples, self-assessments, and planning tools that will help you transform your courses by making incremental changes in different dimensions. The book discusses a continuum from instructor-centered to learner-centered approaches to teaching. It defines components of and discusses implementation examples of learner-centered teaching on five dimensions:

- The function of content
- The role of the instructor
- The responsibility for learning
- The purposes and processes of assessment
- The balance of power

Much of this book is devoted to specific activities you can do to transform your teaching. This book shows that there are many different approaches to transforming teaching to a learner-centered approach. To give you a better idea of what a learner-centered course might look like and how to transform a course, this book uses case studies. You'll learn ways to determine the learner-centered status of your courses. You can use this learner-centered status determination as an assessment tool for educational programs and as a way to plan for transformation. This book also discusses how to overcome challenges to becoming a learner-centered instructor.

Purposes of This Book

Instructors and administrators can use the tools contained in this book as a vehicle to transform courses to be more learner-centered, or as a way to assess the learner-centered status of educational programs or of your own teaching, program assessment, or to document how individuals teach.

Transform Courses to Be More Learner-Centered

Within the last decade many individuals—for example, Doherty, Riordan, and Roth (2002), the authors of the *National Report on Greater Expectations: A New Vision for Learning as a Nation Goes to College* (Association of American Colleges and Universities, 2002), Weimer (2002), and Tagg (2003)—have discussed learner-centered teaching. Although this recent literature defined and described learner-centered teaching, it often is less pragmatic in describing ways to implement the changes that instructors need to make to achieve that goal (Wright, 2006). The primary purpose of this book is to address this shortcoming.

This book defines a practical system for implementing incremental changes to make courses more learner-centered. Using this systematic guide, you will use self-assessment tools to identify the learner-centered status of courses. These tools include a set of rubrics that identify incremental steps to transform a course from instructor-centered to learner-centered in five separate dimensions as well as a Planning for Transformation exercise. A rubric is a written summary of the criteria and different levels or standards for each criterion to evaluate someone or something (Walvoord, 2004). The Planning for Transformation exercise will help you plan how to transform your current approach to a more learner-centered approach while maintaining or increasing the standards of your course. You will have opportunities to apply what you learn by assessing a course of your own and identifying ways in which you can make it more learner-centered. After using the self-instructional guides provided in this book, you should have the necessary skills and new attitudes to use learner-centered teaching effectively. The outcome of these changes should be increased student learning.

For many of us, incorporating a few techniques is an important step within an incremental change process. However, we may be at a loss as to learner-centered techniques. Throughout the book, you will find examples of such techniques. Many are easy to adopt and do not require major changes in the way we teach.

Assess the Learner-Centered Status of Educational Programs or of Your Teaching

Many institutions of higher learning and educational programs claim that they are learner-centered. Because accountability is an important goal in higher education, we need ways to show that we are doing what we say we are doing. This book gives an easy-to-use method for determining the learner-centered status of our institutions or our educational programs. This method includes the set of rubrics that help you identify the status, from instructor-centered to learner-centered, in five separate dimensions and a Documentation to Support the Selected Status form to document your rationale or cite examples to support why you chose the rating you did. The rubrics describe instructor behaviors for each of the five dimensions of learner-centered teaching. You can use the rubrics to show a snapshot of your current implementation of learner-centered teaching. Alternatively, you might use these rubrics in a pre- and post-transformation of changes within an educational program. Individual instructors can use the rubrics to document how their teaching has evolved as they incorporate more learner-centered practices.

Audience

The primary audience for this book is instructors of all disciplines in community colleges, four-year colleges, and universities who are considering transforming their instruction to be learner-centered. This book gives practical help that applies to all disciplines and courses. New instructors who are just deciding how to teach and mid-career instructors who are ready to change their teaching approaches may find this book especially helpful.

The book is particularly useful for instructors of general education courses who are continually challenged to present content in an environment that motivates students to learn, are expected to develop students' abilities to take responsibility for their own learning, and need to facilitate students' abilities to apply their acquired knowledge and skills in other courses. In addition, the book offers suggestions for transforming advanced undergraduate and graduate or professional courses. Further, it's clear that many science and health professions instructors are reluctant to adopt learner-centered approaches because of the required rigor of their courses; this book addresses this concern by describing many examples that come from the sciences in general and the clinical sciences in particular.

Another primary audience is administrators and instructors who are doing assessments of their educational programs or of their own teaching. This book describes an easy-to-use tool that administrators and instructors can use in assessments of educational programs. This tool shows the status of courses or educational programs on the continuum from instructor-centered to learner-centered.

A secondary audience is faculty developers and instructional designers who help instructors at their institutions transform their teaching. These faculty-support people can use the rubrics in one-on-one consultations with instructors or in faculty development workshops to determine instructors' level of comfort with learner-centered teaching practices and their understanding of these practices. The rubrics can serve as stimuli for discussions about how to implement learner-centered approaches in workshops. The application activities given throughout this book work well in such workshops. Ongoing faculty development programs, such as weeklong workshops or a summer institute, can use this book as a basis to transform courses. Faculty learning communities may focus on different dimensions as they work together to change their courses.

Still another audience is graduate students either in higher education courses or in Preparing Future Faculty (PFF) programs. These students can use the techniques and information in this book to design learner-centered courses.

Overview of the Book

You will find that this book is easier to read than it appears at first glance. This is intended to be a workbook or guide as well as resource throughout your transformation process. It follows a consistent pattern. I support the concepts with tables, exhibits, and case studies or examples. I explain all the tables, and I use the same format for all of the rubrics. Exhibits contain worksheets or forms; boxes describe implementation examples or case studies.

Part One: Transforming Teaching to Be More Learner-Centered

Chapter One explains the rationale for why instructors should adopt learner-centered approaches, gives a case example of a learner-centered course, and describes a continuum from instructor-centered to learner-centered on five dimensions. In Chapter Two you will learn how to read and understand the rubrics. Chapter Three shows the ways the rubrics can help you make incremental transitions on the learner-centered continuum.

You will learn how to begin to transform your course toward being more learner-centered. You will also see how to assess educational programs on their status, from instructor-centered to learner-centered.

Part Two: The Five Dimensions of Learner-Centered Teaching

Chapters Four through Eight correspond respectively to the five dimensions of learner-centered teaching: the Function of Content, the Role of the Instructor, the Responsibility for Learning, the Purposes and Processes of Assessment, and the Balance of Power. Each chapter explains the components of the rubric for that dimension and describes implementation examples to foster your understanding of learner-centered teaching. To illustrate the process, this part uses a case example showing how the instructor of a general education course assessed and began to transform the course from instructor-centered to learner-centered. Each chapter ends with an application activity to use with your own course, to help you rate the status of your course on the rubrics. These activities assist your identification of which components you want to transform and how you will transform them.

The implementation examples, set off in boxes, describe specific learner-centered practices. Many of these techniques achieve more than one component of learner-centered teaching either within the same dimension or in other dimensions. These examples, coming from a variety of disciplines and types of courses, should give you ideas for what you can do in your own courses. For example, many of these examples come from the sciences because instructors in these content-rich disciplines often have trouble trying to adopt learner-centered practices. Many other examples come from general education courses because many instructors believe that upper-level or advanced courses are better adapted to incorporate learner-centered practices.

Part Three: Discussion and Conclusion

This part of the book describes a systematic change process for becoming a more learner-centered instructor. It considers large aspects of the transformational process, such as considering what aspects of your course can be learner-centered and how to overcome obstacles. Although we may strive to achieve a total learner-centered approach, it may not be realistic or obtainable in every course. Chapter Nine discusses factors to consider when determining whether a learner-centered approach is appropriate for a particular course. It shows how instructors of lower-level classes or classes with large enrollment can incorporate learner-centered approaches. Chapter Ten discusses strategies for overcoming resistance. It can be difficult to change the way you teach: various people, including yourself, your students, your peers, your chair, and the administrators at your institution may resist change when you begin this transition. Chapter Eleven summarizes the incremental approach, helping you begin to see where you can make changes to gradually transform your teaching to become learner-centered.

If you make changes in several components, a very different teaching-learning-assessment dynamic will emerge in your courses. Therefore, you need an assessment tool to document your progress. You can use these rubrics as this assessment tool to determine the learner-centered status of educational programs or of your own teaching.

The appendices add the following material:

A. Glossary of terms

B. The rubrics, the Planning for Transformation exercise, and the Documentation to Support the Selected Status form

C. Development of the rubrics

Getting the Most Out of This Book

This book will teach you how to determine the learner-centered status of courses and how you can transform courses to be more learner-centered in a systematic and incremental way. You should analyze the present status of one of your courses and think about ways of transforming it in the following order:

1. *Understand and accept the rationale for learner-centered teaching.* Chapter One discusses the rationale for learner-centered teaching by summarizing the supporting literature.

2. *Understand the dimensions and the components within these dimensions.* You will achieve this by reading the chapter explanations.

3. *Complete the application activity, which prepares you to complete the rubric.* The application activities will help you think about the status of your course and possibilities for change.

4. *Complete the rubrics for the course as it is now.*

5. *Decide which components of which dimensions you want to transform.* Your answers to the application activities and on the rubrics should assist you in your selections.

6. *Complete the Planning for Transformation exercise for those components you want to change.*

The more actively you engage with this book, the easier it will be for you to transform your teaching to more learner-centered approaches. Choose a specific course to use as you read the book and complete the steps just outlined. You can discuss the techniques you wish to incorporate with peers in your department. You may want to try out some techniques within the course as you are teaching it. How you engage with the material is a matter of personal style. I recommend that you write your responses to the questions and fill out the answers to the questions given in the application activities. You may also choose to discuss your thoughts with a trusted colleague.

The implementation examples or techniques should help you think about and discuss becoming more learner-centered. After reading about these techniques, you should decide if this technique could work with your courses. Ask yourself, "Can I implement this technique in my teaching?"

Once you understand how to use the rubrics and the planning for transformation exercise, described in Part One, you can read the rest of the book in order, or choose to focus on a specific dimension, or read about the different dimensions in any order you choose.

Acknowledgments

This book represents years of collaboration with many instructors as they tried to become more learner-centered. I want to acknowledge the support and assistance of the instructors and administration of the University of the Sciences in Philadelphia with whom I tested the ideas in this book. I am indebted to over 250 people who offered their ideas and constructive criticisms when they attended my workshops given at the University of the Sciences in Philadelphia and at various professional conferences, including POD, The Teaching Professor, Lilly-East, the Middle States Commission on Higher Education, and Educause. They helped me to define the components and the levels on the rubrics. Many people helped with specific wording and organization of the book. The most notable of these are David Brightman, my wise editor at Jossey-Bass, Janis Fisher Chan, the three external reviewers, Justin Everett, Anne Marie Flanagan, JoAnn Gonzalez-Major, Alison Mostrom, Deirdre Pettipiece, Glenn Rosenthal, and the production staff at Jossey-Bass, especially Cathy Mallon. Salar Alsardary, David Brightman, Janis Fisher Chan, Christine Flanagan, Barbara Cohen-Kligerman, Paula Kramer, Madhu Mahalingam, and Jeanette McVeigh reviewed drafts of chapters for clarity and offered insightful comments. I also want to acknowledge the more than three dozen instructors who willingly shared their examples of learner-centered teaching that I discuss throughout the book. Andrew Peterson, the instructors of the Occupational Therapy program at the University of the Sciences in Philadelphia— especially Paula Kramer, their chair—and Linda Robinson shared their courses to serve as the main case studies in the book.

My sister, Ella Singer, read the entire book for the tiny mistakes I would never see and offered new insights. I also want to thank her for her enthusiasm for this project. Mary Rafferty assisted on the clerical and administrative parts of the book. She contacted every instructor who provided examples and secured their permission.

Finally, I want to express my love and appreciation for my son Noah Kosherick for his patience during the many hours that he did not interrupt me as I worked on this book. I also want to thank my other sons Adam and Barry Kosherick for their love and support.

PHYLLIS BLUMBERG

June 2008

Bala Cynwyd, Pennsylvania

The Author

Phyllis Blumberg has been teaching using learner-centered approaches to first-year college through graduate and medical students for over twenty-five years. Although she has used many learner-centered approaches, in particular she often teaches using problem-based learning. She began and directed one of the early problem-based learning programs for medical students in the 1980s.

Blumberg has worked for thirty years as a faculty developer with instructors in the health sciences and the sciences in general. She has worked with faculty at five universities in United States and Canada on a one-to-one basis to help them change their teaching so their students will learn more. Blumberg is currently the director of the Teaching and Learning Center and professor of social sciences and education at the University of the Sciences in Philadelphia. More than 80 percent of the instructors at her university voluntarily participate in at least one faculty development event or consult with her individually every year. Blumberg is the author of more than fifty articles on active learning, learner-centered teaching, problem-based learning, and program evaluation. She is a frequent presenter at POD, The Teaching Professor, Lilly-East, and other conferences, and she has given workshops at numerous colleges and universities across North America.

Blumberg earned her doctorate in educational and developmental psychology from the University of Pittsburgh, Learning Research and Development Center.

Developing Learner-Centered Teaching

Part One

Transforming Teaching to Be More Learner-Centered

Chapter 1

Introduction

ARE YOU INTERESTED in improving the quality of your students' learning? Do you want your students to be able to better retain what they learned in your courses so that they will be able to apply their knowledge to new situations? Would you like your students to take more responsibility for their learning? Although you may have answered yes to all of these questions, you may not know how to achieve these learning outcomes. This book offers practical suggestions within a systematic framework to help you make changes in how you teach that will enhance your students' learning.

Instructors usually plan courses by deciding what content they will teach and how they will organize the content into lectures. The emphasis on what instructors do often leads to students' being passive learners. Further, instructors and employers complain that students or graduates cannot apply what they previously learned and are unable to learn on their own. For over a decade, literature geared toward college and university instructors (Barr & Tagg, 1995; DeZure, 2000; Fink, 2003; Gardiner, 1994) has called for reform that changes the focus from what *instructors* do to what the *students* are learning. Educators call the traditional method *instructor-centered teaching* and the newer format *learner-centered teaching*. Although this call for action began with isolated individuals, it has gained increasing support from many international and national professional organizations, such as Association of American Colleges and Universities, American Educational Research Association, the National Science Foundation, and the National Research Council.

Learner-centered teaching does not use a single teaching method; rather, it emphasizes a variety of different method types that shift the role of instructors from givers of information to facilitators of student learning or creators of an environment for learning. With all of the ways we have to disseminate information using technology, the instructor should not be the primary source of knowledge for students. In learner-centered teaching, the instructor focuses on what students are learning, how they are learning, and how they can use the learning (Weimer, 2002).

Why Instructor-Centered Approaches Are Not Very Effective

Research shows that many college students fail to engage with the material. Instead, students often memorize material for which they have no understanding—and thus they often do not remember material they studied earlier.

The National Science Foundation (NSF) sees many disadvantages to instructor-centered approaches. According to the NSF, there are unintended consequences of too much emphasis on teaching at the expense of learning, including graduates who are not prepared to solve real-world problems and lack the skills and motivation to continue to learn beyond their formal education. The unintended consequences related to beginning students in the sciences include more students with negative attitudes toward the sciences, technology, engineering, and mathematics (the STEM disciplines) and high attrition rates in these educational programs, especially in the early courses. Although the NSF work focuses on the STEM disciplines, these claims probably apply to other disciplines as well (Springer, Stanne, & Donovan, 1999).

Resistance to Learner-Centered Approaches

Instructors are resistant to changing their instructional methods. Many disciplines are content-rich, and there is a perception that content coverage is very important. Some instructors believe that they cover less material if they use learner-centered approaches. Other instructors also feel that they do not have control over what material they must cover in their courses because their courses or content are prerequisites for more advanced courses. Further pressures for professional program accreditation lead many instructors to believe that they need to continue to use traditional teaching methods.

The choice of terminology can encourage or hinder instructors' acceptance of a teaching approach. The higher-education literature uses several terms to describe the approach that focuses on the learner or student. The first of these, *learner-centered teaching*, places the emphasis on the person who is doing the learning (Weimer, 2002), emphasizes the important interrelationships between instructors and learners (Blumberg, 2004), and focuses on the process of learning. The term *learner-centered teaching* appeals to instructors because it identifies their critical role of teaching in the learning process. A commonly used variation of learner-centered teaching is *learning-centered teaching*. *Learning-centered teaching* focuses on the process of learning. The phrase *student-centered learning* is also used, but some instructors do not like it because it appears to have a consumer or customer satisfaction implication that they feel is not appropriate in educational settings. Acquiring an education, they feel, is not equivalent to purchasing an item. Learning does not come automatically to students simply because they pay tuition. *Student-centered learning* also seems to encourage students to be more empowered and appears to take the teacher out of the traditional critical role. In addition to the preceding reasons, I have chosen *learner-centered teaching* to be more consistent with Weimer's (2002) terminology.

Before I review the strong research evidence for why learner-centered approaches are superior to instructor-centered approaches, I will discuss a case study to help you visualize what a learner-centered course might look like. This case study illustrates how an instructor transformed a traditional course to make it very learner-centered.

Case Study: A Course That Became Learner-Centered

Andrew Peterson (Peterson, 2006) has taught a required management course to more than one hundred pharmacy students each semester for the past ten years. For the first five years, he and guest practitioners lectured to mostly uninterested students who did not see why they needed to take this course. Even though the course was worth four credits, students did not see the value of the material and thus did not routinely attend class. He assessed the students using multiple-choice examinations.

Five years ago, Peterson decided to transform this course to help students see the relevance of the content to their careers. Now he rarely lectures; instead, the students mostly work in small groups and make presentations to the class on the content.

Box 1.1 describes the management course as Peterson teaches it now. Table 1.1 shows the contrasts between the old manner in which he taught the course and the learner-centered ways in which he now teaches it.

Andrew Peterson perceives many advantages to the learner-centered way he now teaches the Pharmacy Systems Management course. As Table 1.1 shows, these advantages include increases in student engagement with the content, learning, personalization, student satisfaction, and students' ability to apply what they learn to other situations. I will be referring to this case study later in this book.

If you agree with him that the transformed methods for teaching this course are superior to the old ways and if you would like to learn how to

---

Box 1.1. Pharmacy Systems Management: A Learner-Centered Course

Pharmacy Systems Management is a required course for pharmacy students. The course introduces students to aspects of management that they are most likely to face in pharmacy practice, including human resource management and purchasing. Students learn to apply these concepts within the context of current pharmacy environments.

After discussions with other instructors, Peterson concluded that the way he assessed students reinforced their notion that this course was not relevant to them. He decided to assess students in ways that are more similar to how pharmacists would use the content of the course. This, he reasoned, might help the students connect the material with their future practice. Thus the first part of the transformation came about with a decision not to give exams. Although this seemed like an easy change, it forced Peterson to review the objectives of the course and of each individual class. He decided that written and oral assessments would more realistically represent what pharmacists actually do.

The review of the daily class objectives led Peterson to create student-management teams representing different types of pharmacies. The students work in their groups to solve problems relating to their type of pharmacy, because pharmacy systems management relies on teamwork and cooperation. For example, in one activity students determine what action the managers would need to take relating to medication errors. The students in a hospital pharmacy group discuss how they could prevent medication errors from occurring or how they would handle the public relations if an error did occur. Several times during the semester, each group presents some of its findings to the rest of the class, which allows students to hear how other types of pharmacies view a particular topic.

There are four required written assignments, several oral presentations, and additional elective assignments during the semester. These assignments assess the students' understanding of the content and help them reflect on their experiences. Two of the four required assignments are self-assessments. The midpoint assessment asks students to describe what they have learned in class so far, assess how well they are performing on their assignments and in their groups, and describe what they intend to do during the second half of the semester to improve (or maintain) their performance. The other required written assignments focus on content.

The instructor grades all assignments using a rubric-scoring sheet. Rubrics are checklists or scoring guides that list the concrete components you are looking for when you grade a student (Suskie, 2004). They also identify different levels of performance within each of these graded components. In this course, students receive the rubric ahead of time; they are encouraged to share their work with their group members and use the rubric as a guide for developing their papers. If a paper does not meet the satisfactory level noted in the rubric, the student must redo the paper until it meets that level. For each redo, there is an associated grade reduction.

The instructor determines grades based on a combination of performances in written assignments, oral presentations, and group participation. The instructor specifies what is required to earn each grade level. For example, to earn a C, the student must successfully complete the four required assignments and at least two oral presentations, plus four other written assignments, and must participate in 50 percent of the group activities.

---

teach in similar ways, read on! In the next sections, I will summarize the reasons why there is widespread support for learner-centered teaching. Then I will review the research evidence that learner-centered approaches lead to better outcomes than traditional instructor-centered approaches.

TABLE 1.1

Contrasts Between Instructor-Centered and Learner-Centered Approaches for the Pharmacy Management Course.

Course characteristics that remain the same	Instructor-centered characteristics of original course	Problems and concerns with the old way course was taught	Changes made	Learner-centered characteristics of the transformed course	Benefits to student learning and other outcomes
Class size: >100 students seated in an auditorium-style classroom	Instructor used no activities in which students interact with material, instructor, or each other.	Students often felt disconnected from faculty. Students tended to remain with their friends and not interact with others students.	Students are organized into twenty groups of six people representing the managers of different types of pharmacies. Students remain with their group throughout the semester.	Instructor routinely uses activities in which students interact with material, instructor, and each other	Instructor gets to know students individually as well as in groups. Students interact with other students with whom they normally would not; they report this is a benefit.
Class schedule: Class meets twice weekly for two-hour session.	Instructor used one approach, that of lectures, throughout the course without focusing on creating an environment for learning or accommodating different learning styles.	Students were not engaged and were bored by the lecture format.	Student groups engage in varied in-class activities. Groups make presentations.	Instructor intentionally uses various teaching/learning methods that are appropriate for student learning goals.	Students enjoy variety of activities done in class.
Type of material students need to learn: Students need to learn abstract, conceptual material,	Instructor used content that helps students build a knowledge base. Instructor allowed students	Students memorized facts; learned content in a superficial way without an emphasis on understanding	Students use active learning strategies in more than two-thirds of the classes. Students teach	In addition to building a knowledge base, instructor uses content to help students: • Evaluate why	Active learning, active engagement in the content promotes a deeper understanding of material.

(Continued)

TABLE 1.1

Contrasts Between Instructor-Centered and Learner-Centered Approaches for the Pharmacy Management Course. (*Continued*)

Course characteristics that remain the same	Instructor-centered characteristics of original course	Problems and concerns with the old way course was taught	Changes made	Learner-centered characteristics of the transformed course	Benefits to student learning and other outcomes
in contrast to scientific, factual content they learn in other classes. Students need to be able to apply information to their careers.	to memorize content. Instructor provided content so students can learn it in isolation, without providing opportunities for them to apply knowledge to new content.	and without personal meaning. Students did not feel material was important to their careers.	each other within their groups. Groups present to the entire class.	they need to learn content • Practice using inquiry or ways of thinking in the discipline • Learn to solve real-world problems Instructor encourages students to transform and reflect on most of the content to make their own meaning out of it. Instructor frames and organizes content so students can learn additional content that is not taught.	Use of groups as managers allows for direct application of material to simulated real-life situations.
Attendance policy: Attendance is optional.	Although attendance was optional, the instructor felt students should attend even when	Class attendance varied from 25% to 75%. Students felt they could memorize	Students are responsible for learning during class through group activities and other active learning processes.	Instructor • Helps students to take advantage of opportunities to learn	Student attendance at all classes increases to nearly 100% on group activity days.

(*Continued*)

TABLE 1.1 (*Continued*)

Course characteristics that remain the same	Instructor-centered characteristics of original course	Problems and concerns with the old way course was taught	Changes made	Learner-centered characteristics of the transformed course	Benefits to student learning and other outcomes
	they were not expected to be active learners. Instructor did not encourage students to take responsibility for their own learning. Instructor extensively used extrinsic motivators to get students to earn grades.	sufficient material to pass exams without coming to class. Poor attendance promoted dissension and dissatisfaction among those students who routinely attended. Often, students would look for "extra credit" for attending, as attendance did not positively improve one's grade (that is, nonattendees could get notes and still do well on tests).	Students cannot get notes from others when they miss active learning activities done in class. Grade directly relates to participation in group activities.	• Fosters an understanding of consequences of not taking advantage of such learning opportunities, like missing class. Instructor inspires and encourages students to become intrinsically motivated to learn.	Students understand learning occurs in class and with peers. Students are accountable for all of their time and their efforts in class. Students see direct application of the material to their careers.
Assessment of students: Must assess students and assign a final grade.	Instructor used only two summative assessments (to make decisions to assign grades). Instructor did not integrate assessment within the learning process.	Promoted "learn and dump" phenomenon. Students did not appear to retain information in later years; often told other faculty "we never learned that."	Exams were eliminated from class. Assessments now include written assignments, group activities, group presentations, in-class assessments, written assessments,	Consistently throughout the learning process, instructor integrates: • Formative assessment • Constructive feedback Instructor mostly	Students feel more relaxed about learning material without the pressure of exams. Multiple assessment strategies allow students to demonstrate ability through various formats.

(*Continued*)

TABLE 1.1

Contrasts Between Instructor-Centered and Learner-Centered Approaches for the Pharmacy Management Course. (*Continued*)

Course characteristics that remain the same	Instructor-centered characteristics of original course	Problems and concerns with the old way course was taught	Changes made	Learner-centered characteristics of the transformed course	Benefits to student learning and other outcomes
	Instructor did not consider peer and self-assessments relevant. Instructor did *not* use • Assignments that are open-ended • Test questions that allow for more than one right answer		and peer and self-assessments. Students contract for their grade by deciding on the amount of elective work they will do.	integrates assessment within the learning process. Instructor encourages students to use peer and self-assessments routinely. Instructor uses • Mastery (students redo assignments until they reach acceptable level). • Contract grading (students contract for their grade based on how much acceptable work they do) to determine what grade students will earn. Instructor routinely uses assignments that are open-ended.	Students retain information and use it in other courses.

Widespread Support for Learner-Centered Teaching

There is a logical progression from knowing the advantages of learner-centered approaches, to accepting this approach, to making changes in your teaching. The support for why you should implement learner-centered teaching comes from numerous sources, including national educational reform task forces, research on student learning outcomes, accreditation standards, and educational and psychological research.

The increasing importance given to a national survey of college students' engagement in their educational activities highlights the focus on student learning. The National Survey of Student Engagement (NSSE) is a measure of educational quality and indicates the kinds of learning environments that the students encounter. The swift growth in the number of institutions of higher education using this survey is a testament to the widespread acceptance of learner-centered teaching (Ewell, 2001). Results from 972 colleges and universities surveying more than 844,000 students have led the NSSE researchers to develop five benchmarks of effective educational practices: raising the level of academic challenge, using active and collaborative learning, fostering meaningful student-faculty interactions, creating enriching educational experiences, and establishing a supportive campus environment (National Survey of Student Engagement [NSSE], 2005). All of these benchmarks are consistent with learner-centered teaching.

Student engagement through learner-centered approaches leads to desirable student outcomes. The benefits of learner-centered education include increased motivation for learning and greater satisfaction with school; these outcomes lead to greater academic achievement (Slavin, 1990; Johnson, 1991; Maxwell, 1998). Students in learner-centered programs differ from students in more instructor-centered programs in some concrete and specific ways (Blumberg, 2004); namely, they

- Know why they need to learn content

- Have a self-awareness of their learning abilities and how they acquire knowledge (Association of American Colleges and Universities, 2002)

- Can use knowledge to solve problems (Fink, 2003)

- Have the ability to continue to learn throughout their lives. (Association of American Colleges and Universities, 2002), as they can retrieve and evaluate information that they need to learn (Doherty, Riordan, & Roth, 2002)

- Can communicate their knowledge outside the classroom (Fink, 2003)

The assessments of student learning outcomes are fundamental to the current accreditation process for institutions of higher education and for professional programs. Student learning outcomes form a "common currency" with which one can judge the equivalence and value of various learning experiences (Middle States Commission on Higher Education, 2003b). This focus on the assessment of student learning is congruent with learner-centered teaching (Middle States Commission on Higher Education, 2003b).

Educational and Psychological Research Supports Learner-Centered Teaching

What psychologists and educators have discovered about learning and the learning process forms a strong rationale for implementing learner-centered teaching. A joint task force of the American Psychological Association and the Mid-Continent Regional Educational Laboratory integrated this research into the fourteen learner-centered psychological principles (Lambert & McCombs, 2000). Alexander and Murphy (2000) further summarized these learner-centered principles into the following five domains:

- The knowledge base
- Strategic processing and executive control
- Motivation and affect
- Development and individual difference
- Situation or context

I summarize this research here to enable you to use it as you transform your teaching and to help you describe why you made the changes you made.

The Knowledge Base

Current knowledge is the foundation on which students can build future knowledge (Alexander & Murphy, 2000). Learning is a constructive process that involves building links between new information and experiences onto the individual's existing knowledge base. These links may add to, modify, or reorganize existing knowledge. In order to learn, each person needs to construct or make his own meaning of knowledge (Alexander & Murphy, 2000). Therefore you, as an instructor, cannot construct knowledge for your students. When students do not integrate new knowledge with prior knowledge, they cannot use this knowledge in the future even in situations just slightly different from the one in which they learned it.

Often when students just memorize material they are not establishing links to prior knowledge (Alexander & Murphy, 2000).

Prior knowledge is a good predictor of future learning. For example, children's religious affiliation influenced how they understood and recalled information contained in texts about religious practices (Lipson, 1983). When prior knowledge is flawed or misleading, it interferes with one's ability to learn correct information. For example, when scientific facts or theories do not support commonplace notions of science, students do not change their beliefs about how the world functions. Therefore, one of the mainstays of good science instruction is that students must confront their misconceptions about the world in order to learn science (Svinicki, 2004).

Knowledge is domain- or discipline-specific and multifaceted. Novices' organization of knowledge is different from an expert's organization of this knowledge. What is clear to you as a content expert in your field is often not clear to your students. In addition, students can be novices in some disciplines while being expert or intermediate in other domains (Alexander & Murphy, 2000).

Strategic Processing and Executive Control

Strategic processing means that a person's mental actions and executive control are self-regulating or that the person is monitoring his or her mental actions. Psychologists sometimes group these under the terms *general cognitive* or *meta-cognitive strategies*. In addition to having a knowledge base, successful learners think about their own learning and assess how successful they are as learners. They consciously use different thinking strategies in different learning situations (Alexander & Murphy, 2000). Throughout higher education, you can expose students to different learning strategies and allow them to practice them.

Students who think about their own thinking (a practice called *meta-cognition* by psychologists) learn better than students who do not employ this strategy. Regardless of your discipline, you can foster meta-cognition by encouraging students to monitor their thinking. You can ask questions about your students' thought processes as they conduct their work (Alexander & Murphy, 2000). This is similar to mathematics instructors asking students to show their work and not just the answers. You can ask students to explain what they do when they cannot find the answer or cannot solve the problem.

Researchers found that college students use a combination of three different approaches to their learning: deep, surface, and strategic (Ramsden, 2003).

Surface learning is learning in isolation; it often employs rote memorization of facts. Students easily forget what they studied through surface learning because they did not make the content meaningful to them. *Deep learning* contrasts sharply with surface learning because in deep learning the students connect what they are presently learning to their own experiences. They make connections between a theory and real-world examples. Students organize the information when they are engaged in deep learning. As you might suppose, psychologists advocate for deep learning. *Strategic learning* is doing whatever it takes to pass the course or get a good grade, such as doing assignments according to how previous successful students did them. Retention varies with strategic learning approaches, depending on what the students do.

Students may use different learning approaches depending on what instructors or their educational programs demand of them. Survey results show that as students enter medical school, they largely use surface and strategic learning approaches. There are two major forms of the preclinical or classroom phase of medical education: one form relies largely on lectures to cover the material, the other uses facilitated small-group discussions of patient cases. There are few lectures in the latter programs and these students often read the material on their own. Evidence from many different medical programs in North America, Europe, and Australia indicates that students in these small-group discussion programs use deep learning. Their peers in the lecture-based programs, some even in the same school but in different tracks, continue to use surface and strategic approaches to learning (Blumberg, 2000).

Motivation and Affect

Motivation relates to how needs and desires direct thoughts and behaviors. Affect, a related construct, refers to the feelings or emotions that people have. Affect also influences thoughts and behaviors (Alexander & Murphy, 2000).

The effort that students invest in the learning process greatly influences the quality and quantity of their learning. Conclusive research evidence supports these observations. This research shows that personal involvement, intrinsic motivation, and personal commitment lead to more learning. People who have a positive self-concept, who set realistically high goals for themselves, and who think that school is relevant to them do better in school than those who do not have these characteristics (Alexander & Murphy, 2000).

Research supports common educators' beliefs that motivational constructs such as confidence and control over learning influence learning and achievement. Beliefs about one's own competency or ability to succeed, called *self-efficacy*, correlate with grades. Much research evidence shows that confident students try harder, are more engaged in their learning and thinking, and ultimately do perform better than students with less self-efficacy. Further, students who believe that they have control over their learning are more likely to be more actively engaged in their academic work and work harder, achieving higher grades than do students who do not believe they have control over their learning (Pintrich, 2003).

Just as knowledge is domain- or discipline-specific, so is a student's motivation to learn discipline- or task-specific. Students' interests vary among their courses. When students perceive a course to be not relevant to their interests or their careers, they are less likely to be motivated to excel in the course. As a learner-centered instructor, you try to find ways for students to connect students' personal interests to the overall course goals. For example, in a twentieth-century literature course, students can select from a list of novels for their own reading. Students very interested in war can read appropriate war novels, whereas others might choose books that look at a local culture of the same period.

Development and Individual Differences

Human development is a process that considers common and unique characteristics of people at the same age. Individual differences encompass variations among humans regardless of age. This domain considers the roles of both nature and nurture in learning (Alexander & Murphy, 2000).

Although most people think of development as a process limited to preschool, primary, or secondary school students, college students continue to develop. For example, Perry (1999) felt that college students go through four phases of how they understand knowledge and accept alternative perspectives.

There are important individual differences in learning. Students have different capacities for learning that are a function of prior experience and heredity. By the time students enter college they have developed their own preferences for how they like to learn. As students may not be aware of those learning preferences, asking students to take one of the many different self-assessment inventories can be very insightful. A commonly used one is the Kolb Inventory of Cognitive Styles, which places people on four axes: feeling, watching, thinking, and doing. The Myers-Briggs Type Indicator that places people along four continua of introversion/extraversion, thinking/feeling, sensing/intuition, and perceiving/judging is the foundation for the Kolb Inventory of Cognitive Styles (Bean, 1996). Although the Myers-Briggs is a personality inventory, researchers have found that the personality types also predict learning preferences. For example, depending on where students fall on these continua on the Kolb or the Myers-Briggs Inventories, they prefer and excel at different types of writing assignments (Jensen & DiTiberio, 1989).

Situation or Context

How students learn, the situation, and the context all greatly influence what they learn. Theories of learning highlight the roles of active engagement and social interaction in the students' own construction of knowledge (Bruner, 1966; Kafai & Resnick, 1996; Piaget, 1963; Vygotsky, 1978). People learn better when they interact and collaborate with others throughout the instructional task. In collaborative and cooperative learning situations, students can see and appreciate the perspectives of others. These situations also facilitate reflective thinking that can promote better learning (Lambert & McCombs, 2000). The social context of learning is an integral part of the learning process, not merely a background context that the student encounters (Resnick, 1991).

A meta-analysis review of research literature indicates that many students, especially those in the sciences and engineering or technology disciplines, learn best through active, small-group activities. Small-group learning is particularly effective in the early courses to reduce the attrition rates of students desiring to major in the discipline or for those nonmajors who want to gain literacy in that discipline. The positive gains associated with small group learning are significantly greater for students who are part of underrepresented groups in higher education, female, or both (Springer, Stanne, & Donovan, 1999).

The instructor plays essential roles in creating the learning situation or context. Rather than being the person who gives the information, the instructor's primary role is to be a guide or facilitator of learning by creating environments for student learning. In fact, when instructors encourage students to discuss the material, students perform better than they do after simply listening to lectures. Research shows that personal involvement, intrinsic motivation, and personal commitment lead to more learning (Alexander & Murphy, 2000). Through the creation of learning environments, you develop active learning situations for your students.

Active learning can take many forms, but it always actively engages the students in the learning process. Active learning requires, among other things, that the students perform meaningful learning activities and think about what they are doing (Bonwell & Eison, 1991). Small-group discussions, requiring students to use inquiry to solve problems individually, and reflection or journal writing are common examples of active learning (Bean, 1996). There is a great deal of research supporting active learning, including a meta-analysis of the effectiveness of active learning. The results from 480 engineering students enrolled in twenty-three different courses employing both active learning and lecture methods at six different universities showed significantly greater learning gains for those students enrolled in the active learning courses (Prince, 2004).

Summary of the Research Evidence

When we consider all that psychologists and educational researchers know about how people learn, we have strong evidence that should lead us to adopt learner-centered approaches instead of instructor-centered approaches. One consistent recommendation of all of this research is the need to shift the emphasis from what *you* do to what the *students* do to learn.

When the focus becomes student learning, colleges attain higher rates of student retention and have better-prepared graduates than those students who were more traditionally trained (Matlin, 2002; Sternberg & Grigorenko, 2002). This body of research is the foundation of the learner-centered approaches discussed in this book. Many of the components discussed in this book parallel the points in this review of the literature. Here is a summary of the relevant, major points of this research:

- Students need to create their own understanding of material by connecting it with what they already know (Alexander & Murphy, 2000).
- Successful students are actively involved in their own learning, monitor their thinking, think about their learning, and assume responsibility for their own learning (Lambert & McCombs, 2000).
- Knowledge of learning preferences can lead to success in college because individual differences interact with teaching and learning methods in ways that can be helpful or hindering (Bean, 1996; Grasha, 1996; Lambert & McCombs, 2000).
- Personal involvement, intrinsic motivation, confidence in one's abilities to succeed, and a perception of control over learning lead to more learning and higher achievement in school (Alexander & Murphy, 2000).
- Learning is a social process; in comparison studies between students in lecture and active learning courses, there are significantly more learning gains in the active learning courses (Springer et al., 1999).

Application of This Research to Support Teaching

Although the psychological literature builds a strong case for learner-centered teaching, it is abstract and hard to translate into classroom or online educational practices. Maryellen Weimer, in her 2002 book *Learner-Centered Teaching*, discussed five practices that need to change to achieve this type of teaching. This organizational scheme brings all of the previous research and literature into a more applied focus for instructors. She broadly labeled these five practices as the Function of Content, the Role of the Instructor, the Responsibility for Learning, the Purposes and Processes of Assessment, and the Balance of Power. The next section of this chapter explains these five practices or dimensions of learner-centered teaching.

The Five Dimensions of Learner-Centered Teaching

Here is an overview of the five dimensions of learner-centered teaching.

- *The function of content* in learner-centered teaching includes giving students a strong knowledge foundation, the ability to apply the content, and the ability to learn more independently. Students need an understanding of why they need to learn the content, and they need to be actively engaged in their learning.

- *The role of the instructor* focuses on helping students learn. Instructors should not just disseminate information. Instead, they should create an environment in which students can learn. The teaching and learning methods that instructors use should be appropriate for student learning goals.

- *The responsibility for learning* shifts from the instructor to the students. Instructors should proactively assist their students to take responsibility for their own learning by creating situations that motivate students to accept this responsibility. Further, instructors should guide students to acquire skills that will help them learn in the future. When students assume responsibility for their own learning, they become self-directed, lifelong learners who are aware of their own abilities to learn.

- *The purposes and processes of assessment* shift from only assigning grades to include providing constructive feedback to assist student improvement. Learner-centered teaching integrates assessment with feedback as a part of the learning process.

- *The balance of power* shifts so that the instructor shares some decisions about the course with the students, such that the instructor and the students collaborate on course policies and procedures. Learner-centered teaching maintains an appropriate balance of power between the instructor and the students by giving students opportunities to learn and some control over expressing perspectives and their methods of learning and assessment.

Contrasts Between Instructor-Centered and Learner-Centered Approaches

Contrasts between instructor-centered approaches and learner-centered approaches further explain each of the five dimensions. These contrasts between these two approaches illustrate differences in what you as an instructor do. In addition, your behaviors lead to differences in what you expect your students to do. Table 1.2 contrasts instructor-centered approaches with learner-centered approaches on one essential component of each of these five dimensions of learner-centered teaching.

TABLE 1.2

Contrasts Between Instructor-Centered and Learner-Centered Approaches on Each of the Five Dimensions of Learner-Centered Teaching.

Dimension	Definition of this dimension	An essential component	Instructor-centered approach	Learner-centered approach
The Function of Content	Content includes building a knowledge base, how the instructor and the students use the content.	Level to which students engage in content.	Instructor allows students to memorize content.	Instructor encourages students to transform and reflect on most of the content to make their own meaning out of it.
The Role of the Instructor	An essential role of the instructor is to assist students to learn.	Instructor uses teaching and learning methods appropriate for student learning goals.	Instructor • Does not have specified learning goals *and/or* • Uses teaching and learning methods that conflict with learning goals	Instructor intentionally uses various teaching and learning methods that are appropriate for student learning goals.

(Continued)

TABLE 1.2

Contrasts Between Instructor-Centered and Learner-Centered Approaches on Each of the Five Dimensions of Learner-Centered Teaching. (*Continued*)

Dimension	Definition of this dimension	An essential component	Instructor-centered approach	Learner-centered approach
The Responsibility for Learning	Students should assume greater responsibility for their own learning over time.	*Responsibility for learning should rest with the students.*	Instructor assumes *all* responsibility for student learning (provides content to memorize, does not require students to create their own meaning of content, tells students exactly what will be on examinations).	Instructor provides increasing opportunities for students to assume responsibility for their own learning, leading to achievement of stated learning objectives.
The Purposes and Processes of Assessment	There are additional purposes and processes of assessment beyond assigning grades.	Formative assessment (giving feedback to foster improvement).	Instructor • Uses only summative assessment (to make decisions to assign grades) • Provides students with no constructive feedback	Consistently throughout the learning process, instructor integrates • Formative assessment • Constructive feedback
The Balance of Power	The balance of power shifts so that the instructor shares some decisions about the course with the students.	Flexibility of course policies, assessment methods, learning methods, and deadlines.	Instructor mandates all policies and deadlines. *or* Instructor does not adhere to policies.	Instructor is flexible on most • Course policies • Assessment methods • Learning methods • Deadlines *and* Instructor always adheres to what instructor has agreed to with the students.

An Incremental Approach

As Table 1.2 shows, the contrast in teaching methods between the instructor-centered and learner-centered approaches is quite large. Just listing the learner-centered approaches may not suggest ways to change your own teaching. The dimension "The Responsibility for Learning" shown in Table 1.2 illustrates this contrast. Most instructors believe that students should assume responsibility for their own learning, but their behavior and that of their students do not always support this philosophy. Instructors may not know how to help students assume increasing responsibility for their own learning.

The methods we use to teach are quite varied; therefore, our teaching is necessarily at different levels of transitioning from instructor-centered to learner-centered. Further, because it is easier to make gradual changes in our teaching, this book proposes an incremental approach to transforming courses to be more learner-centered. This book discusses how you can make changes in your teaching gradually by changing only a few components within these five dimensions of learner-centered teaching at a time. Even these small steps often have a significant impact on the overall learner-centeredness of a course. Furthermore, small steps in one component often have spillover effects on other dimensions.

Moving from Instructor-Centered to Learner-Centered Teaching

Incremental steps allow you to make changes gradually as you make a transition from where you are now toward learner-centered teaching. The incremental approach used in this book describes two levels of transitioning for each component of each of the five dimensions of learner-centered teaching. This incremental approach makes the transformation process more manageable.

For example, Table 1.3 shows the incremental steps between the instructor-centered and learner-centered approaches on the essential component, the level to which students engage in content from the Function of Content dimension. Similar incremental steps exist for each of the other components. The two levels of transitioning, "lower" and "higher," show small incremental steps, which are easier to implement. The last column on the right describes a learner-centered approach or the goals that you should be aiming for when transforming a course.

The instructor's expectations and the way in which the instructor assesses the students determine the level to which students engage in the

TABLE 1.3

Incremental Transitions from Instructor-Centered to Learner-Centered Teaching on the Level to Which Students Engage in Their Learning.

The Function of Content

Component	Employs *instructor-centered* approaches →	→ Transitioning to learner-centered approaches →		Employs *learner-centered* approaches
		Lower level of transitioning	**Higher level of transitioning**	
Level to which students engage in content	Instructor allows students to memorize content.	Instructor provides content so students can learn material as given to them without transforming or reflecting on it.	Instructor assists students to transform and reflect on *some* of the content to make their own meaning out of *some* of it.	Instructor encourages students to transform and reflect on *most* of the content to make their own meaning out of it.

content. In an instructor-centered approach, the instructor would allow the students to memorize facts, such as formulas or dates in history, without their having any meaning, and to later recall them on a test. At the lower level of transitioning, the instructor provides the content so that the students can actively learn it, perhaps by providing them with questions whose answers come directly from the textbook or the lectures. At the higher level of transitioning, the instructor provides activities that help students transform some of the content to make their own meaning out of it. For example, the instructor might ask the students to develop a chart or graph to summarize some material in the text. Finally, with a learner-centered approach, the instructor would expect the students to develop associations between what they read or heard in class and their own lives or real-world phenomena, thus forming their own meaning from all of the content. For example, the instructor could ask students to write journals reflecting on their reading. When students engage in the content at this level, they are more likely to remember it and be able to use it later.

Using Rubrics to Identify Incremental Steps Toward Learner-Centered Teaching

Table 1.4 is a rubric that shows the four levels between instructor-centered and learner-centered approaches on one essential component of each of the five dimensions of learner-centered teaching. Rubrics are matrices that

TABLE 1.4

Incremental Transitions from Instructor-Centered to Learner-Centered Teaching on One Component of Each of the Five Dimensions of Learner-Centered Teaching.

Dimension	An example of one component of this dimension	Instructor-centered approach →	→ Transitioning to learner-centered approaches →		Learner-centered approach
			Lower level of transitioning	Higher level of transitioning	
The Function of Content	Level to which students engage in content	Instructor allows students to memorize content.	Instructor provides content so students can learn material as given to them without transforming or reflecting on it.	Instructor assists students to transform and reflect on *some* of the content to make their own meaning out of *some* of it.	Instructor encourages students to transform and reflect on *most* of the content to make their own meaning out of it.
The Role of the Instructor	Teaching and learning methods appropriate for student learning goals	Instructor • Does *not* have specified learning goals *or* • Uses teaching and learning methods that conflict with learning goals	Instructor : • Uses teaching and learning methods without regard for student goals • Does not use active learning activities	Instructor uses *some* teaching and learning methods that are appropriate for student learning goals.	Instructor intentionally uses *various* teaching and learning methods that are appropriate for student learning goals.
The Responsibility for Learning	Responsibility for learning should rest with the students	Instructor assumes *all* responsibility for student learning (provides content to memorize; does not require students to create their own meaning of content; tells students exactly what will be on examinations).	Instructor assumes *most* responsibility for student learning (provides detailed notes of content to be learned and reviews content to be examined while helping students learn the material and meet objectives).	Instructor provides *some* opportunities for students to assume responsibility for their own learning.	Instructor provides *increasing* opportunities for students to assume responsibility for their own learning, leading to achievement of stated learning objectives.

(Continued)

TABLE 1.4

Incremental Transitions from Instructor-Centered to Learner-Centered Teaching on One Component of Each of the Five Dimensions of Learner-Centered Teaching. (*Continued*)

Dimension	An example of one component of this dimension	Instructor-centered approach →	→ Transitioning to learner-centered approaches →		Learner-centered approach
			Lower level of transitioning	Higher level of transitioning	
The Purposes and Processes of Assessment	Assessment within the learning process	Instructor • Sees assessment as less important than teaching *and* • Does not integrate assessment within the learning process	Instructor *minimally* integrates assessment within the learning process.	Instructor *somewhat* integrates assessment within the learning process.	Instructor *mostly* integrates assessment within the learning process.
The Balance of Power	Flexibility of course policies, assessment methods, learning methods, and deadlines	Instructor • Mandates all policies and deadlines *or* • Does not adhere to policies	Instructor • Is flexible on *a few* course policies, assessment methods, learning methods, and deadlines *and* • Infrequently adheres to these flexible decisions	Instructor • Is flexible on *some* course policies, assessment methods, learning methods, and deadlines *and* • Somewhat adheres to what was agreed upon	Instructor • Is flexible on *most* course policies, assessment methods, learning methods, and deadlines *and* • Always adheres to what instructor has agreed to with the students

identify (1) important traits or components and (2) levels of performance within each of these components (Walvoord, 2004). Many instructors, such as the pharmacy management instructor described earlier in this chapter, use rubrics to grade student assignments efficiently and objectively (Suskie, 2004). I use rubrics in another way throughout this book, to show how you can determine the learner-centered status of courses. Further, these rubrics show you how you can identify incremental steps in course transformation from instructor-centered to learner-centered approaches.

In the example given in Table 1.4, I have included only one essential component for each dimension of learner-centered teaching. In reality, experience tells us that each dimension is complex and is composed of more than one component. Through discussions with over 250 instructors and faculty developers, and a review of the literature on learning and learner-centered teaching, I have identified between four and seven major components of each of these five dimensions and developed a separate rubric for each of the five dimensions. Each of five rubrics corresponds to a different dimension of learner-centered teaching according to Weimer's (2002) ideas and contains specific components of the dimension. In the rest of the book, you will find detailed descriptions of the rubrics and the components, and implementation examples for each of these components. Each step of the rubrics explains what instructors can do to make their courses more learner-centered; the instructor's perspective is the focus throughout. You will have many opportunities to practice using the rubrics.

Table 1.5 shows the rubric for one of these dimensions, that of the Role of the Instructor. The rubric format is similar to the one already shown, with the component named or described in the column on the left column and four levels of transformation, from instructor-centered to learner-centered.

Using Rubrics at the Beginning of a Change Process

You can use the rubrics as a self-assessment tool at the beginning of a change process toward learner-centered teaching. First, the rubrics allow you to determine your status on the learner-centered continuum. Second, they help you identify specific components you might want to change. Third, the rubrics suggest incremental changes you can make on these components to transform your teaching.

Transforming your overall approach to teaching a course may take several years, whereas moving from one level to the next on a specific criterion on a rubric within a dimension is a realistic short-term goal. Chapter Three discusses the transformation process I propose in more detail. This transformation process to make courses more learner-centered is not an easy one, and you are likely to encounter a variety of obstacles along the way, but the results are worth the effort. Chapter Ten, Strategies for Overcoming Obstacles and Resistance, offers specific ways for you to overcome these obstacles. Although being a learner-centered instructor should be your goal, it is not necessary or practical to be learner-centered on every component.

TABLE 1.5

The Rubric for the Role of the Instructor Dimension of Learner-Centered Teaching.

The Role of the Instructor

Component	Employs *instructor-centered* approaches →	→ Transitioning to learner-centered approaches →		Employs *learner-centered* approaches
		Lower level of transitioning	**Higher level of transitioning**	
1. Creation of an environment for learning through (1) organization and (2) use of material that accommodates different learning styles	Instructor uses the same approach or approaches throughout the course even if the students are not learning.	Instructor does not focus on creating a learning environment, but students do learn.	Instructor creates a learning environment through use of one out of the two subcriteria.	Instructor creates a learning environment by using both subcriteria: through organization and use of material that accommodates different learning styles.
2. Alignment of the course components: objectives, teaching or learning methods, and assessment methods—for consistency	Instructor does *not* align objectives, teaching or learning methods, and assessment methods.	Instructor • *Minimally* aligns objectives, teaching or learning methods, and assessment methods *or* • Aligns two out of the three course components	Instructor *somewhat* aligns objectives, teaching or learning methods, and assessment methods.	Instructor explicitly, coherently, and consistently aligns objectives, teaching or learning methods, and assessment methods.
3. Teaching or learning methods appropriate for student learning goals	Instructor • Does *not* have specified learning goals *or* • Uses teaching and learning methods that conflict with learning goals	Instructor • Uses teaching and learning methods without regard for student learning goals • Does not use active learning activities	Instructor uses *some* teaching or learning methods that are appropriate for student learning goals.	Instructor intentionally uses *various* teaching or learning methods that are appropriate for student learning goals.

(Continued)

TABLE 1.5 (*Continued*)

The Role of the Instructor

| Component | Employs *instructor-entered* approaches → | → Transitioning to learner-centered approaches → | | Employs *learner-centered* approaches |
		Lower level of transitioning	**Higher level of transitioning**	
4. Activities involving student, instructor, and content interactions	Instructor uses no activities in which students actively interact with material, or instructor, or each other.	Instructor uses a *few* activities in which students actively interact with material, or instructor, or each other.	Instructor uses *some* activities in which • Students actively interact with material, or instructor, or each other *or* • There are some three-way interactions	Instructor *routinely* uses activities in which students actively interact with material, and instructor, and each other.
5. Articulation of SMART objectives: • **S**pecific • **M**easurable • **A**ttainable • **R**elevant • **T**ime oriented	Instructor • Articulates vague course objectives *and/or* • Does not articulate objectives in syllabus	Instructor articulates in syllabus course objectives that do not have all five attributes of SMART objectives.	Instructor articulates SMART objectives in syllabus but does not refer to them throughout the course.	Instructor articulates SMART objectives in syllabus and regularly refers to them throughout the course.
6. Motivation of students to learn (intrinsic drive to learn versus extrinsic reasons to earn grades)	Instructor extensively uses extrinsic motivators to get students to earn grades.	Instructor • Provides *limited* opportunities for students to become intrinsically motivated to learn • Uses extrinsic motivators to get students to earn grades	Instructor provides *some* opportunities for students to become intrinsically motivated to learn.	Instructor inspires and encourages students to become intrinsically motivated to learn.

Choosing a Course to Transform

You will have a better idea of how to become a learner-centered instructor if you apply what you learn about the transformation process to a course of your own. As you read the book, you will find opportunities to evaluate the status of the course—the degree to which it is currently instructor-centered or learner-centered—and then to identify incremental steps for transforming it.

Before proceeding, choose the course on which you will work; to describe it, complete the worksheet given in the following application activity. For purposes of helping you understand this book, I recommend that you choose a course that meets these criteria:

- You are very comfortable with the course content and enjoy teaching it.
- The course is not in your own research area; if it is, you may be too close to the material to allow the course to become learner-centered.
- You have taught the course at least three times and expect to continue teaching it on a regular basis.
- You feel that you can improve the course so that students learn more or achieve better outcomes.

Using Rubrics to Determine Status of Educational Programs or for Teaching Dossiers

You can also use the rubrics as a program assessment tool to show the status of your curriculum or to show the changes that you and your colleagues have made toward becoming more learner-centered. If you and your fellow instructors were to do this before implementing changes and then afterward, you would be able to look at the changes your educational program made over time. Individual instructors can use the rubrics to document how their teaching has evolved as they incorporate more learner-centered approaches. These rubrics could be placed in teaching dossiers for promotion or when applying for new positions. You could include a rubric in your annual evaluation of your teaching. Chapter Three will further discuss this use of the rubrics.

Chapter Summary

This chapter introduced the concept of learner-centered teaching through a case study of a course that the instructor transformed from instructor-centered to learner-centered. The chapter described the advantages of learner-centered approaches and reviewed the literature that strongly suggests the use of learner-centered teaching. Next, the chapter contrasted instructor-centered teaching with learner-centered teaching, explaining the idea of incremental steps between these two approaches. Rubrics were introduced; for the purpose of this book, these contain checklists identifying the components to consider when determining whether a course is instructor-centered or learner-centered. The rubrics also identify levels of performance or incremental steps within each of these components. The rubrics relate to Weimer's (2002) five dimensions of learner-centered teaching—the Function of Content, the Role of the Instructor, the Responsibility for Learning, the Purposes and Processes of Assessment, and the Balance of Power—which you will use as you read the rest of the book to determine how to transform a course of your own.

APPLICATION ACTIVITY

Choosing a Course to Transform

Pick a course that you want to analyze and think of how you can transform this course to be more learner-centered. You will be analyzing this course for most of the rest of this book.

Choose a course based on the criteria listed in the section "Choosing a Course to Transform."

Describe the Course Demographics

Course name and number_____

Type of course: classroom _____ laboratory _____ seminar _____ online _____ service-learning or field experience _____ other _____

Size of course: fewer than 20 students _____ 21–59 students _____ 60–150 students _____ more than 150 students _____

Level of the course: developmental (remedial) _____ general education _____ upper level undergraduate _____ graduate _____ professional _____

Continuing learning or in-service _____

Other special considerations (for example, you team teach the course with another instructor or you teach this course only in summer school—a short, intensive time)

Do you want to start by making small changes, perhaps just adding separate techniques? Yes _____ No _____

Alternatively, do you perhaps want to be more integrative in your transformation by making more unified changes? Yes _____ No _____

Chapter 2

Understanding the Rubrics

AS YOU SAW in Chapter One, the rubrics are matrices that state the components of the dimensions of learner-centered teaching and the incremental standards or levels on the continuum from instructor-centered to learner-centered. The rubrics help you determine the learner-centered status of a course and suggest possible incremental transformations.

This chapter provides an overview of the rubric formats, explains how to read the rubrics, and describes the phrases commonly used in the rubrics.

Reading the Rubrics

A separate rubric summarizes each of the five dimensions of learner-centered teaching: the Function of Content, the Role of the Instructor, the Responsibility for Learning, the Purposes and Processes of Assessment, and the Balance of Power. The rubrics for all five dimensions have the same format—typified in Table 2.1, for the Function of Content—for ease of comprehension. Appendix B lists all five rubrics.

Here is an explanation of the rubric format:

- The top row shows the name of the dimension—in this case, "The Function of Content."

- The first column on the left lists the components of the dimension, which are numbered. There will be four to seven components for each dimension. As you can see, the four components for the Function of Content are as follows:

  1. Varied uses of content

  2. Level to which students engage in content

  3. Use of organizing schemes

  4. Use of content to facilitate future learning

- Each cell to the right of the instructor-centered level contains suggestions for incremental changes, with two levels of transitioning to the learner-centered level on the right.

Although the labels for these four continuum levels are the same on all five rubrics, the actual descriptors within the components vary. For example, look

TABLE 2.1

The Rubric for the Function of Content Dimension of Learner-Centered Teaching.

The Function of Content

Component	Employs *instructor-centered* approaches →	→ Transitioning to learner-centered approaches →		Employs *learner-centered* approaches
		Lower level of transitioning	**Higher level of transitioning**	
1. Varied uses of content				
In addition to building a knowledge base, instructor uses content to help students:	Instructor uses content that helps students build a knowledge base.	In addition to building a knowledge base, instructor uses content to help students:	In addition to building a knowledge base, instructor uses content to help students:	In addition to building a knowledge base, instructor uses all four subcriteria in the following ways to help students:
• Know why they need to learn content		• Recognize why they need to learn the content	• Identify why they need to learn content	• Evaluate why they need to learn content
• Acquire discipline-specific learning methodologies, such as how to read primary source material			• Use discipline-specific learning methodologies with instructor's assistance	• Acquire discipline-specific learning methodologies
• Use inquiry or ways of thinking in the discipline			• Use inquiry or ways of thinking in the discipline with the instructor's assistance	• Practice using inquiry or ways of thinking in the discipline
• Learn to solve real-world problems	Instructor and content help students solve problems.	• Apply content to solve problems with instructor's assistance	• Learn to apply content to solve real-world problems with instructor's assistance	• Learn to solve real-world problems
	or	*or*	*or*	
	Instructor uses any one or none of the four subcriteria for uses of content.	Instructor uses any two of the four subcriteria for uses of content.	Instructor uses any three of the four subcriteria for uses of content.	

TABLE 2.1 (*Continued*)

The Function of Content

| Component | Employs *instructor-centered* approaches → | → Transitioning to learner-centered approaches → | | Employs *learner-centered* approaches |
		Lower level of transitioning	Higher level of transitioning	
2. Level to which students engage in content	Instructor allows students to memorize content.	Instructor provides content so students can learn material as it is given to them without transforming or reflecting on it.	Instructor assists students to transform and reflect on *some* of the content to make their own meaning out of *some* of it.	Instructor encourages students to transform and reflect on *most* of the content to make their own meaning out of it.
3. Use of organizing schemes	Students learn content without a clearly defined organizing scheme provided by instructor.	Instructor provides *limited* organizing assistance.	Instructor provides *some* organizing schemes to help students learn content.	Instructor provides and uses organizing schemes to help students learn content.
4. Use of content to facilitate future learning	Instructor provides content so students can learn it in isolation, without providing opportunities for them to apply knowledge to new content.	Instructor provides students with limited opportunities to apply knowledge to new content.	Instructor frames content so students can see how it can be applied in the future.	Instructor frames and organizes content so students can learn additional content that is not taught.

at the fourth component on the Function of Content rubric, "Use of Content to Facilitate Future Learning." If you read across the continuum from left to right, you see that the levels range from instructor-centered ("Instructor provides content so students can learn it in isolation, without providing opportunities for them to apply knowledge to new content") to learner-centered ("Instructor frames and organizes content so students can learn additional content that is not taught") with two intermediate steps in between.

- Items with bullets describe different aspects of a component. For example, the first component of the Function of Content, "Varied uses of content," has four aspects:

  - Know why they need to learn content.

  - Acquire discipline-specific learning methodologies, such as how to read primary source material.

- Use inquiry or ways of thinking in the discipline.

- Learn to solve real-world problems.

- Because each dimension is a separate rubric, the list of components for each dimension begins with 1.

- Most of the information you will need to understand the component is contained in the name of the component column. Sometimes the learner-centered column contains additional clarifying or descriptive information.

- Read the rubrics horizontally across the page, considering one component or one row at a time.

- The arrows in the second row of the rubric indicate the direction toward which you are striving.

A Closer Look

Focusing on one component at time will help you consider what kinds of changes you might make in a course to make it more learner-centered. For example, Table 2.2 highlights component 3 of the Function of Content rubric, "Use of organizing schemes."

When you read this component, first notice that you will be thinking about organizing schemes. An organizing scheme is a discipline-specific conceptual framework that helps students integrate the material (Bransford, Brown, & Cocking, 2000). For example, some of the organizing schemes in the biological sciences are the structure-function relationship, the cellular basis of all life, and evolution. Individual differences regarding cognition, affect, and behavior in organisms, especially humans, form an organizing

TABLE 2.2

Component 3 of the Function of Content Dimension.

The Function of Content

Component	Employs *instructor-centered* approaches →	→ Transitioning to learner-centered approaches →		Employs *learner-centered* approaches
		Lower level of transitioning	**Higher level of transitioning**	
3. Use of organizing schemes	Students learn content without a clearly defined organizing scheme provided by instructor.	Instructor provides *limited* organizing assistance.	Instructor provides *some* organizing schemes to help students learn content.	Instructor provides and uses organizing schemes to help students learn content.

scheme in psychology. Instructors can use organizing schemes as a way to help students understand and integrate the content. In an instructor-centered approach, you would teach without discussing any organizing schemes. For example, you might teach each chapter in an introductory course as a separate unit without showing how the units relate to each other. In the lower level of transitioning, you might use organizing schemes to define the objectives of the course but not discuss them further. In the higher level of transitioning, you might discuss how each unit relates to the organizing schemes. In a learner-centered approach you would integrate the organizing schemes into your teaching and learning activities and ask students to use them on examinations.

Notes on Interpreting the Rubric Levels

As you read the rubrics, you will find that there are several different types of rubric levels, depending on the nature of a specific component. The following definitions will help guide your interpretations.

Quantitative gradations. For some components, the rubrics differentiate the levels in a component by providing gradations, such as from *not used/none* through *few/minimally/limited* to *some/partially* and finally *most/consistently.* Table 2.3, which shows Component 4 from the Role of the

---

TABLE 2.3

Example of Quantitative Gradations on a Row of a Rubric.

The Role of the Instructor

Component	Employs *instructor-centered* approaches →	→ Transitioning to learner-centered approaches →		Employs *learner-centered* approaches
		Lower level of transitioning	**Higher level of transitioning**	
4. Activities involving student, instructor, content interactions	Instructor uses no activities in which students actively interact with material, or instructor, or each other	Instructor uses *few* activities in which students actively interact with material, or instructor, or each other	Instructor uses *some* activities in which students actively interact with material, or instructor, or each other. or There are some three-way interactions.	Instructor *routinely* uses activities in which students actively interact with material, and instructor, and each other

TABLE 2.4

A Guide to Interpreting Quantitative Gradations on the Rubrics.

| Component | Employs *instructor-centered* approaches → | → Transitioning to learner-centered approaches → | | Employs *learner-centered* approaches |
		Lower level of transitioning	**Higher level of transitioning**	
Terms	Rarely/infrequently/none or not at all	Few/minimally/limited	Some (somewhat, sometimes)/Partially	Routinely/consistently/throughout/most
Frequency of this type of activity throughout course	Used <10% of the time	Used 10 to 44% of the time	Used 45 to 79% of the time	Used >80% of the time
Example using the interaction component referred to in Table 2.3.	Instructor demonstrates how to do problem sets in class before or after students work on similar problems.	Students hand in solutions to three problem sets solved as homework. Instructor grades solutions and provides some feedback. Students work individually.	Students hand in solutions to problems they solved as homework. Instructor provides feedback on their solutions and encourages them to talk one-to-one with the instructor. Students work together on solutions 50% of the time and work individually on 50% of the assignments.	Throughout the course, the students work in small groups to solve problems based upon content. Instructor circulates among the groups, answers questions, and asks probing questions. Occasionally the instructor calls students together for a mini-demonstration or explanation. There are no other lectures.

Instructor rubric, provides an example of quantitative gradations, using the terms *no, a few, some,* and *routinely* to indicate the level to which an instructor employs learner-centered approaches in activities that involve student/instructor/content interactions.

Where you place your ratings along the continuum is a subjective judgment, depending on the specifics of the course. Table 2.4 offers a rough guide to the meaning of these quantitative gradations.

Qualitative gradations. For some components, the levels differ qualitatively. Table 2.5, depicting Component 5 of the Purposes and Processes of

TABLE 2.5

Example of Qualitative Gradations on a Rubric.

The Purposes and Processes of Assessment

| Component | Employs *instructor-centered* approaches → | → Transitioning to learner-centered approaches → | | Employs *learner-centered* approaches |
		Lower level of transitioning	Higher level of transitioning	
5. Justification of the accuracy of answers	Instructor • Determines accuracy of answers *and* • Does not allow students to ask why they got answers wrong	Instructor allows students to ask why they got answers wrong.	Instructor allows students to justify their answers when they do not agree with those of instructor.	Instructor encourages students to justify their answers when they do not agree with those of instructor.

Assessment rubric, shows an example. For qualitative gradations, the focus is on different types of instructor behaviors or different ways the instructor help students learn. For example, at the instructor-centered level, the teacher's opinion about correct answers is unquestioned. At the lower level of transitioning, the instructor allows students to ask why an answer is marked incorrect, but does not give credit for other answers. With the higher level of transitioning, the instructor might allow students to write justifications for answers the instructor marked as wrong and give the students credit for reasonable justifications. With the learner-centered approach, an instructor might give students a blank piece of paper to use in conjunction with multiple-choice tests, encourage them to write justifications for some of their answers, and give them credit for a reasonable justification when an answer differs from the one the instructor chose as correct.

Gradations involving subcriteria. For some components of some rubrics, the students' attainment of increasing number of specific skills equals the gradation level. A course is considered learner-centered on those components when the instructor helps students become proficient in all of the skills, at a higher or lower level of transitioning when the instructor helps them acquire only some of the skills, and instructor-centered when the instructor helps them acquire none of the skills. The subcriteria or skills are not a hierarchy.

Table 2.6, depicting Component 6 from the Responsibility for Learning rubric, shows subcriteria. As you can see, in an instructor-centered course,

---

TABLE 2.6

Example of Gradations Involving Subcriteria on a Rubric.

The Responsibility for Learning

Component	Employs *instructor-centered* approaches →	→ Transitioning to learner-centered approaches →		Employs *learner-centered* approaches
		Lower level of transitioning	**Higher level of transitioning**	
6. Information literacy skills: a. Framing questions b. Accessing sources c. Evaluating sources d. Evaluating content e. Using information legally (as defined by the Association of College and Research Libraries)	Instructor does not help students acquire information literacy skills.	Instructor helps students acquire two of the five information literacy skills.	Instructor helps students acquire four of the five information literacy skills.	Instructor facilitates students to become proficient in all five information literacy skills.

---

the instructor does not help students acquire any of the five information literacy skills. At the lower or higher level of transitioning, the instructor helps students become proficient at only some of these skills. In a learner-centered course, the instructor helps students become proficient in all five of these information literacy skills.

Instructors may emphasize different information literacy skills in different courses, depending on the learning goals. Table 2.7 depicts how occupational therapy instructors planned a curriculum so that their students develop these skills at different points (Kramer, Ideishi, Kearney, Cohen, Ames, Shea, et al., 2007). Once the students have developed these skills, they should continue using them correctly. Students participate in two years of general education first (referred to here as Y 1–2) and then three years of professional education (referred to here as Y 3–5).

Table 2.8 shows that the instructors in this curriculum expect the students to be at different levels in their development of information literacy skills depending on their year of the program. General education courses

TABLE 2.7

Where Students Learn and Use Information Literacy Skills in an Occupational Therapy Curriculum.

Information Literacy Skills	Framing questions in a researchable way	Accessing appropriate sources	Evaluating sources consulted	Evaluating information	Using information legally, including proper citations and paraphrasing
Where in the curriculum the students learn this skill	Y1, 2 through Y4 Comment: How the question is asked gets more refined.	Y3 Comment: They learn about professional occupational therapy resources.	Y4 Comment: They learn criteria for evaluating sources.	Y4, Y5 Comment: They learn how to evaluate clinical references in relation to specific cases.	Y1, Y2 through Y3 Comment: They learn how to paraphrase properly, how to use citations properly.

TABLE 2.8

The Development and Use of Information Literacy Skills During an Occupational Therapy Curriculum.

The Responsibility for Learning

Component	Employs *instructor-centered* approaches →	→ Transitioning to learner-centered approaches →		Employs *learner-centered* approaches
		Lower level of transitioning	Higher level of transitioning	
6. Information literacy skills (framing questions, accessing and evaluating sources, evaluating content, using information legally as defined by the Association of College and Research Libraries)	Instructor does not help students acquire information literacy skills.	Instructor helps students acquire two of the five information literacy skills.	Instructor helps students acquire four of the five information literacy skills.	Instructor facilitates students to become proficient in all five information literacy skills.
Where students are expected to acquire and use these skills		Y1, Y2, Y3		Y4, Y5

are at the lower level of transitioning because students should be proficient in two out of the five information literacy skills. Although students in the first professional year should be proficient in three of these skills, they are still in the lower level of transitioning, as they do not yet have proficiency in four out five skills required for the higher level of transitioning. Courses in the final two years of the professional program are at the learner-centered level because the students should be proficient in all five information literacy skills.

Guidelines for Using the Rubrics

When you use the rubrics to evaluate the current level of your courses, keep the following in mind:

- Courses can be at many different levels within each dimension of learner-centered teaching.

- On each rubric, consider each component (each horizontal row) separately as you think about how you teach this course. Read across the entire line before making a decision on which level is appropriate.

- For the components that have bulleted points embedded within a row, consider each point separately.

- As you go through the components, ask yourself how you employ each specific component or whether it is absent in your teaching. Try to think of an example of the way you implement the component and think about why you believe the course is at a certain level for that component.

  - For the components with quantitative gradations, decide how often you employ this technique, then mark the appropriate level.

  - For the components with qualitative gradations, think about which level most accurately describes the way in which you employ the component.

- For each specific component, circle or check the appropriate level on that horizontal row.

- Do not assign an overall score within each dimension or across the dimensions. Do not count the number of learner-centered or instructor-centered characteristics that your course has.

- Even as a learner-centered instructor, you should not expect all of your courses to be at the highest level on every component of all dimensions. Factors that influence the learner-centeredness of a course include the level of the students, the size and organization of the class, and the content itself. Chapter Nine discusses the ways in which these criteria influence the components for each dimension.

Chapter Summary

This chapter explained how to read and understand the formats of the rubrics relating to the five learner-centered dimensions. Each dimension contains four to seven separate components—the horizontal rows of the rubrics. Each rubric identifies four incremental levels, from instructor-centered to learner-centered. This chapter explained how you should assign a rating on a row of the rubrics.

APPLICATION ACTIVITY

Before you proceed to the next chapter, in which you will read about ways to plan for change, complete this application activity to make sure you understand how to assign levels within rows or components of the rubric.

Comprehension check. Here is the scenario: The instructor of a writing intensive course tells her students how long it will take her to grade each essay and return it with comments. Given this instructor's knowledge of how long it takes her to grade each essay and how many essays she has to grade, she is generally able to return the essays according to this announced schedule.

In the rubric excerpt shown in Table 2.9, assign the appropriate level for this course on Component 6, "Timeframe for feedback" of the Purposes and Processes of Assessment dimension.

TABLE 2.9

Comprehension Check on the Rubrics.

The Purposes and Processes of Assessment

| Component | Employs *instructor-centered* approaches → | → Transitioning to learner-centered approaches → | | Employs *learner-centered* approaches |
		Lower level of transitioning	Higher level of transitioning	
6. Timeframe for feedback	Instructor does not provide a timeframe for feedback. *or* Instructor does not return tests or does not grade assignments.	Instructor • Provides a timeframe for feedback, without seeking students' input *and* • Usually follows the timeframe for providing feedback	Instructor • Provides a timeframe for feedback, with students' input *and* • Usually follows the timeframe for providing feedback.	Instructor and students • Mutually agree on a timeframe for feedback *and* • Always follow the timeframe for providing feedback

(Continued)

Suggested level. I would place this course at the lower level of transitioning because the instructor establishes the timeframe for feedback and usually follows it. The difference between the two levels of transitioning is whether the instructor seeks students' input. If she were to discuss the timeframe for feedback with the students and ask them if that timeframe is appropriate, the course would be at the higher level of transitioning on this component. In a learner-centered approach, the instructor and the students would mutually agree on the timetable for getting feedback. The instructor would explain that one of the reasons it is important for the students to agree on the timeframe for feedback is that they should incorporate the instructor's feedback into their next essay. Thus this feedback timeframe also influences the dates when their assignments are due.

Applying the Comprehension Check to Your Own Course

In the purposes and processes of assessment rubric excerpt shown in Table 2.9, rate the appropriate level of your course on Component 6, "Timeframe for feedback." Use Table 2.9 to rate your own course as well. Circle the appropriate level or mark it with an X.

Please explain why you selected this level.

Chapter 3

Tools for Facilitating Change and Assessment

YOU CAN USE the rubrics for self-assessment and as an assessment tool for others to see. As a self-assessment tool, you can use them to identify the learner-centered status of your courses as you begin a change processes, or to measure your progress over time toward becoming a learner-centered instructor. You can use the rubrics as part of a larger assessment of educational programs or of your teaching that you will share with others. Depending on your intended use, you will complete one of two additional forms. The first is the Planning for Transformation exercise—a worksheet that will help you decide where and how to begin the course transformation process. The second is the Documentation to Support the Selected Status form, used for sharing your rubric assessments with others. This chapter describes these forms and shows a completed version of each for the Pharmacy Management course discussed in Chapter One.

Using the Rubrics to Begin the Transformation Process

When you use the rubrics to evaluate the current level of your courses to identify starting points for change, keep the following in mind:

- These ratings are self-assessments or perceptions. You do not need to ask your peers or students to rate your course.

- In some cases, an entire component may not appear to be relevant. Instead of rejecting this component outright, however, consider the criteria and identify the reasons it is not appropriate for your course. This decision-making process may help you see this course differently or think about potential areas of transformation.

Selecting Components You Will Transform

Once you identify the status of your course by completing the five rubrics, you can begin to think about how you could transform it to become more learner-centered. Start the transformation process gradually, by selecting two or three components you would like to transform so that they become more learner-centered. The goal is *not* to transform your course to be learner-centered on all components on every dimension.

The components you choose to transform can be in the same dimension or in separate dimensions of learner-centered teaching. Consider your choices carefully, however, because the future direction of your course depends on which components you pick to transform. For example, the instructor in the case study in Chapter One wanted only to make his assessments more relevant to his students' careers. Yet because of this decision, he ended up totally transforming his course. In an attempt to engage students more actively in their own learning, you could end up changing how you spend most of your class time, from lectures to small-group activities.

Your philosophy of teaching, the nature of the course, the culture of your department and your institution, and the requirements of your students' educational programs will influence your selection of components to transform. For example, the culture of your department or your institution may make implementing some learner-centered approaches easier than attempting other practices.

There are many possible ways to select components to think about changing. One way is to list the ideas that occur to you as you complete the rubrics. You might list the components that made you think, "I never thought about it before, but I could do that." Next, consider the overall weaknesses that you and other instructors collectively notice about students in your educational programs. Could you help the students overcome these weaknesses by using more learner-centered approaches? Also, consider what components you would feel more comfortable changing and which changes you think your students are more likely to accept. On the other hand, if you really want to transform your course to be more learner-centered, choose components that are not a natural or easy choice. As a challenge, as you work through this book, you might consider components that are a stretch for you, the way instructors in your discipline usually teach, or use a different philosophy of teaching.

After you identify the components you want to change, you will plan how to transform them using the Planning for Transformation exercise described in the next section of this chapter.

Using the Planning for Transformation Exercise

The Planning for Transformation exercise provides an organized way to think about how to begin transforming your course. Once you have answered the questions on the planning exercise, you will have a document to guide you through the change process.

The exercise has five sections:

- In the first, you will describe the status of the component you want to change and its present level.

- In the second, you will describe your planned changes.

- The third section, perhaps the most important, asks a series of tactical questions. Answering these questions completely will improve your chances of a successful change.

- In the fourth section, you will consider the outcomes of your change.

- Finally, because transforming a course can be an incremental and iterative process, the fifth section asks you to think about your plans beyond this cycle of transformation.

A note of caution: the Planning for Transformation exercise appears simple. Many of the questions, however, require a great deal of thought, and the more attention you give to your answers, the more successful your transformation process is likely to be. As you begin transforming your course, you can return to your answers on the exercise to ensure that you have considered all the aspects that you need to address. Then, once you have implemented your changes, you can review the form to determine whether you have achieved your desired changes.

Exhibit 3.1 presents the Planning for Transformation exercise form. I include a completed exercise form in this chapter (see Exhibit 3.2) to help you see how you can use the form and how much detail you might include. You will have opportunities to complete the Planning for Transformation exercise for the components you want to transform in the next section of the book.

Using the Rubrics in a Formal Assessment

Many institutions of higher learning and educational programs claim that they are learner- or learning-centered. Because accountability is an important goal in higher education, we need ways to show that we are doing what we say we are doing. The rubrics for the five dimensions of learner-centered teaching can be an assessment tool to show the learner-centered status of our institutions or our educational programs. Individual instructors can show that they are teaching in a learner-centered manner with the rubrics. We can use the rubrics to show a snapshot of our current implementation of learner-centered teaching. Alternatively, we might use these

EXHIBIT 3.1

The Planning for Transformation Exercise

Date _____

A. Status of your course now

  1. Dimension of learner-centered teaching:

  2. Component:

  3. Current level:

     ❏ Instructor-centered

     ❏ Lower level of transitioning

     ❏ Higher level of transitioning

     ❏ Learner-centered

  4. Briefly describe your current implementation (to document your baseline prior to transformation).

B. Desired changes:

  1. Describe the desired changes you wish to make for this component in the near future.

  2. What is the level you want to achieve with this/these changes?

     ❏ Instructor-centered

     ❏ Lower level of transitioning

     ❏ Higher level of transitioning

     ❏ Learner-centered

C. Tactical planning questions:

  1. What do you need to do, decide, or learn about prior to making changes?

  2. What obstacles or challenges do you need to overcome to implement this change successfully? (Resistance may come from your philosophy of teaching, your chair, your peers, your students, or the culture of your institution.)

  3. Identify specific strategies (such as learning about successful implementations, trying a small pilot implementation, explaining to your students and other instructors why you are making these changes) for overcoming each obstacle or challenge.

(Continued)

4. What resources (such as time, money, student assistants, or computer software) would help you implement your change?

5. What do you need to do to get your students to accept this change? (Possibilities include repeated explanations for why you are doing what you are doing or having the activity count in the final grade.)

D. Outcomes of the change:

1. In what ways will implementing this change influence other aspects of your course to be more learner-centered? (For example, when you incorporate various teaching or learning methods that are consistent with your student learning goals [Component 3 of the Role of the Instructor dimension], most likely the students will more actively engage in the content [Component 2 of the Function of Content dimension].)

2. In what ways (such as increased learning) will your students benefit from this change? How will the students behave differently (such as increased participation in class or greater engagement with the content)?

3. In what ways will you benefit from this change? (For example, more enjoyment of teaching, more satisfaction that your students are learning more, anticipation of fewer student complaints.)

E. Possible future changes:

1. What is the optimal level for this component for this course?
    ❑ Instructor-centered
    ❑ Lower level of transitioning
    ❑ Higher level of transitioning
    ❑ Learner-centered

2. In the long term, what additional changes, if any, might you make to further transform this component to reach this optimal level of the learner-centered approach?

EXHIBIT 3.2

The Planning for Transformation Exercise for the Pharmacy Management Course Described in Chapter One

Date: Spring 2002

A. Status of your course now

   1. Dimension of learner-centered teaching: *Purposes and Processes of Assessment*

   2. Component: *4. Authentic assessment (what practitioners/professionals do)*

   3. Current level:

      ☑ Instructor-centered

      ❏ Lower level of transitioning

      ❏ Higher level of transitioning

      ❏ Learner-centered

   4. Briefly describe your current implementation (to document your baseline prior to transformation).

      I use two multiple-choice examinations that do not reflect how my students will use this information in their practice. This is the opposite of authentic assessment.

B. Desired changes:

   1. Describe the desired changes you wish to make for this component in the near future.

      a. I would like to eliminate the use of multiple-choice exams and allow the students to begin to make judgments about people and process relevant to contemporary pharmacy practice. To do this, I need to change the form of assessment that would allow me to see how the students make decisions and what their reactions are to given situations, and I need to determine how they might proceed in resolving real-life problems in pharmacy. When I eliminate the multiple-choice exams, I will be using more authentic assessments as well as authentic learning opportunities.

      b. I will also need to use groups to allow students to interact as a management team and make decisions in that type of environment.

   2. What is the level you want to achieve with this/these changes?

      ❏ Instructor-centered

      ❏ Lower level of transitioning

      ❏ Higher level of transitioning

      ☑ Learner-centered

(Continued)

C. Tactical planning questions:

1. What do you need to do, decide, or learn about prior to making changes?

    a. I need to determine the types of decisions pharmacists need to make in real life, such as about personnel, product, and mode of drug distribution. I also need to see if these types of decisions are consistent among dimensions, such as community pharmacy, hospital pharmacy, and in the pharmaceutical industry and drug companies.

    b. My decision to include authentic assessment led me to conclude that I need to incorporate more authentic learning opportunities so that the students can practice these same skills. I will need to rethink some of the classes so that students can practice these skills prior to the assessments.

    c. I need to plan more group activities.

2. What obstacles or challenges do you need to overcome to successfully implement this change? (Resistance may come from your philosophy of teaching, your chair, your peers, your students, or the culture of your institution.)

    One of the primary obstacles is how my colleagues will react to a no-exam course. Explaining the grading system to the students will also be a challenge.

    Last, the workload associated with evaluating these assessments.

3. Identify specific strategies (such as learning about successful implementations, trying a small pilot implementation, explaining to your students and other instructors why you are making these changes) for overcoming each obstacle or challenge.

    a. Regarding the instructor resistance, I will be working with key instructors, as identified with my chair, to educate them on the change and the rationale for it. This will help to allay any fears that I am making this an "easy" course.

    b. With the students, I will dedicate time in the beginning of class to review the grading scheme, and just before midpoint I will give them a printout of their progress and again review the scheme. I will also make myself available, in person and via e-mail, to students who have questions.

    c. Last, I will engage some graduate student instructors to help with the grading, and student workers and secretaries to manage the paperwork itself.

4. What resources (such as time, money, student assistants, or computer software) would help you implement your change?

    I will need two or three hours per week of secretarial (or student worker) help to manage the paperwork. In addition, I will need four to six hours of graduate student instructors' help every ten days to help grade the assessments.

5. What do you need to do to get your students to accept this change? (Possibilities include repeated explanations for why you are doing what you are doing and having the activity count in the final grade.)

(Continued)

I will explain to the students that management does not occur in isolation and that much of it occurs from group input and decision making. However, to be an effective decision maker, one must have the information on hand before the meeting. This is why completing the assignments before the group activity is important. Further, both the individual performance and the group performance count in the final grade.

D. Outcomes of the change:

1. In what ways will implementing this change influence other aspects of your course to be more learner-centered? (For example, when you incorporate various teaching and learning methods that are consistent with your student learning goals [Component 3 of the Role of the Instructor dimension], most likely the students will more actively engage in the content [Component 2 in the Function of Content dimension].)

    By putting the responsibility on students' completing work before group activities (rather than cramming for an exam), I will enhance the first two components of the Responsibility for Learning dimension—that is, responsibility for learning and learning-to-learn skills.

2. In what ways (such as increased learning) will your students benefit from this change? How will the students behave differently (such as increased participation in class or greater engagement with the content)?

    I expect that students will have a greater level of class participation (and attendance) and be more interested in the learning the subject matter if they see why they need to learn it.

3. In what ways will you benefit from this change? (For example, more enjoyment of teaching, satisfaction that your students are learning more, anticipation of fewer student complaints.)

    I will get fewer complaints over grades and unfair test questions and more interaction with the students. I hope that through making the changes I will be able to make a large class feel like a small one.

E. Possible future changes:

1. What is the optimal level for this component for this course?

    ❏ Lower level of transitioning

    ❏ Higher level of transitioning

    ☑ Learner-centered

2. In the long term, what additional changes, if any, might you make to further transform this component to reach this optimal level of the learner-centered approach?

    Eliminating examinations forces me to rethink the entire course. The use of authentic assessments will occur in class as well as in assignments. Therefore, students will engage in different types of learning activities in class.

    Once I decided to use authentic assessment and team activities, I realized that I could eliminate most of the lectures. Students in teams can discuss the content that I usually cover in a lecture.

rubrics in a pre- and post-intervention of changes. If you are sharing these rubrics with others for individual or program assessment purposes, you will need to provide supporting evidence, such as through examples or explanations of your rationale, to justify your judgments. The Documentation to Support the Selected Status form (see Exhibit 3.3) gives you the vehicle to show why you made these decisions.

Using Rubrics to Determine the Status of Educational Programs

You might do this assessment as part of an accreditation self-study or as the assessment for an educational intervention grant. If you were assessing the impact of an educational intervention to teach instructors about learner-centered approaches, you would use these rubrics as a baseline before a curriculum change project, then again to measure changes made after the in-service activities. Instructors can use the rubrics to communicate how their approaches to teaching led to a culture of learner-centered teaching. If all instructors completed the rubrics for the courses in an educational program, you could summarize the overall status of these courses by counting the number of courses at each level on each component. You could show the total number of courses at each level of each component or you could show the range on each of the levels for courses in the educational program. You could look at the learner-centeredness by level in the curriculum. For example, you might show that lower-level courses are at a lower level of learner-centeredness whereas more advanced courses use more learner-centered approaches, as is the case in Table 2.8. The second model, described in Chapter Nine, is a summary of the learner-centered status for another dimension of this educational program. You would use the Documentation to Support the Selected Status form to complete this assessment.

Using Rubrics as an Assessment Tool for Teaching Dossiers

Individual instructors can use the rubrics to document how their teaching has evolved as they incorporate more learner-centered practices. You could include a copy of the rubrics along with your student evaluation of your teaching. These rubrics could be placed in teaching dossiers for promotion or when applying for new positions. Here again you would include examples as evidence to support your claims about the status of your teaching.

Supporting Your Rubrics Determinations

You show your rationale of your selection on the rubrics and supporting examples on the Documentation to Support the Selected Status form. Include enough detail so that other people who are not familiar with your course will understand what you and your students do. You might want to include some further supporting evidence such as statements from your syllabus, or learning assignments or activities or products that the students develop. These might be included as an appendix to this form. Exhibit 3.3 shows the Documentation to Support the Selected Status form. You will complete this form if you are doing an assessment for the purposes of educational program evaluation, or as part of a teaching dossier. Refer to the rubrics as you complete the form. (If you are completing the rubrics for the purposes of beginning to transform your teaching, you can skip this form.)

To increase the reliability of ratings, two people can independently rate the same course. You can do this in one of several ways. A peer who is familiar with your course can review the course materials that you use and ask you clarification questions when necessary. Then that person can use the rubrics to determine, independently, the learner-centered status of your course. You and your colleague can compare the ratings and reach a consensus on the appropriate level. The other way you can add to the reliability of your rubric ratings is to have another instructor review the examples and rationale that you provide on the Documentation to Support the Selected Status form. That person can determine whether your ratings are appropriate. The two of you can discuss any differences in rating and together revise the rating on the rubrics.

The development process for the rubrics gives them face validity. First, I chose components and the levels within the rubrics based on the literature on learner-centered teaching. Next, a total of over 250 faculty developers and instructors, in many different disciplines and teaching at all levels in higher education, offered feedback and validation. This cycle of feedback and corrections validated the components and the rubrics.

Exhibit 3.4 shows how the instructor of the pharmacy management course described in Chapter One completed the Documentation to Support the Selected Status form.

EXHIBIT 3.3

The Documentation to Support the Selected Status Form

Name: Date:

What are you assessing?

Course Name(s) _____

Educational Program Name_____

Other_____

Purpose of this assessment:

Note: Because this form is the same for all components, I include, as a sample, the beginning of the form for the components for the Function of Content dimension of learner-centered teaching here. Appendix B contains the complete form for all components for all dimensions.

The Function of Content

Component 1. *Varied uses of content*

In addition to building a knowledge base, instructor uses content to help students: know why they need to learn content, acquire discipline-specific learning methodologies such as how to read primary source material, use inquiry or ways of thinking in the discipline, learn to solve real-world problems.

Current level:

❑ Instructor-centered

❑ Lower level of transitioning

❑ Higher level of transitioning

❑ Learner-centered

Rationale for or example to support level chosen:

(Continued)

Component 2. Level to which students engage in content

Current level:

    ❏ Instructor-centered

    ❏ Lower level of transitioning

    ❏ Higher level of transitioning

    ❏ Learner-centered

    Rationale for or example to support level chosen:

Component 3. Use of organizing schemes

Current level:

    ❏ Instructor-centered

    ❏ Lower level of transitioning

    ❏ Higher level of transitioning

    ❏ Learner-centered

    Rationale for or example to support level chosen:

Component 4. Use of content to facilitate future learning

Current level:

    ❏ Instructor-centered

    ❏ Lower level of transitioning

    ❏ Higher level of transitioning

    ❏ Learner-centered

    Rationale for or example to support level chosen:

EXHIBIT 3.4

The Documentation to Support the Selected Status Form for the Pharmacy Management Course

Name: *Andrew Peterson*   Date: *December 11, 2007*

What are you assessing?

Course Name(s) *Pharmacy Systems Management*

_____

Educational Program Name_____

Other_____

Purpose of this assessment:

To document my progress toward becoming a learner-centered teacher after I changed my course. This is a post-intervention assessment.

The Function of Content

Component 1. *Varied uses of content*

In addition to building a knowledge base, instructor uses content to help students know why they need to learn content, acquire discipline-specific learning methodologies such as how to read primary source material, use inquiry, or ways of thinking in the discipline, learn to solve real-world problems.

Current level:

❏ Instructor-centered

❏ Lower level of transitioning

☑ Higher level of transitioning

❏ Learner-centered

Rationale for or example to support level chosen:

I explain why students need to learn the content and then they use the content within the context of different types of pharmacy practice. I introduce them to the broader context of pharmacy practice and show them how this content is relevant and how it is used. Students use discipline-specific inquiry skills to solve real-world problems such as used in the recruitment process for employees or resolving personnel conflicts.

I do not assist the students to develop discipline-specific learning methodologies such as how to read primary source material. I assume that my students already know how to read primary source material as they are in their second year of professional education.

Component 2. *Level to which students engage in content*

Current level:

❏ Instructor-centered

❏ Lower level of transitioning

❏ Higher level of transitioning

☑ Learner-centered

(Continued)

Rationale for or example to support level chosen:

The students use active learning strategies consistently throughout the course. Students come to class prepared, having already done assignments, and then use the material in class to learn more. They engage with each other and the content consistently throughout the class.

Component 3. Use of organizing schemes

Current level:

❑ Instructor-centered

❑ Lower level of transitioning

❑ Higher level of transitioning

☑ Learner-centered

Rationale for or example to support level chosen:

I divide the course into three modules of personnel management, product management, and drug use/policy. I talk about these modules on the first day of class and discuss them as we move from one module to the next. I see these three topics as organizing schemes for this course, but the students probably do not realize this. I do not incorporate them actively as ways to organize their learning.

Component 4. Use of content to facilitate future learning

Current level:

☑ Instructor-centered

❑ Lower level of transitioning

❑ Higher level of transitioning

❑ Learner-centered

Rationale for or example to support level chosen:

As we cover material, I help them to see that there are many other possibilities and things to learn. For example, we practice different models of conflict resolution. However, the students know that there are many other types of conflicts and situations. I hope the models I provide will allow them to learn how to solve conflicts in the future.

The Role of the Instructor

Component 1. Creation of an environment for learning through organization and use of material that accommodates different learning styles

Current level:

❑ Instructor-centered

❑ Lower level of transitioning

❑ Higher level of transitioning

☑ Learner-centered

(Continued)

Rationale for or example to support level chosen:

I give students many different resources to learn from, including print and electronic materials. They can learn in different ways. However, I have organized the material to make it easier to learn. My three modules also help organize the material the students need to learn. Through the different types of optional assignments that students do to earn higher grades, I accommodate different learning styles.

Component 2. *Alignment of the course components: objectives, teaching or learning methods, and assessment methods for consistency*

Current level:

❑ Instructor-centered

❑ Lower level of transitioning

❑ Higher level of transitioning

☑ Learner-centered

Rationale for or example to support level chosen:

I realized that I did not have an aligned course when I decided that I wanted to eliminate exams. My small group learning activities that also count as part of their grades bring the course into alignment. My main objective is that students develop the knowledge and skills to be managers of pharmacy practices. They practice these skills throughout the course. I embed assessments in their learning activities.

Component 3. *Teaching or learning methods appropriate for student learning goals*

Current level:

❑ Instructor-centered

❑ Lower level of transitioning

❑ Higher level of transitioning

☑ Learner-centered

Rationale for or example to support level chosen:

I plan a variety of different types of activities to meet the learning goals of being able to use abstract material related to pharmacy practice, and they need to be able to apply this information to their careers. Students work in teams, give presentations, and do practical tasks as they would in pharmacy practice.

Component 4. *Activities involving student, instructor, content interactions*

Current level:

❑ Instructor-centered

❑ Lower level of transitioning

❑ Higher level of transitioning

☑ Learner-centered

Rationale for or example to support level chosen:

Throughout the semester, the students work in small groups on activities relating to the content of the course. They present to each other on their application of the content.

(Continued)

Component 5. Articulation of SMART objectives (SMART = Specific, Measurable, Attainable, Relevant, Time-oriented)

Current level:

❏ Instructor-centered

☑ Lower level of transitioning

❏ Higher level of transitioning

❏ Learner-centered

Rationale for or example to support level chosen:

My objectives are attainable and relevant.

Some are specific and others are broad.

I am not always able to measure them. For example, it is hard to measure their ability to apply what they learned to their career.

They are not time-oriented except I expect the students to meet them by the end of the semester.

Component 6. Motivation of students to learn (intrinsic drive to learn versus extrinsic reasons to earn grades)

Current level:

❏ Instructor-centered

❏ Lower level of transitioning

❏ Higher level of transitioning

☑ Learner-centered

Rationale for or example to support level chosen:

Students have written on the course evaluation forms, "This course inspired me to learn more about management" and "I am more interested in retail pharmacy now." A few students want to specialize in managed care pharmacy after taking this course.

The Responsibility for Learning

Component 1. Responsibility for learning

Current level:

❏ Instructor-centered

❏ Lower level of transitioning

❏ Higher level of transitioning

☑ Learner-centered

(Continued)

Rationale for or example to support level chosen:

I use grading rubrics in which the standards rise during the semester, and the grading criteria also gets more complicated. The students get these rubrics in advance and I tell them that they will be taking more responsibility for their learning as the course progresses. Midway through the semester the students have to write what they need to do to improve in the class and how they are going to achieve these objectives. They realize that they need to take on more responsibilities to do well in the second half of the class.

Component 2. Learning-to-learn skills or skills for future learning

Current level:

❑ Instructor-centered

❑ Lower level of transitioning

☑ Higher level of transitioning

❑ Learner-centered

Rationale for or example to support level chosen:

I direct them to develop some learning-to-learn skills such as time management, self-monitoring, and goal setting. I do not teach them some of these skills for further learning, such as how to do independent reading in this discipline. The entire class does not develop these skills by the end of the semester.

Component 3. Self-directed, lifelong learning skills

Current level:

❑ Instructor-centered

❑ Lower level of transitioning

☑ Higher level of transitioning

❑ Learner-centered

Rationale for or example to support level chosen:

Through the self-assessments and discussions, the students realize their own abilities to learn.

I do not work with the students to develop lifelong learning skills.

Component 4. Students' self-assessment of their learning

Current level:

❑ Instructor-centered

❑ Lower level of transitioning

❑ Higher level of transitioning

☑ Learner-centered

Rationale for or example to support level chosen:

I require two large self-assessments of their learning assignments. I relate why this is an important skill to develop to the content of the course.

(Continued)

Component 5. Students' self-assessment of their strengths and weaknesses

Current level:

❏ Instructor-centered

❏ Lower level of transitioning

❏ Higher level of transitioning

☑ Learner-centered

Rationale for or example to support level chosen:

Students assess themselves and their peers on content mastery, clarity of explanations, group participation, and their presentations throughout the course.

Component 6. Information literacy skills of (a) framing questions, (b) accessing and (c) evaluating sources, (d) evaluating content, (e) using information legally

Current level:

❏ Instructor-centered

❏ Lower level of transitioning

☑ Higher level of transitioning

❏ Learner-centered

Rationale for or example to support level chosen:

I help the students learn to frame questions, evaluate the content, and use information legally and ethically.

I give them all the material they need to read, so they do not get any practice accessing sources. Students learn to evaluate sources in terms of what kinds of information they can learn from these sources. They do not evaluate whether a source is reliable or not, as I give them only reliable sources.

The Purposes and Processes of Assessment

Component 1. Assessment within the learning process

Current level:

❏ Instructor-centered

❏ Lower level of transitioning

❏ Higher level of transitioning

☑ Learner-centered

Rationale for or example to support level chosen:

All aspects of the course combine learning and assessment. For example, students work on activities in small groups that require application of the reading. I grade these assignments. There are no separate examinations.

(Continued)

Component 2. Formative assessment

Current level:

❑ Instructor-centered

❑ Lower level of transitioning

❑ Higher level of transitioning

☑ Learner-centered

Rationale for or example to support level chosen:

I give feedback continuously. I give students formative feedback through the grading rubrics on their group activities, their written assignments, and presentations. Peers give each other formative, constructive feedback on group activities and presentations.

Component 3. Peer and self-assessment

Current level:

❑ Instructor-centered

❑ Lower level of transitioning

❑ Higher level of transitioning

☑ Learner-centered

Rationale for or example to support level chosen:

Prior to the students handing in assignments for me to grade, they are encouraged to get feedback from their peers. Students assess themselves and their peers on presentations and group performance and participation.

Component 4. Demonstration of mastery and ability to learn from mistakes

Current level:

❑ Instructor-centered

❑ Lower level of transitioning

☑ Higher level of transitioning

❑ Learner-centered

Rationale for or example to support level chosen:

Students can redo the four written assignments, group activities, and the final group presentation if they do not get a good enough grade.

They cannot redo the optional assignments if they are not good enough.

(Continued)

Component 5. *Justification of the accuracy of answers*

Current level:

❑ Instructor-centered

❑ Lower level of transitioning

☑ Higher level of transitioning

❑ Learner-centered

Rationale for or example to support level chosen:

I invite students if they do not agree with my grading to discuss their perspectives with me. They can justify their answers when they do not agree with mine. I will regrade a paper if I see their perspective as correct.

Component 6. *Timeframe for feedback*

Current level:

❑ Instructor-centered

❑ Lower level of transitioning

☑ Higher level of transitioning

❑ Learner-centered

Rationale for or example to support level chosen:

I explain that they will get feedback on an assignment before they need to hand in the next assignment like the previous one. They agree to my timetable on assignments.

Although I try very hard to follow my timetable, I do not always get my papers back on time.

Component 7. *Authentic assessment*

Current level:

❑ Instructor-centered

❑ Lower level of transitioning

❑ Higher level of transitioning

☑ Learner-centered

Rationale for or example to support level chosen:

All assessments in this course are authentic. For example, the students have to choose an automation system for their type of pharmacy and justify their choice. They have to write a memo to a director of a pharmacy about a potential medical error, citing the criteria for the medication error.

(Continued)

The Balance of Power

Component 1. Determination of course content

Current level:

❏ Instructor-centered

❏ Lower level of transitioning

☑ Higher level of transitioning

❏ Learner-centered

Rationale for or example to support level chosen:

The students have choices in the type of content they learn in the optional assignments. They can explore topics that interest them in these optional assignments. They are not able to pick completely new areas to learn additional content.

Component 2. Expression of alternative perspectives

Current level:

❏ Instructor-centered

❏ Lower level of transitioning

❏ Higher level of transitioning

☑ Learner-centered

Rationale for or example to support level chosen:

In class discussions, the students can disagree with me. When that happens, I set up a point-counterpoint discussion. For example, we discuss what a profession is. Sometimes they name occupations as professions that I do not agree are professions. They need to justify their perspective and then the class as a whole makes the decision.

Component 3. Determination of how students earn grades

Current level:

❏ Instructor-centered

❏ Lower level of transitioning

❏ Higher level of transitioning

☑ Learner-centered

Rationale for or example to support level chosen:

Students determine the grade they get by the amount of optional assignments they do at a competent level. I use mastery grading for the required assignments. If they do not do a competent job, they can redo the assignment until they demonstrate mastery.

(Continued)

Component 4. Use of open-ended assignments

Current level:

❏ Instructor-centered

❏ Lower level of transitioning

❏ Higher level of transitioning

☑ Learner-centered

Rationale for or example to support level chosen:

All assignments and small group activities are open-ended.

Component 5. Flexibility of course policies, assessment methods, learning methods, and deadlines

Current level:

❏ Instructor-centered

❏ Lower level of transitioning

❏ Higher level of transitioning

☑ Learner-centered

Rationale for or example to support level chosen:

When students ask for an extension, I say if you will give me a better product later, I will take the assignment late. I also ask the students to give me feedback on the due dates, and I can adjust them if they have other big deadlines at the same time.

If a student is struggling after the first few assignments, I talk to the student to find out how I can be flexible with policies to help that student to succeed. I offer these students additional ways to earn points. Students can choose how they want to learn.

Component 6. Opportunities to learn

Current level:

❏ Instructor-centered

❏ Lower level of transitioning

❏ Higher level of transitioning

☑ Learner-centered

Rationale for or example to support level chosen:

On the student evaluations of the course and on some of the final self-assessments of their learning, students tell me that they now see the importance of coming to class prepared and participating in discussions. Some students have remarked that the course policies helped them take advantage of opportunities to learn instead of finding ways to short circuit the learning process. Since I changed the class to be more learner-centered, not one student has said to me, "Did I miss anything in class?"

Chapter Summary

This chapter discussed two different reasons to use the rubrics: as a tool to begin the change process and as a tool for use in a more formal assessment of an educational program or of teaching. The Planning for Transformation exercise provides an organized way to think about how to begin transforming a course and serves as a document to guide you through the change process. You would complete the Documentation to Support the Selected Status form as part of an educational program or personal assessment of the learner-centered status.

In the next part of the book, we will consider each of the five dimensions of learner-centered teaching in more detail and provide implementation examples.

APPLICATION ACTIVITY

Note: In this activity you will think about possible components you might want to transform later as you read the next section.

Refer to the rubrics in Appendix B to complete this activity. Using the course you chose in Chapter One for possible transformation, consider what components you might want to change. Your choices might change as you read the next section of the book.

1. Considerations for choosing the components of the five dimensions you want to change:

    a. What components of the dimensions do you would feel most comfortable changing?

    b. What components of the dimensions do you think the students will accept?

    c. Which components, if you change how you teach, would help your students to overcome weaknesses observed in many students?

    d. As you read the rubrics, especially the learner-centered explanations on the components, did you say to yourself, "I could do that, but I never thought about it before"? List those components.

(Continued)

e. If you really want to make large transformational changes that are not natural to the way you teach, list the components that are a big stretch or challenge to the way you teach now.

f. Which components, if any, did you list repeatedly in your answers to the preceding questions?

2. Answer the following questions for each component listed in question 1f, which is your tentative list of possible components to change:

a. If your course is not at the appropriate level of learner-centeredness for this component, can you transform it? Yes _____ No _____

b. Does your philosophy of teaching foster or inhibit a change with this component? Yes _____ No _____

c. Is a change with this component feasible with the type of course you are teaching? Yes _____ No _____

d. Will the culture of your department and your institution support a change in the component? Yes _____ No _____

3. Pick two or three components you would like to plan how to change based on your answers to the preceding questions. This is a tentative list. As you read the examples given in the next section, you will have a better idea of which components you will want to transform.

Possible components to transform

Dimension _____

Component _____

Dimension _____

Component _____

Dimension _____

Component _____

The Five Dimensions of Learner-Centered Teaching

Introduction to the Learner-Centered Dimensions

In Part One of this book, I explained the concept of using rubrics as a tool to evaluate the status of a course on the continuum from instructor-centered to learner-centered for the five learner-centered dimensions. Part Two will facilitate your in-depth comprehension of each dimension and show you how to transform your teaching.

Each chapter in Part Two examines one of the five dimensions in more detail and provides examples of learner-centered teaching for each component. To illustrate the process of transforming a course to be more learner-centered, throughout the next five chapters I discuss a case example of a general education course, Psychology 101, described at the end of this introduction. I will refer to this course, repeatedly.

Throughout these chapters, you can test your understanding by marking the appropriate cells on the rubrics to indicate your rating of the Psychology 101 course on the instructor-centered to learner-centered continua. Then you will read an explanation of how I rated each component of the dimension for this course in the section labeled "Analysis of the Psych 101 Course." Following my analysis of the current status of this course, the psychology instructor completed the Planning for Transformation exercise for a few components of each dimension to suggest ways she could transform this course.

Each chapter ends with an application activity or reflection questions to answer with your own course. These are intended to help you determine the current level of your course on each dimension and begin thinking about which components you want to transform. After you have completed the rubrics for all five dimensions and answered the questions on the Planning for Transformation exercise, you will have a well-developed plan for how to transform your course to be more learner-centered.

The chapters include many suggestions for ways in which you can change your courses to achieve learner-centered teaching. When transforming your own course, I recommend that you make only a few changes at a time—a few changes can have a large impact. If you want to make more substantial changes, I recommend that you rethink the course entirely rather than just adding different isolated techniques.

Suggested Process for Transformation

I suggest that you pursue the following process as you begin to transform your course. You should do the first five steps separately for each dimension of learner-centered teaching, and for the last two steps integrate your thinking from all five dimensions:

1. Understand the descriptions of the dimensions and their components. You will achieve this by reading the explanations given in these chapters.

2. Complete the application activity at the end of the chapter. Completing these questions will help you think about the status of your course and possible ways you might want to transform it.

3. Complete the rubric for each dimension of learner-centered teaching. You should identify the current status of your course for each component.

4. Decide which components you might want to transform. Refer back to the suggestions for selecting components in Chapter Three.

5. Complete the Planning for Transformation exercise only for those dimensions that you are considering changing. You may have a few components that you want to transform in one dimension, or these components may be in different dimensions. You should complete a form for every component you may want to transform.

6. Review all of your suggested changes from the Planning for Transformation exercises from the five dimension chapters. You can group them or prioritize them. Then choose a few changes you want to make.

7. Begin to change how you teach. You may want to start with a few easy-to-implement changes as you plan for changes that are more comprehensive.

Pace yourself as you read, and go through these steps slowly to avoid becoming overwhelmed by the rubrics, questions, and planning for transformation exercises. You may want to engage in these steps over several months. Remember, I am advocating for incremental changes.

Although each rubric describes four incremental levels, from an instructor-centered to a learner-centered course, you do not need to make the transition using every level. These levels help you identify the status of your course and guide you to make the transition gradually. However, you are free to skip the transitioning level or levels on a component and change your course to be learner-centered in one step.

A note about the rubrics and forms for your use in these chapters: The first chapter in this part—Chapter Four, The Function of Content—will give excerpted parts of the rubrics as you read about the components. The repetition of the excerpted parts of the rubrics should help you to learn how to interpret and use the rubrics. The later chapters in this part of the book will refer to these materials without actually including them repeatedly. Copy the rubric forms and Planning for Transformation exercise presented in Appendix B as many times as you want to actively engage with the book. You are allowed to copy these forms for your own use, provided you include the proper reference to this book.

Case Example: Psychology 101

Psych 101 is a survey, general education course. Most of the approximately one hundred students who take the class each semester are in their first or second years. The course enrolls mostly nonmajors, but it also serves as the introductory course for students wanting to major in psychology. It is a typical example of an instructor-centered course that could become more learner-centered.

This course features many common characteristics of large survey courses. Lectures and brief demonstrations emphasize the content covered in the textbook. Students also participate in small-group, active learning activities that count as part of the grade. The multiple choice, midterm, and final exam count for about 50 percent of the grade. There are frequent quizzes to keep the students current with the material.

Course Objectives

The course syllabus states,

> *Students will be able to recognize and/or describe both verbally and in the written mode:*

1. Fundamental concepts and theories that form the empirically supported knowledge base for cognition, affect, and behavior

2. The methods used by psychologists in studying both mental processes and behavior of humans and other species

3. Individual differences regarding cognition, affect, and behavior in organisms, especially the human species

The syllabus also lists transdisciplinary skills that the instructor expects the students to acquire during general education courses, such as communication skills and teamwork skill development.

Course Organization and Design

At the beginning of the semester, the instructor places study guides—one for each chapter of the text—onto an online course management system. Each study guide includes learning objectives, key concepts, and questions that the instructor requires the students to answer. Students can also access examination outlines through the online course management system.

Questions in the study guide are typically of a factual nature, such as these:

> *Describe the general process of classical conditioning as demonstrated by Pavlov's experiments.*
>
> *Define* operant conditioning *(how does it differ from classical conditioning?).*
>
> *Define* reinforcement, positive reinforcement, *negative reinforcement.*
>
> *Define* punishment.

There are also some thought questions, such as "Why do you suppose psychologists have an interest in human biology?"

The instructor generally lectures on the material that corresponds to assigned chapters in the required textbook. After each class meeting, she puts her detailed lecture notes on the online course management system for the students to access. She does not discuss the content objectives as overriding themes. Further, she does not model how to use the transdisciplinary general education skills.

Intra-teach Sessions

Eight times during the course, after the instructor has completed her lectures on the material covered in a few chapters, the students engage in Intra-teach, an active learning exercise used by instructors in various disciplines in higher education. For about thirty minutes, groups of two or three students review the content of the chapters by discussing study questions provided to them in advance. Immediately following the Intra-teach session, the students individually take a quiz requiring short written answers. All of the questions come directly from the study guide that students just discussed in the Intra-teach. There are no make-ups for missed quizzes.

Student Expectations and Course Policies

Course policies, listed in the syllabus that students receive on the first day of class, state that students must attend class regularly and be punctual, turn off all electronic gadgets in the classroom, and check the online course management system frequently for emails or announcements. The syllabus also states:

> *This course adheres to the university policies for Student Disabilities Support Services, make-up examinations, academic integrity which means no tolerance of academic dishonesty including fabrication, cheating, or plagiarism.*

> *Students are expected to read the textbook prior to the lecture. All students are encouraged to study regularly, not just before examinations, study actively, comparing, contrasting, and organizing and participate actively in class.*

Assessment of Student Learning

The following assess student learning:

- Eight short-answer quizzes (following the Intra-teach sessions) that all together count for 48 percent of the student's grade
- Two two-hour multiple-choice examinations (the midterm and the final), each consisting of forty to sixty multiple-choice questions, together counting for 52 percent of the grade

Students can earn additional points for the effectiveness of the Intra-teach sessions and for participation in all of the sessions. When students miss an Intra-teach session, they lose points.

- For each Intra-teach session, if the members of a pair or triad all receive a score of B or better on an individual quiz, each earns one effectiveness point.
- Students can earn a maximum of five participation points for taking part in all Intra-teach sessions.
- Students will lose one point for each session missed in addition to getting a zero on the quiz.

Final grades are determined using the following formula:

(0.24 × score on the midterm examination) + (0.28 × score on the final examination) + (0.48 × average quiz scores) + Effectiveness Points +/− Participation Points = Final Grade

Chapter 4

The Function of Content

THINK ABOUT THE WAY you plan your courses. If you are like most instructors, you focus on the content to be covered, and that content largely determines how you teach the course. For example, the Psych 101 instructor in the case example described in the Introduction to Part Two designed her course to follow the chapters of the textbook and then planned lectures and assignments to convey that material.

In a typical instructor-centered course, the focus is on covering the content and helping students to build a knowledge base, or use content to solve problems, or both. In fact, many instructors consider that one of their essential roles is to cover material or give students a knowledge base in the discipline. When the material in a discipline increases, instructors are likely to feel pressured to cover more material. Yet this emphasis on content coverage may not help the students understand the content, why they need to know it, and how to use it in the future.

In contrast, the learner-centered instructor helps the students engage with the content and apply the material, in addition to building a knowledge base. Learner-centered instructors help the students learn why they need to know the content, convey an appreciation of the value of content to students, and help them to learn new content in the future. They help students learn, think, and solve real problems within the discipline. Content becomes both a desired end product and a means to other desired ends, including helping students use the content to solve problems in the discipline, apply it to new situations, or make predictions of future events or consequences.

The Function of Content Components

The rubric for the Function of Content dimension, presented in Table 4.1, shows the continuum from instructor-centered to learner-centered approaches for the four main components. Courses that are in transition from instructor-centered to learner-centered have fewer of the learner-centered characteristics on each component. Instructor-centered approaches focus on building a large knowledge base, perhaps at the expense of the students' ability to use it or to engage in a meaningful way with the content.

TABLE 4.1

The Rubric for the Function of Content Dimension of Learner-Centered Teaching.

The Function of Content

Component	Employs *instructor-centered* approaches →	→ Transitioning to learner-centered approaches →		Employs *learner-centered* approaches
		Lower level of transitioning	**Higher level of transitioning**	
1. Varied uses of content In addition to building a knowledge base, instructor uses content to help students:	Instructor uses content that helps students build a knowledge base.	In addition to building a knowledge base, instructor uses content to help students:	In addition to building a knowledge base, instructor uses content to help students:	In addition to building a knowledge base, instructor uses all four subcriteria to help students in the following ways:
• Know why they need to learn content		• Recognize why they need to learn the content	• Identify why they need to learn content	• Evaluate why they need to learn content
• Acquire discipline-specific learning methodologies (such as how to read primary source material)			• Use discipline-specific learning methodologies with instructor's assistance	• Acquire discipline-specific learning methodologies
• Use inquiry or ways of thinking in the discipline			• Use inquiry or ways of thinking in the discipline with the instructor's assistance	• Practice using inquiry or ways of thinking in the discipline
• Learn to solve real-world problems	Instructor and content help students solve problems	• Apply content to solve problems with instructor's assistance	• Learn to apply content to solve real-world problems with instructor's assistance	• Learn to solve real-world problems
	or Instructor uses any one or none of the four subcriteria for uses of content	*or* Instructor uses any two of the four subcriteria for uses of content	*or* Uses any three of the four subcriteria for uses of content	

(Continued)

TABLE 4.1 (*Continued*)

The Function of Content

Component	Employs *instructor-centered* approaches →	→ Transitioning to learner-centered approaches →		Employs *learner-centered* approaches
		Lower level of transitioning	**Higher level of transitioning**	
2. Level to which students engage in content	Instructor allows students to memorize content.	Instructor provides content so students can learn material as it is given to them without transforming or reflecting on it.	Instructor assists students to transform and reflect on *some* of the content to make their own meaning out of *some* of it.	Instructor encourages students to transform and reflect on *most* of the content to make their own meaning out of it.
3. Use of organizing schemes	Students learn content without a clearly defined organizing scheme provided by instructor.	Instructor provides *limited* organizing assistance.	Instructor provides *some* organizing schemes to help students learn content.	Instructor provides and uses organizing schemes to help students learn content.
4. Use of content to facilitate future learning	Instructor provides content so students can learn it in isolation, without providing opportunities for them to apply knowledge to new content.	Instructor provides students with limited opportunities to apply knowledge to new content.	Instructor frames content so students can see how it can be applied in the future.	Instructor frames and organizes content so students can learn additional content that is not taught.

Component 1: Varied Uses of Content

Look across the third row of Table 4.1, "1. Varied uses of content," for the levels of transitioning for this component. Note the four subcomponents, which describe additional functions of content beyond knowledge or skills acquisition. Students often fail to grasp the additional functions of content because they spend so much time concentrating on building a strong knowledge base. Perhaps some of the problem rests with the instructors. To help students grasp these additional functions of content, instructors need to teach explicitly using these other functions.

At the learner-centered level of this component, the instructor uses content to help students to acquire and use all four of these additional functions of content. The two transitioning levels and the instructor-centered level offer some flexibility in terms of which of the four components the instructor uses. If the instructor employs three out of the four subcomponents, this would be rated at the higher level of transitioning; two out of four would mean that the course was at the lower level of transitioning; use of one or none of the four would place it at the instructor-centered level.

Let us look more closely at each of the subcomponents of Component 1.

- *Know why they need to learn content.* How many times have we heard our students complain, "Why do I have to take this course? I want to be a _____." For example, at my university, the pharmacy majors wonder why they need to learn biology, chemistry, and English composition. First, the two science disciplines are the building blocks for study in their own intended major. And second, as instructors, we know that all of our students need to be able to write clearly. The problem is that we do not convey this appreciation of the value of content to our students. This lack of understanding of why content should be learned is especially common in general education courses, as evidenced by the comments made by first-year students at my university. This concern continues beyond general education. Once the instructor of the pharmacy management course described in Chapter One changed how he taught the course, his students gained an appreciation for the value of content in the course. Previously they had questioned why they needed to learn the content.

Students fail to understand why they need to take advanced courses that are outside their major's department. For example, instructors who plan curricula for chemistry majors require that they take several advanced mathematics courses. The students may not see the value in these courses, yet chemists often use advanced mathematics to solve problems in their own discipline. Students may not be able to transfer what they learned in one discipline to another unless the connections are clear and explicit, because chemistry, physics, and engineering students rarely take courses taught by mathematicians that focus on the relevance of the mathematics to their own discipline. Box 4.1. describes how a mathematician teaches advanced chemistry students how to solve chemistry problems using higher-level mathematics.

Box 4.1. Learner-Centered Example of Know Why They Need to Learn Content

Lia Vas teaches an advanced mathematics course for chemistry majors (Vas, 2005). This elective course for chemistry students helps students learn to apply mathematics to chemistry. The mathematics instructor teaches the content using a unifying theme that helps the students understand why they need to learn this material. The unifying theme is that it is easier to solve problems in one discipline by translating them into a different discipline, solving them in the other discipline, and then translating the solution back into the original setting and discipline. The presentation of complex mathematical concepts through concrete examples and applications in chemistry stimulates students' interest in learning the concepts. The context helps the students master the concepts and see how they can use mathematics to solve chemistry problems.

Note: There are subtle distinctions in how the instructor uses the "know why they need to learn" content. At the learner-centered level, instructors assist students to evaluate why they need to learn content. At the higher level of transitioning, the instructor helps the students identify why they need to learn the content, and at the lower level of transitioning, the instructor helps the students recognize why they need to learn the content.

- *Acquire discipline-specific learning methodologies, such as how to read primary source material.* As a learner-centered instructor, you explicitly assist students to acquire the learning skills that are necessary to learn more of this discipline in the future. Some of these learning skills are reading, writing, and speaking appropriately in the discipline. Depending on the level and type of the course, the specific learning skills vary. For example, in introductory courses you may need to show your students explicitly how to read textbooks, especially how to read the figures and tables or how to cite sources accurately. In more advanced courses, you may need to discuss how to read the primary literature in the discipline. Box 4.2. shows an example of how you can teach students to read the primary literature in the social, natural, and clinical sciences.

- *Use inquiry or ways of thinking in the discipline.* As we know, scientists think differently from historians. Students, especially novices, do not recognize these ways of using inquiry or thinking in specific disciplines. Their lack of understanding of the ways in which experts in specific disciplines use evidence or construct arguments can lead to a lack of understanding of the content; therefore instructors need to help students practice using inquiry or ways of thinking in our disciplines. One method of doing that is to give them problem-solving exercises

---

Box 4.2. Learner-Centered Example of Acquire Discipline-Specific Learning Methodologies

Jeanette McVeigh (2005) developed an online assignment to teach students in the natural, clinical, and social sciences how to read the primary literature in these disciplines. The instructor downloaded the actual text of sections of journal articles as a PDF file for students to read, developed commentary about the selections, and placed this commentary together with links to the relevant sections of the articles on an online course management system. She also prepared questions for students, to ensure that they met the objectives of finding information in appropriate places in a scientific article.

The students read the assignment online, click on the appropriate sections of the article as they go through the assignment, and answer the instructor's questions. The questions help students to reflect on the importance of the structure of the articles and to learn where they can find specific information such as previous literature or implications for future research.

Box 4.3. Learner-Centered Example of Use Inquiry or Ways of Thinking in the Discipline

In their general chemistry course, Madhu Mahalingam, Frederick Schaefer, and Elisabeth Morlino (2006) use small-group problem-solving exercises during recitations to develop the students' problem-solving and inquiry skills. Instead of using the usual format for recitation classes, in which instructors answer questions or go over problems, these chemistry instructors changed all of the recitation classes into group problem-solving sessions. These activities develop problem-solving skills in chemistry, improve understanding of concepts introduced in the lecture, give students opportunities to use inquiry in chemistry, and enable students to develop skills to communicate scientifically among themselves. The instructors developed problem-solving exercises that promote discussion within the groups or require predictions. Since the instructors introduced these group problem-solving sessions, the number of students failing or just passing has gone down.

---

that help develop inquiry skills. Box 4.3 describes how instructors in a general chemistry course give students opportunities to use inquiry in chemistry.

- *Learn to solve real-world problems.* One characteristic that distinguishes novices from experts is that experts use content to solve real problems. Novices seldom do this. Because of the importance of learning to solve problems in a discipline, it is likely that problem solving will be one of the subcomponents that an instructor employs. Therefore the rubric shows the application of content to solve real problems in the discipline on all levels. Note that there are subtle distinctions in how the instructor uses problem solving at the four levels. Moreover, it is not an essential characteristic of the two transitioning levels or at the instructor-centered level.

Box 4.4. Learner-Centered Example of Learn to Solve Real-World Problems

Philip Gehrman (2006) uses service-learning to help his students apply what they learned in his course to meet a real community need. The content focuses on the theories of how people change their behaviors and reduce their risk of diseases. For example, a common behavioral change targeted in these theories is quitting smoking.

Gehrman's students developed a health promotion campaign for children based on theories of health and behavior change that they studied in the class. Combining the content of his class with what they learned in developmental psychology, students conducted the campaign, which focused on nutrition and exercise, at an alternative inner city school that had no health curriculum. The campaign had to be appropriate to the local conditions in the neighborhood of the elementary school. For example, the college students developed an exercise program that students could do at local playgrounds rather than at private fitness clubs.

Instructors can require students to solve real problems within the context of a course. The instructor can use case vignettes or simulations, or the students can go beyond the classroom or laboratory to solve actual problems confronting agencies or corporations. Often students engage in these experiences through fieldwork, practicum, or internships. One way students can solve real-world problems in the context of a course is through service-learning. Service-learning is course-embedded work, done to benefit the community, that uses the content from the course. When students engage in service-learning, they apply the content from the course to solve real-world problems in the community. Box 4.4 discusses the service-learning part of a psychology course in which students apply theories to develop a health promotion campaign for elementary school students.

Component 2: Level to Which Students Engage in Content

The level of engagement with course material influences how well students learn the content. When students learn content by memorizing it without attaching meaning, they usually forget it quickly. To remember and be able to use content, students must engage with the content to create their own meaning for it. Table 4.2 shows the level to which students engage in content.

In learner-centered courses, students develop understanding by making their own associations with new content, developing their own examples of a concept, putting concepts into their own words, or reflecting on the meaning of the content. When students reflect on content, they apply it to their own lives or real-world situations. Reflection is more than summarizing someone else's words; it includes the student's own perspectives.

TABLE 4.2

Level to Which Students Engage in Content.

The Function of Content

Component	Employs *instructor-centered* approaches →	→ Transitioning to learner-centered approaches →		Employs *learner-centered* approaches
		Lower level of transitioning	**Higher level of transitioning**	
2. Level to which students engage in content	Instructor allows students to memorize content.	Instructor provides content so students can learn material as it is given to them without transforming or reflecting on it.	Instructor assists students to transform and reflect on *some* of the content to make their own meaning out of *some* of it.	Instructor encourages students to transform and reflect on *most* of the content to make their own meaning out of it.

Box. 4.5. Learner-Centered Example of Level to Which Students Engage in Content

Russell Moulds (2005) requires students to write personal marginal notes on their reading of essays, helping students relate to and react to their reading assignments. This practice helps students think critically about the material, forces them to analyze their points, and encourages them to substantiate their claims about the validity of points raised in the essay. Before the first marginal note assignment, Moulds shows his students samples of his own marginal annotations and explains them. Annotations might include personal challenges to the reading, further examples, references to other sources, personal experiences that relate to the reading, ideas on applications, personal reactions to the reading, and ideas of how these concepts compare or contrast with other concepts. Then he requires his students to make a few brief marginal annotations on some of their required reading assignments. The students hand in their books, with their names clearly identified, at the end of the class in which they discuss the reading. Moulds checks to see that the students have completed their annotated notes and gives them feedback. He has found that class discussion improves on the days following an annotation assignment because students are more prepared.

Through engagement with the content, students might think of common examples of the concept. For example, students might apply the theme of loneliness discussed in a nineteenth-century novel to contemporary situations of loneliness. The example in Box 4.5 shows how students create their own meaning from reading assignments.

TABLE 4.3

Use of Organizing Schemes.

The Function of Content

| Component | Employs *instructor-centered* approaches → | → Transitioning to learner-centered approaches → | | Employs *learner-centered* approaches |
		Lower level of transitioning	Higher level of transitioning	
3. Use of organizing schemes	Students learn content without a clearly defined organizing scheme provided by instructor.	Instructor provides *limited* organizing assistance.	Instructor provides *some* organizing schemes to help students learn content.	Instructor provides and uses organizing schemes to help students learn content.

Component 3: Use of Organizing Schemes

An organizing scheme is a discipline-specific overriding theme or a conceptual framework of the course or the discipline that helps experts integrate much of the material (Bransford, Brown, & Cocking, 2000). Students, especially those in introductory courses, often do not perceive these organizing schemes, so instructors need to describe them explicitly and show students how to use them in their studies. Instructors can use organizing schemes as a way to help students understand and integrate the content. Knowing how to use organizing schemes makes it easier for students to comprehend the discipline instead of simply memorizing isolated facts. The description of how the Psych 101 course can become more learner-centered, presented later in this chapter, gives an implementation example for this component. Table 4.3 shows the different ways instructors use organizing schemes.

Component 4: Use of Content to Facilitate Future Learning

A universal purpose of education is to prepare students to apply the content in the future. As shown in Table 4.4, learner-centered approaches take this one step further. Here the instructor actively frames content so that students are able to see how they can apply it to learn new content once the course is over. When instructors give students the desire to continue learning and the tools to learn more about the discipline on their own, students should be able to continue learning in a discipline when the

TABLE 4.4

Use of Content to Facilitate Future Learning.

The Function of Content

Component	Employs *instructor-centered* approaches →	→ Transitioning to learner-centered approaches →		Employs *learner-centered* approaches
		Lower level of transitioning	**Higher level of transitioning**	
4. Use of content to facilitate future learning	Instructor provides content so students can learn it in isolation, without providing opportunities for them to apply knowledge to new content.	Instructor provides students with limited opportunities to apply knowledge to new content.	Instructor frames content so students can see how it can be applied in the future.	Instructor frames and organizes content so students can learn additional content that is not taught.

Box 4.6. Learner-Centered Example of Use of Content to Facilitate Future Learning

Timothy Cudd (2003) teaches a physiology course to future veterinarians. Bodily function and dysfunction are very complex issues because there are almost limitless ways in which the various cells, organs, and organ systems of the body can become dysfunctional. One of the basic principles that Cudd emphasizes is that when one component dysfunctions, it influences other components within the same organ system and in other organ systems. He wants his students to be able to predict the impact of a specific malfunction on other components of the body. To achieve these objectives, students practice making these predictions in four different settings: in class, in the lab, in homework assignments, and on tests. Each of these predictions involves a novel physiological malfunction or a different animal. The students get feedback on how they did throughout the course and get better at making these predictions as the course progresses.

course is over. For example, students would be able to continue to read and write poetry after a first-year English course. Box 4.6 describes a graduate-level physiology course for future health professionals in which the instructor uses content to help students learn new content. In this course, the instructor's goal is to equip students with the ability to apply basic physiological knowledge of organ systems to predict physiological responses to diseases or therapies.

Content as an End and a Means to an End

As referred to earlier, the learner-centered functions of content mean that content is both an end in itself and a means to other ends. This transformation of the use of content can be difficult for both instructors and students. It is much more time consuming for students to learn how to learn the content and make their own meanings of it than for you to cover it yourself. Students are not efficient in this process, and you know that you do a better job of explaining or summarizing the material than the students can. Although the students are inefficient in their learning, active engagement in the process of learning content ultimately leads to greater mastery of the discipline.

Even though it is time consuming for you to make content a means to an end as well as an end in itself, you do not have to drop significant amounts of content from your course. Once you show students how to learn the material, they will be able to acquire more of it on their own. For example, you do not need to repeat in class most of the material that is in the textbook or in required reading assignments. Instead, you might discuss only the most confusing parts in class. You can assist students to comprehend the material in the text on their own by giving them study guides that help them to identify the key concepts and problem-solving questions or questions that help them reflect on what they read, thus saving class time for problem solving and application activities.

Analysis of the Psych 101 Course for the Function of Content

To test your understanding of the components for the Function of Content, identify the status of our case example, Psych 101 (described at the end of the Introduction to this part of the book) on this dimension. Use a copy of the rubric for the Function of Content dimension in Appendix B to indicate your ratings. Mark or circle the appropriate cells to indicate your rating on the learner-centered to instructor-centered continuum for this rubric. When you are finished, compare how you rated the case study with how I rated the status of this course. In Table 4.5, which appears after the following individual component explanations, I have boldfaced the criterion that matches my rating for each component.

The following are my ratings for the Psych 101 course and my explanation for these ratings:

Component 1. Varied Uses of Content

- *Rating:* Employs instructor-centered approaches; the instructor uses content that helps students build a knowledge base, and instructor and content help students solve some problems, *or* instructor uses any one or none of the four subcriteria for uses of content.

As the course objectives state, this course focuses on building a basic knowledge base in psychology. To acquire the content, the students attend lectures and read the textbook. The instructor does not cover the content in a learner-centered way because the focus is on knowledge acquisition and not on the other functions of content. The majority of the questions in the study guides for the Intra-teach sessions and the examinations are factual, and only a few require application or problem solving. (Intra-teach sessions use a small-group review of material followed by a quiz taken individually on that material. For more details on the Intra-teach technique, see the case study description of the Psych 101 course.)

Component 2: Level to Which Students Engage in Content

Rating: Employs lower level of transitioning; the instructor provides content so students can learn material as it is given to them without transforming or reflecting on it.

- The instructor uses demonstrations and exercises that help students to understand the material, but she is the one who is making the material meaningful. The students are not transforming much of this material themselves.
- For the most part, the students' learning activities—including the preparation for the Intra-teach, preparation for quizzes and examinations, and small-group discussions in the Intra-teach sessions—require the students to learn definitions and concepts explained in the lectures and textbook. These activities do not require the students to create their own meaning of the content.
- Although there are a few thought or opinion questions that would require the students to create their own interpretations of the material, this is not the focus of these activities.
- The preparation of the answers to the questions on the study guide and the small-group discussions during the Intra-teach sessions do foster active learning of the material.

Component 3: Use of Organizing Schemes

Rating: Employs instructor-centered approaches; students learn content without a clearly defined organizing scheme provided by the instructor.

The syllabus objectives state two possible organizing schemes:

The students will be able to recognize and describe the methods used by psychologists in studying both mental processes and behavior of humans and other species.

The students will be able to recognize and describe individual differences regarding cognition, affect, and behavior in organisms, especially the human species.

The instructor does not discuss these objectives as overriding themes, nor does she explicitly use these organizing themes to help the student organize their study and learn the content. Instead, she focuses on the details of the content contained in the individual chapters of the textbook.

Component 4: Use of Content to Facilitate Future Learning

Rating: Employs lower level of transitioning; the instructor provides students with limited opportunities to apply knowledge to new content.

The instructor does not frame and organize content so students can learn additional content that she does not teach.

- The instructor provides limited opportunities to apply knowledge to new content in the following ways:

  - She gives demonstrations of how the concepts work in the lectures so the students do not learn the content in isolation.

  - She provides a few thought questions in the chapter study guides that allow opportunities to apply knowledge to new content.

- The active learning technique Intra-teach is a good example of the application of a fundamental psychological principle covered in Psych 101. Although the instructor uses the Intra-teach technique, she does not show explicitly how it is an application of human learning principles, including integration of materials into a context. Therefore it is unlikely that the students realize this application of the content. She could frame the content of human learning around the application of these principles by way of the Intra-teach, which the students already use.

Table 4.5 summarizes my ratings of the Psych 101 course on the Function of Content dimension.

TABLE 4.5

Ratings (in bold) for the Psych 101 Course on the Function of Content Dimension.

The Function of Content

Component	Employs *instructor-centered* approaches →	→ Transitioning to learner-centered approaches →		Employs *learner-centered* approaches
		Lower level of transitioning	**Higher level of transitioning**	
1. Varied uses of content				
In addition to building a knowledge base, instructor uses content to help students:	**Instructor uses content that helps students build a knowledge base.**	In addition to building a knowledge base, instructor uses content to help students:	In addition to building a knowledge base, instructor uses content to help students:	In addition to building a knowledge base, instructor uses all four subcriteria to help students in the following ways:
• Know why they need to learn content		• Recognize why they need to learn the content	• Identify why they need to learn content	• Evaluate why they need to learn content
• Acquire discipline-specific learning methodologies (such as how to read primary source material)			• Use discipline-specific learning methodologies with instructor's assistance	• Acquire discipline-specific learning methodologies
• Use inquiry or ways of thinking in the discipline			• Use inquiry or ways of thinking in the discipline with the instructor's assistance	• Practice using inquiry or ways of thinking in the discipline
• Learn to solve real-world problems	**Instructor and content help students solve problems** *or* **Instructor uses any one or none of the four subcriteria for uses of content**	• Apply content to solve problems with instructor's assistance *or* Instructor uses any two of the four subcriteria for uses of content	• Learn to apply content to solve real-world problems with instructor's assistance *or* Uses any three of the four subcriteria for uses of content	• Learn to solve real-world problems

(Continued)

TABLE 4.5 (*Continued*)

The Function of Content

Component	Employs *instructor-centered* approaches →	→ Transitioning to learner-centered approaches →		Employs *learner-centered* approaches
		Lower level of transitioning	**Higher level of transitioning**	
2. Level to which students engage in content	Instructor allows students to memorize content.	**Instructor provides content so students can learn material as it is given to them without transforming or reflecting on it.**	Instructor assists students to transform and reflect on *some* of the content to make their own meaning out of *some* of it.	Instructor encourages students to transform and reflect on *most* of the content to make their own meaning out of it.
3. Use of organizing schemes	**Students learn content without a clearly defined organizing scheme provided by instructor.**	Instructor provides *limited* organizing assistance.	Instructor provides *some* organizing schemes to help students learn content.	Instructor provides and uses organizing schemes to help students learn content.
4. Use of content to facilitate future learning	Instructor provides content so students can learn it in isolation, without providing opportunities for them to apply knowledge to new content.	**Instructor provides students with limited opportunities to apply knowledge to new content.**	Instructor frames content so students can see how it can be applied in the future.	Instructor frames and organizes content so students can learn additional content that is not taught.

Transforming the Psych 101 Course to Be More Learner-Centered

After analyzing the status of her course, the Psych 101 instructor decided she could transform the following components: (1) a subcomponent of "the varied uses of content," (2) "level to which students engage in content" and (3) "use of organizing schemes." She completed the Planning for Transformation exercise for each component, as shown in Exhibits 4.1, 4.2, and 4.3.

EXHIBIT 4.1

The Planning for Transformation Exercise 1 for the Function of Content Component 1

A. Status of your course now   Date: 2-27-07

   1. Dimension of learner-centered teaching: *The Function of Content*

   2. Component: 1. *In addition to building a knowledge base, instructor uses content to help students practice using inquiry or ways of thinking in the discipline*

   3. Current level:

      ☑ Instructor-centered

      ❑ Lower level of transitioning

      ❑ Higher level of transitioning

      ❑ Learner-centered

   4. Briefly describe your current implementation (to document your baseline prior to transformation).

      The focus of the course is on factual and conceptual knowledge. Students learn the material as presented in the lectures or the textbook. They do not need to use psychological inquiry to get an A in the course.

B. Desired changes:

   1. Describe the desired changes you wish to make for this component in the near future.

      a. *Change many of the questions in the study guide to include more questions that require inquiry and to apply the basic principles of psychology. The students will use these questions on the Intra-teach and quizzes.*

      b. *Include more inquiry questions on the midterm and final.*

   2. What is the level you want to achieve with this/these changes?

      ❑ Instructor-centered

      ❑ Lower level of transitioning

      ☑ Higher level of transitioning

      ❑ Learner-centered

C. Tactical planning questions:

   1. What do you need to do, decide, or learn about prior to making changes?

      I would like to see how other instructors of general education courses use inquiry successfully.

      [Author's note: Box 4.3 offers an example of how that general chemistry course uses inquiry to help students learn the content better.]

      I need to change some of the questions in the study guides and on the examinations.

   2. What obstacles or challenges do you need to overcome to successfully implement this change? (Resistance may come from your philosophy of teaching, your chair, your peers, your students, or the culture of your institution.)

      Developing these new inquiry questions will take time.

   3. Identify specific strategies (such as learning about successful implementations, trying a small pilot implementation, explaining to your students and other instructors why you are making these changes) for overcoming each obstacle or challenge.

      I will have to find the time to make these changes. I can develop them over time, incorporating them iteratively.

(Continued)

4. What resources (such as time, money, student assistants, or computer software) would help you implement your change?

   I might consult the instructor's manual for some questions or look at other general psychology resources that I am not currently using with this course.

5. What do you need to do to get your students to accept this change? (Possibilities include repeated explanations for why you are doing what you are doing or having the activity count in the final grade.)

   When I explain the study guides, I will explain that there are different types of questions: factual ones and ones that require inquiry. When I help students review for the midterm and final examinations, I will explain that a large percent of the questions will require inquiry.

D. Outcomes of the change:

   1. In what ways will implementing this change influence other aspects of your course to be more learner-centered? (For example, when you incorporate various teaching or learning methods that are consistent with your student learning goals [Component 3 of the Role of the Instructor dimension], most likely the students will more actively engage in the content [Component 2 of the Function of Content dimension].)

      By requiring students to use inquiry more in the course, they might gain a greater understanding of why they need to learn the content and they might be able to use content to facilitate future learning; both are parts of Component 1 of the Function of Content.

   2. In what ways (such as increased learning) will your students benefit from this change? How will the students behave differently (such as increased participation in class or greater engagement with the content)?

      The students should learn the material better and be able to use the concepts more.

   3. In what ways will you benefit from this change? (For example, more enjoyment of teaching, satisfaction that your students are learning more, anticipation of fewer student complaints.)

      Satisfaction that the students are learning more.

E. Possible future changes:

   1. What is the optimal level for this component for this course?
      - ❏ Instructor-centered
      - ❏ Lower level of transitioning
      - ❏ Higher level of transitioning
      - ☑ Learner-centered

   2. In the long term, what additional changes, if any, might you make to further transform this component to reach this optimal level of the learner-centered approach?

      Many questions in the study guide and on the examinations could pose real-life situations and require the students to use psychological concepts to explain the situation or predict future behaviors. I would have to change the focus of the course from fact acquisition to inquiry and ways of thinking in psychology. I am not ready to make this big a change now.

      I could adapt group problem-solving exercises used in a general chemistry course to my recitation classes. I am not ready to make this change either.

      [Author's note: Box 4.3 offers an example of how that general chemistry course uses inquiry to help students learn the content better.]

EXHIBIT 4.2

The Planning for Transformation Exercise 2 for the Function of Content Component 2

A. Status of your course now   Date: 2-27-07

   1. Dimension of learner-centered teaching: *The Function of Content*

   2. Component: 2. *Level to which students engage in content*

   3. Current level:

      ❏ Instructor-centered

      ☑ Lower level of transitioning

      ❏ Higher level of transitioning

      ❏ Learner-centered

   4. Briefly describe your current implementation (to document your baseline prior to transformation).

      Students learn the content as presented. They can answer questions by reading the textbook or from their lecture notes. They do not have to make their own meaning out of most of the material; they can just use the instructor's examples.

B. Desired changes:

   1. Describe the desired changes you wish to make for this component in the near future.

      As homework assignments, require students to develop concept maps (Novak, 1998) to summarize the material in each chapter. Concept maps are graphic representations of content to show how the material is related and integrated. I would also like to discuss some of the student-generated concept maps in class.

      [Author's note: See a definition and discussion of concept maps later in this chapter.]

   2. What is the level you want to achieve with this/these changes?

      ❏ Instructor-centered

      ❏ Lower level of transitioning

      ❏ Higher level of transitioning

      ☑ Learner-centered

C. Tactical planning questions:

   1. What do you need to do, decide, or learn about prior to making changes?

      I need to teach my students how to create concept maps. Therefore, I need to reorganize how I spend my time while covering the material in the first chapter. I need to use at least one class session to demonstrate to the students how to develop a concept map and then create one for the material in the first chapter in class.

      I will have to plan how to teach the creation of concept maps, and if I want my students to use the university's computer software to create them, I probably will have to teach the students how to use this software also.

   2. What obstacles or challenges do you need to overcome to successfully implement this change? (Resistance may come from your philosophy of teaching, your chair, your peers, your students, or the culture of your institution.)

      I will have to replan the class schedule because I am adding at least one class instructing my students on how to create concept maps. This is not a trivial obstacle because I already feel the semester is too packed.

(Continued)

3. Identify specific strategies (such as learning about successful implementations, trying a small pilot implementation, explaining to your students and other instructors why you are making these changes) for overcoming each obstacle or challenge.

   As I plan the course schedule for when I teach the course next, I can make the adjustments required. I may have to eliminate one or two lectures or the emphasis I place on some content.

   As a pilot this semester, I will teach my teaching assistant how to do concept maps. I will see how much time it takes to teach how to do concept maps, and I'll get feedback on how well I teach it.

4. What resources (such as time, money, student assistants, or computer software) would help you implement your change?

   The university owns a general site license for computer software for developing concept maps. I will download the software onto my computer, and I will have to learn how to use it.

5. What do you need to do to get your students to accept this change? (Possibilities include repeated explanations for why you are doing what you are doing or having the activity count in the final grade.)

   I will teach my students how to develop concept maps as a way to show the relationships among the concepts in chapter one of the textbook.

   To encourage students to make meaningful concept maps, I will count these homework activities in the final grade.

D. Outcomes of the change:

1. In what ways will implementing this change influence other aspects of your course to be more learner-centered? (For example, when you incorporate various teaching or learning methods that are consistent with your student learning goals [Component 3 of the Role of the Instructor dimension], most likely the students will more actively engage in the content [Component 2 of the Function of Content dimension].)

   The additional requirements of constructing concept maps would move the course to become more learner-centered on the Role of the Instructor dimension, Component 3, "Teaching or learning methods appropriate for student-learning goals."

2. In what ways (such as increased learning) will your students benefit from this change? How will the students behave differently (such as increased participation in class or greater engagement with the content)?

   The student-generated concept maps will show an increased understanding of the content.

   The students should do better on the examinations because of this increased understanding.

3. In what ways will you benefit from this change? (For example, more enjoyment of teaching, satisfaction that your students are learning more, anticipation of fewer student complaints.)

   Increased satisfaction that the students are learning more.

E. Possible future changes:

1. What is the optimal level for this component for this course?

   ❏ Instructor-centered

   ❏ Lower level of transitioning

   ❏ Higher level of transitioning

   ☑ Learner-centered

2. In the long term, what additional changes, if any, might you make to further transform this component to reach this optimal level of the learner-centered approach?

   I will evaluate the effectiveness of implementing concept maps before making any additional changes. I might incorporate the use of them into classroom activities.

EXHIBIT 4.3

The Planning for Transformation Exercise 3 for the Function of Content Component 3

A. Status of your course now   Date: 2-27-07

   1. Dimension of learner-centered teaching: *The Function of Content*

   2. Component: 3. *Use of organizing schemes*

   3. Current level:

     ☑ Instructor-centered

     ❏ Lower level of transitioning

     ❏ Higher level of transitioning

     ❏ Learner-centered

   4. Briefly describe your current implementation (to document your baseline prior to transformation).

     Although I refer to possible organizing schemes in my objectives, I do not use them to organize the course. I do not use the organizing schemes to help the student learn the material.

B. Desired changes:

   1. Describe the desired changes you wish to make for this component in the near future.

     I will employ these schemes explicitly in my teaching, so that I can explain much of the content within this course. For example, I can use the third course objective, "Individual differences regarding cognition, affect, and behavior in organisms, especially the human species," to show students how to approach the study of human development, personality, abnormal psychology, and intelligence. All of these topics represent different chapters in the textbook. The first objective, "Fundamental concepts and theories that form the empirically supported knowledge base for cognition, affect, and behavior" refers to other organizing schemes, but does not explicitly state them. These concepts and theories are the biological basis of behavior and the dynamic interplay between the individual and the environment. I could use these concepts and theories as organizing schemes with many examples in the course. It would be helpful if I explain why these schemes organize the content and show students how to use them in different ways. This might foster students' seeing the big picture of why they are studying psychology instead of concentrating on the definitions.

   2. What is the level you want to achieve with this/these changes?

     ❏ Instructor-centered

     ❏ Lower level of transitioning

     ☑ Higher level of transitioning

     ❏ Learner-centered

C. Tactical planning questions:

   1. What do you need to do, decide, or learn about prior to making changes?

     a. *Plan what content relates to which organizing scheme.*

     b. *Ask the students to incorporate these organizing schemes into their concept maps.*

(Continued)

c. *Decide how to teach using these organizing schemes. This will require completely replanning my lectures and finding new examples. Therefore, I see this as long-term transformation.*

[Author's note: Box 4.7 offers a description of how a biology instructor uses organizing schemes.]

2. What obstacles or challenges do you need to overcome to successfully implement this change? (Resistance may come from your philosophy of teaching, your chair, your peers, your students, or the culture of your institution.)

I will have to replan my lectures for each chapter to discuss these organizing schemes. I need to reorganize how I spend my time while covering the material in the each chapter. This will require a complete revision of my lectures.

3. Identify specific strategies (such as learning about successful implementations, trying a small pilot implementation, explaining to your students and other instructors why you are making these changes) for overcoming each obstacle or challenge.

I will need to find the time to redo the focus of my lectures from facts to an integrated approach using organizing schemes. I can change the focus of my lectures iteratively. For example, I could redo my lectures for one chapter this semester and plan to reorganize the lectures for a few more chapters the next time I teach it.

4. What resources (such as time, money, student assistants, or computer software) would help you implement your change?

I need time to reorganize the lectures on each chapter so that I will have time to discuss explicitly the organizing schemes that relate to that content.

I will look at other textbooks to see if the authors organize the material around schemes.

I could review the literature on teaching general psychology according to organizing schemes.

5. What do you need to do to get your students to accept this change? (Possibilities include repeated explanations for why you are doing what you are doing or having the activity count in the final grade.)

We need to discuss why organizing schemes help people to understand psychology and teach using these schemes more consistently. This will probably help the students make more sense out of the course, so it should be easy for them to accept this change.

D. Outcomes of the change:

1. In what ways will implementing this change influence other aspects of your course to be more learner-centered? (For example, when you incorporate various teaching or learning methods that are consistent with your student learning goals [Component 3 of the Role of the Instructor dimension], most likely the students will more actively engage in the content [Component 2 of the Function of Content dimension].)

Potentially this change could make the course more learner-centered in several other components of the Function of Content, including Component 1, "Know why they need to learn content" and "Use inquiry or ways of thinking in the discipline," and Component 4, "Use of content to facilitate future learning"

The change can make my course more learner-centered on Component 1 of the Role of the Instructor dimension, "Creation of an environment for learning."

(Continued)

2. In what ways (such as increased learning) will your students benefit from this change? How will the students behave differently (such as increased participation in class or greater engagement with the content)?

   The students will use these organizing schemes successfully in their concept maps and in their answers to quiz and examination questions. The students will learn more and be able to use the concepts more.

3. In what ways will you benefit from this change? (For example, more enjoyment of teaching, satisfaction that your students are learning more, anticipation of fewer student complaints.)

   I will be satisfied that my students are learning more, and I may get fewer student complaints about their grades.

E. Possible future changes:

   1. What is the optimal level for this component for this course?

      ❑ Instructor-centered

      ❑ Lower level of transitioning

      ❑ Higher level of transitioning

      ☑ Learner-centered

   2. In the long term, what additional changes, if any, might you make to further transform this component to reach this optimal level of the learner-centered approach?

      If I use these organizing schemes consistently throughout the course, then the course will be at the learner-centered level; if I use them only as an introduction to the course, then it will be at the lower level of transitioning. I may make this transition in how I organize the material gradually and may be at the higher level of transitioning while I teach some of the course emphasizing these schemes in my daily teaching.

      Even though this will take much rethinking and replanning of the course, this change has great potential for major improvements in the course. This is a worthwhile long-term goal for changing this course.

Concept Maps

A *concept map* is a graphic representation of the content specifically showing the relationships among the concepts, such as cause and effect, consequences, or a series of events (Novak, 1998). Some people also call this a *knowledge map* or *graphic organizer*. Commonly used concept maps include flowcharts, tables, or figures with arrows. Students can create them individually or in groups, by hand or by using computer programs.

You can download a free tool for making concept maps at http://cmap.ihmc.us/download. The creation of concept maps forces students to engage in the material to make it meaningful to them, because they are making the associations among the concepts. (In Chapter Five, on the Role of the Instructor, I will describe how a biology instructor [Mostrom, 2007] uses concepts maps to facilitate student learning.)

[*Author's note:* In her response to C1, the instructor states "I would like to see how other instructors of general education courses use inquiry successfully," and in her response to E2 she adds, "I could adapt group problem-solving exercises used in a general chemistry course to my recitation classes." Box 4.3 offers an example of how that general chemistry course uses inquiry to help students learn the content better.]

Note: As you can see, these Planning for Transformation exercise examples include several different ways the psychology instructor could make her course more learner-centered. I provide these different methods as illustrations and examples for you to consider when planning transforming your own courses. I would recommend that the Psych 101 instructor—or any other instructor—not make *all* of these changes, or at least not make them all at once.

Box 4.7. Learner-Centered Example of Use of Organizing Schemes

Another general education instructor, Lois Peck (2007), uses the organizing schemes of her own discipline, biology, to teach content. Biologists agree that ten schemes organize and explain all of the biological sciences. Some of these schemes are the structure-function relationship, the cellular basis of all life, evolution, and the importance of heredity, explained by DNA.

Peck focuses on these schemes throughout her teaching in general biology. Her introductory unit in this course explains all of these schemes.

She explicitly tells the students that as they read the textbook or study they should think what scheme this content exemplifies and describe how this theme applies to this content. Then she uses the schemes to introduce each separate content area in the course and emphasizes the schemes within her teaching. This explicit instruction on the schemes of the biological sciences helps the students to organize their study and not be overwhelmed by the thousands of terms used in a general biology course.

Chapter Summary

You can use learner-centered approaches on the Function of Content dimension for all levels of courses and all types of disciplines. In addition to helping the students acquire a strong knowledge base, as a learner-centered instructor, you will

- Help students evaluate why they need to learn content
- Explicitly assist students to acquire the learning skills necessary to learn more of this discipline in the future
- Focus on how to apply the material to solve problems
- Teach students how to use the content in the future
- Focus on ways to get the students actively engaged in making the content meaningful to them
- Use the time you interact with the students very differently
- Change your assignments and the nature of your assignments

The focus of this chapter is on *what* you teach; the next chapter focuses on *how* you teach. The next chapter, on the Role of the Instructor, describes how you plan and conduct courses differently to facilitate the students' ability to use the content.

The application activities that close each dimension chapter help you determine where your course is on that dimension's continuum and help you begin to think how you will transform your course to be more learner-centered. First, answer the following questions related to the main components and subcomponents of the Function of Content rubric. After answering the questions, you should be able to complete the rubric easily. Your answers should also prepare you to select two or three components that you can transform.

APPLICATION ACTIVITY

Component 1: Varied Uses of Content

Think about why and how students learn the content in your course.

- Why do students at the level of your course learn the content in this discipline?

- Do you explicitly and consistently discuss why students need to learn this content?

- If yes, describe what you do. Can you include more explicit and consistent discussions on why they should learn this content?

- If no, how could you do this?

Think about discipline-specific learning methodologies.

- What discipline-specific learning methodologies—such as how to read a textbook for introductory courses (especially graphic representations), or how to read primary source material in the discipline, or how to write reports in your discipline—are important for your students to be able to do to succeed in your course?

- Do you explicitly and consistently instruct your students or model with them how to use these discipline-specific learning methodologies?

- If yes, describe what you do and whether you could do more of this.

- If no, how could you do this?

(Continued)

Think about the ways of thinking in this discipline:

- What are the ways of thinking in this discipline?

- Do you explicitly and consistently instruct your students or model with them how to use inquiry or ways of thinking in your discipline?

- If yes, describe what you do and if you could do more of this.

- If no, how could you do this?

Think about solving real-world problems in your discipline.

- How do experts solve real-world problems in your discipline?

- Do you explicitly and consistently instruct your students or model with them how to solve real-world problems in your discipline?

- If yes, describe what you do and whether you could do more of this.

- If no, how could you do this?

(*Continued*)

Component 2: Level to Which Students Engage in Content

Think about the level to which your students engage with the content in your course.

- How do excellent students engage with the content to transform and reflect on it to make their own meaning out of it?

- Do you explicitly and consistently instruct your students or model with them how to engage with the content to make meaning out of it?

- If yes, describe what you do and whether you could do more of this.

- If no, how could you do this?

Component 3: Use of Organizing Schemes

Think about the use of organizing schemes in your course.

- What are organizing schemes for your discipline?

- Do you explicitly and consistently instruct your students using these organizing schemes?

- If yes, describe what you do and whether you could do more of this.

- If no, how could you do this?

(*Continued*)

Component 4: Use of Content to Facilitate Future Learning

Think about your use of content in your course to facilitate future learning.

- What content do you want your students to be able to use to facilitate future learning?

- Do you explicitly and consistently show your students how and under what conditions they will use this content in the future?

- If yes, describe what you do and whether you could do more of this.

- If no, how could you do this?

Completing the Function of Content Rubric for Your Course

Keep your answers to the preceding questions in mind as you complete the Function of Content rubric, found in Appendix B, for your course.

- Read across the entire row before deciding which level is appropriate.
- For each specific component, circle or mark the appropriate level in the row.
- If you decide that the learner-centered level is not appropriate for your course on a component or subcomponent, think of a rationale or justification for that decision.

Planning for Transformation

After you complete the rubric, select two or three specific components that you might want to change. Then copy and complete a Planning for Transformation exercise, found in Appendix B, for each of those components.

Chapter 5

The Role of the Instructor

THINK ABOUT THE way you teach your courses. Traditionally, many university instructors convey information largely through lecturing to the students. For example, the Psychology 101 instructor in our case example spent the majority of class time giving lectures and demonstrations on the material covered in the textbook.

In a typical instructor-centered course, the instructor's focus is on conveying material clearly. The instructor lectures; the students listen and take notes on what the instructor says. The students tend to be passive; they do not interact with the instructor or their peers, and they may even be disengaged in the classroom. The instructor may or may not consider matching the goals of the course with the way he or she teaches or what the students do.

In contrast, the learner-centered instructor considers the students' learning goals for the course and then plans teaching or learning methods that help students meet these goals. As a learner-centered instructor, you will focus on creating an environment in which your students can learn, because one of your most essential roles is to help students learn. When you develop an environment for learning, you will spend more time planning what you expect students to do. Designing a learning environment is also more creative than planning lectures. The case study in Box 5.1 describes how an instructor of English composition purposely creates a larger environment for learning. As a learner-centered instructor, you will consider the individual differences in learning among your students. You will use different methods so that you can accommodate these individual differences. You will encourage students to interact with you and their peers in learning activities. If you are successful as a learner-centered instructor, your students will be intrinsically motivated to learn.

The Role of the Instructor Components

The rubric for the Role of the Instructor dimension, presented in Table 5.1, shows the continuum from instructor-centered to learner-centered approaches for six components. Instructor-centered approaches focus on what the instructor does, usually at the expense of the students being motivated to learn.

Box 5.1. Learner-Centered Example of Creating an Environment for Learning

Christine Flanagan (2007) explicitly tries to create an environment for science students to learn English composition and literature. She believes that students do not see the relevance of these subjects to their own lives; therefore she incorporates real-world experiences throughout her teaching. She takes her students outside the classroom to experience something and then helps them to see how such an experience relates to reading literature and writing English compositions. For example, in a freshman English composition class she asks her students to interview someone who has an interesting story to tell, research the background behind that story, and write a composition about this story.

Flanagan incorporates the usual objectives of a freshman English course into these activities; she instructs her students in the use of proper citations and paraphrasing for this project.

Flanagan also involves her students in an oral history project that is ongoing at a local senior citizens' center. Students write essays about the people's life stories. She hopes that through her incorporation of real-world experiences, including their own, into their education, the students will become curious to learn more. By broadening the definition of where learning occurs and what students should write about, she successfully creates an environment in which students can learn.

TABLE 5.1

The Rubric for the Role of the Instructor Dimension of Learner-Centered Teaching.

The Role of the Instructor

Component	Employs *instructor-centered* approaches →	→ Transitioning to learner-centered approaches →		Employs *learner-centered* approaches
		Lower level of transitioning	**Higher level of transitioning**	
1. Creation of an environment for learning through (1) organization and (2) use of material that accommodates different learning styles	Instructor uses the same approach or approaches throughout the course even if the students are not learning.	Instructor does not focus on creating a learning environment, but students do learn.	Instructor creates a learning environment through use of one out of the two subcriteria.	Instructor creates a learning environment by using both subcriteria: through organization and use of material that accommodates different learning styles.

(Continued)

TABLE 5.1 (*Continued*)

The Role of the Instructor

Component	Employs *instructor-centered* approaches →	Transitioning to learner-centered approaches →		Employs *learner-centered* approaches
		Lower level of transitioning	**Higher level of transitioning**	
2. Alignment of the course components—objectives, teaching or learning methods, and assessment methods—for consistency	Instructor does *not* align objectives, teaching or learning methods, and assessment methods	Instructor • *Minimally* aligns objectives, teaching or learning methods, and assessment methods *or* • Aligns two out of the three course components	Instructor *somewhat* aligns objectives, teaching or learning methods, and assessment methods.	Instructor explicitly, coherently, and consistently aligns objectives, teaching or learning methods, and assessment methods.
3. Teaching or learning methods appropriate for student learning goals	Instructor • Does *not* have specified learning goals *or* • Uses teaching and learning methods that conflict with learning goals	Instructor • Uses teaching and learning methods without regard for student learning goals *and/or* • Does not use active learning activities	Instructor uses *some* teaching or learning methods that are appropriate for student learning goals.	Instructor intentionally uses *various* teaching or learning methods that are appropriate for student learning goals.
4. Activities involving student, instructor, content interactions	Instructor uses no activities in which students actively interact with material, or instructor, or each other.	Instructor uses a *few* activities in which students actively interact with material, or instructor, or each other.	Instructor uses *some* activities in which • Students actively interact with material, or instructor, or each other *or* • There are some three-way interactions	Instructor *routinely* uses activities in which students actively interact with material, and instructor, and each other.
5. Articulation of SMART objectives: • **S**pecific • **M**easurable • **A**ttainable • **R**elevant • **T**ime oriented	Instructor • Articulates vague course objectives *and/or* • Does not articulate objectives in syllabus	Instructor articulates in syllabus course objectives that do not have all five attributes of SMART objectives.	Instructor articulates SMART objectives in syllabus but does not refer to them throughout the course.	Instructor articulates SMART objectives in syllabus and regularly refers to them throughout the course.

(*Continued*)

TABLE 5.1

The Rubric for the Role of the Instructor Dimension of Learner-Centered Teaching. (*Continued*)

The Role of the Instructor

Component	Employs *instructor-centered* approaches →	→ Transitioning to learner-centered approaches →		Employs *learner-centered* approaches
		Lower level of transitioning	Higher level of transitioning	
6. Motivation of students to learn (intrinsic drive to learn versus extrinsic reasons to earn grades)	Instructor extensively uses extrinsic motivators to get students to earn grades.	Instructor • Provides *limited* opportunities for students to become intrinsically motivated to learn • Uses extrinsic motivators to get students to earn grades	Instructor provides *some* opportunities for students to become intrinsically motivated to learn.	Instructor inspires and encourages students to become intrinsically motivated to learn.

Component 1: Creation of an Environment for Learning

Instructors can proactively help students to learn by creating a learning environment through the organization and use of material. People learn differently. For example, some people learn from reading; others like to hear the material presented; still others learn by doing. Some people learn from pictures, diagrams, or matrices; others want to think about concrete examples. The learner-centered instructor creates a learning environment that accommodates different learning styles through the organization and use of material. This material could be the choice of readings or the plan of the course. When instructors use different learning styles or offer options for how students can complete assignments, they make it easier for students to master the material in the course.

Instructors can accommodate these individual learning style preferences through giving students choices in their learning process or encouraging different types of student products. The example given in Box 5.2 discusses an extra-credit assignment that accommodates learning style differences and does not require you to make any changes in the way you teach.

Box 5.2. Learner-Centered Example of Accommodating Different Learning Styles

Karen Tietze (2007) created an extra-credit bingo card assignment for a content-rich science course. Tietze developed many different types of assignments that she specified on the cells on the bingo card. For example, she allowed the students to either create a twenty-word crossword puzzle of the major concepts used, develop a thirty-second computer animation of a concept, write the answers to sets of lecture objectives, create a novel student learning activity, develop a graphic to explain a concept, or find a mistake in the textbook. The students had the opportunity to earn five extra-credit points on their final grade by completing the assignments in any vertical, horizontal, or diagonal line on the card. The entire class chose to participate, and 97 percent of the students completed at least one row. Tietze also found that the students did better on the tests when she used the bingo extra-credit assignment, probably because the students were spending more time on the content because of doing the bingo assignments.

Component 2: Alignment of the Course Components

This component refers to how consistently all aspects of the course are aligned. Alignment means that all major aspects of a course—including the goals of the course, the teaching or learning methods, and the assessment of student learning—are integrated and consistent (Biggs, 1999; Fink, 2003). Current best-practices models in higher education suggest that courses should be aligned. At my university, when an instructor seeks approval for a course in the general education program, the instructor needs to include a three-column table that shows the correspondence among the course objectives, the teaching or learning methods, and the assessment methods.

Instructors can classify the level of their course objectives, such as on Bloom's taxonomy of objectives (Bloom, 1956), into low for knowledge acquisition, medium for application or analysis, and high for evaluation or problem solving. They would also classify the aspects of the course, such as the teaching or learning methods and assessment methods, as requiring knowledge acquisition, application, or problem solving. In aligned courses, the level of the teaching or learning activities and assessment would be consistent with the level of these objectives. Aligned courses may require all low-level learning facts or all high-level evaluating situations. Aligned courses lead to maximum student learning.

To illustrate alignment or aspects of nonalignment, create tables to compare the level of your objectives, teaching or learning methods, and

TABLE 5.2

Alignment of Levels of Objectives, Teaching or Learning Methods, and Assessment Methods.

What level is each of the following?	Aspect is not included in the course	Low level (knowledge or comprehension)	Medium level (application or analysis)	High level (synthesis or evaluation)
Objective				
Teaching or learning methods				
Assessment methods				

assessment methods such as shown in Table 5.2. Use a separate table for each course objective and its corresponding teaching or learning methods, and assessment methods. Mark, by briefly describing it, the appropriate cell for the objectives, the teaching or learning methods, and the assessment methods. Objectives may fall into more than one category. This is also true for the teaching or learning and assessment methods.

Next, for each objective, draw a line or lines connecting the cells you marked in the columns for the three levels. If you can draw a straight, vertical line connecting all rows, on all of the tables for your course, you have an aligned course. A diagonal line or two means that you do not have an aligned course. Instructors have nonaligned courses when there are lofty goals for a course, but the assessments require only recall of information.

Box 5.3 presents an example of an aligned course.

Box 5.3. Learner-Centered Example of Alignment of the Course Components

Heather Reynolds's (2004) urban ecology course is an example of an aligned course. She has three main types of objectives for the course: knowledge and skill acquisition, application of these to solve real-world problems, and the development of a civic ethic and environmental stewardship values. She aligns the objectives, learning methods, and assessment through a variety of learning activities. For example, text readings and lectures present key concepts; assignments to construct fact sheets develop skills and foster the knowledge; and service-learning projects in the community allow students to both apply knowledge and skills and develop a sense of civic ethic and environmental stewardship. This instructor's syllabus describes each type of assignment or assessment and provides some rationale. She thinks it would help her students if she were more explicit about this alignment in her syllabus.

Component 3:   Teaching or Learning Methods Appropriate for Student Learning Goals

Teaching or learning methods are the active learning activities that instructors use with their students. These teaching or learning methods may be in class, online, or required homework assignments or projects. There are hundreds of different teaching or learning methods, and instructors should select those that are appropriate for the student learning goals. Student learning goals describe what the student should be able to know, do, or value because of learning in the course. To facilitate learning, teaching or learning methods need to be congruent with the student learning goals. For example, if learning goals state that students should be able to use data to evaluate evidence and make predictions of consequences, the instructor would select teaching or learning methods whereby the students would practice using data sets to predict consequences. This might be a project requiring students to test data, evaluate their answers, and report on future consequences.

This book describes many learner-centered teaching or learning methods. For example, in the urban ecology course just referred to, the instructor uses a service-learning project (service-learning is work done to benefit the community that uses the content from the course), reading, a poster presentation, written reports, and reflections in addition to demonstrations in class. Box 5.4 discusses other teaching or learning methods that are appropriate for the student learning goals in another course.

Box 5.4. Learner-Centered Example of Teaching or Learning Methods Appropriate for Student Learning Goals

Bernard Brunner's (2006) introductory physics course is an example of using multiple teaching or learning methods to fit the course objectives. The course objectives include knowledge and skill acquisition, their application to solve real-world physics problems, and the ability to use physics principles in other settings.

To achieve these goals, Brunner intentionally employs a combination of three different teaching or learning methods, including Just-in-Time Teaching (JiTT) (Novak, Patterson, Gavrin, & Christian, 1999), small-group discussions of problems, and audience-response system keypads. In JiTT, the instructor posts several thought-provoking questions or problems on the course website the day before the instructor covers the material in class. Students answer the questions or solve the problems, write a rationale for their answers, and send their responses electronically to the instructor before the class that will cover this content. In class, after a brief lecture on the material, the students are again asked to answer the JiTT questions, only this time they respond using their individual keypads (sometimes referred to as clickers) that are part of the audience-response system. If the majority of the class does not get the answer right, they discuss the problem or question in groups of four students. After a short discussion, the students respond again using their keypads. This iterative process of discussion and answering the question continues until a majority of the students get the answer right.

Component 4: Activities Involving Student, Instructor, Content Interactions

Research indicates that more learning occurs in social situations than alone (Kafai & Resnick, 1996). Students can learn from interacting with each other and with the instructor. Students interact with the content by actively doing something with it—such as working in small groups to solve problems—rather than just hearing about it or reading it. The combination of social interactions and actively engaging with the content leads to increased learning.

Box 5.5 describes how a biology instructor gets her students to interact with her, each other, and the content.

You can use a simple diagram to plot interactions. Place these categories of instructor, student, and content in a diamond configuration, such as shown in Figure 5.1. Use arrows to show interactions. A single-headed arrow shows one-way communication, such as when an instructor is lecturing to the students. A double-headed arrow indicates two-way interactions, such as between students when they are using content materials in a small-group discussion. If no interaction occurs, do not place an arrow between them.

Box 5.5. Learner-Centered Example of Activities Involving Student, Instructor, and Content Interactions

Alison Mostrom (2007) structures all of the classes in her upper-level ecology course around small groups of students creating concept maps (Novak, 1998) of their reading of the required primary and secondary literature and textbook. Concept maps are graphic representations particularly showing the relationship among the concepts, such as cause and effect, consequences, or a series of events (for more on concept maps, see Chapter Four). She uses a three-day process to create concept maps for each article they read. Prior to the first class on a topic, Mostrom requires her students to carefully read the assigned readings and outline the main aspects of the topic that they will analyze. She suggests that they pay attention to hierarchies and the interrelations among subcomponents of the topic.

In class on the first day of this process, the small groups of students begin to develop a concept map of the topic. On the second day, the groups refine their maps and begin to develop a short written summary of their concept maps. On the last day devoted to an article, the students do their final editing and complete their finished products. The groups then present their maps to each other. Throughout these classes, the instructor circulates among the groups of students to assist them, pointing out misconceptions or questioning their assumptions. The students individually edit their maps and summaries as homework between classes.

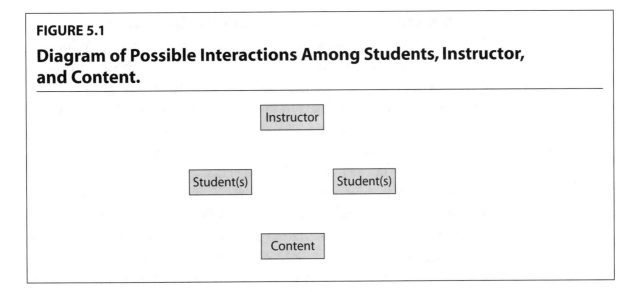

FIGURE 5.1

Diagram of Possible Interactions Among Students, Instructor, and Content.

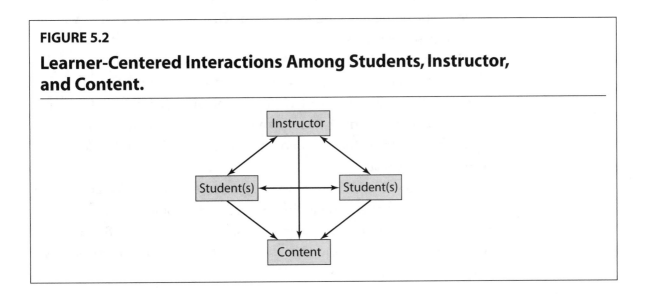

FIGURE 5.2

Learner-Centered Interactions Among Students, Instructor, and Content.

A map of learner-centered courses on this component, such as the ecology course described in Box 5.5, would have double-headed arrows between the instructor and each of the student categories and a single-headed arrow from the instructor and each of the student categories to the content, as shown in Figure 5.2.

Component 5: Articulation of SMART Objectives

Objectives should specify student-learning goals or student-learning outcomes. SMART objectives are the most specific types of objectives because they describe five conditions. SMART stands for specific, measurable, attainable, relevant or realistic in terms of results expected, and time oriented. *Specific* objectives are concrete and use action verbs. *Measurable* objectives may be numeric in terms of a quantity or descriptive in terms of a quality. *Attainable* objectives are feasible and appropriately limited in scope to that which is in your control and influence. *Relevant* and realistic results include products the students develop or skills they can demonstrate. *Time* oriented means that there is a target date for completion and perhaps even for the intermediate steps. A SMART objective, describing changes in the student, will state what changes will result (specific), how much change is expected (measurable), who or what will change (attainable), where the change will occur (relevant), and when the change will occur (timeframe). They assist us in determining whether we are meeting the needs of our students, planning teaching or learning activities, and assessing whether we met these objectives.

Here is an example of a SMART objective: By the end of the curriculum and methods course, preservice students preparing to teach elementary education will develop interactive lesson plans to increase their future students' ability to write coherent and accurate book reports. These book reports will describe the plot and characters of the books the elementary school students read.

To develop a SMART objective, start with an action verb that describes what you want your students to do. This verb should express a directly measurable action, such as *evaluate, predict,* or *analyze.* Then fill in the rest of the objective by answering how, why, and when you want the students to be able to do this action.

Component 6: Motivation of Students to Learn

Intrinsically motivated students learn because they want to learn; that is, they have an intrinsic drive to learn versus extrinsic reasons to earn grades. Although these students often earn excellent grades in their courses, the grades themselves do not motivate them to learn. These students may go well beyond the requirements of a course because the subject matter interests them. For example, in a literature course the intrinsically motivated students read additional books by authors of books required for the course. Unlike these students, many other students require external motivators to get them to learn. Common extrinsic motivators include rules such as participation policies, required reading assignments, and grades.

Box 5.6. Learner-Centered Example of Motivation of Students to Learn

Jeegisha Patel (2006) teaches a course in which the preprofessional health care students apply therapeutic knowledge to patient cases. In the past, each student was responsible for making a presentation on a care plan for a specific patient once or twice during the semester. Following the presentation, the students were supposed to discuss the rationale for their therapeutic choice. She noticed that the majority of students did not participate in the class discussion and demonstrated the therapeutic knowledge only when they were presenting. Patel wanted to help the students to be more motivated to learn and to apply therapeutic knowledge to patients. In addition, she wanted her students to retain the material better.

In place of case presentations, Patel instituted weekly games to discuss patient care and care plans. She and one of the students collaboratively develop a game for the rest of the students to play. Students and instructor developed games using television quiz show formats, classic board games, or party games. Patel found that the game format aroused student interest and participation. Students consistently came more prepared for class and expressed how much they appreciated learning the content.

Many of us who teach have found that some of our students have increasingly less intrinsic motivation to learn and spend few out-of-class hours preparing for their courses. We have responded by instituting more rules, such as requiring class attendance, and by relying more on extrinsic motivators, such as giving points for class participation (Weimer, 2002). The more instructors provide these extrinsic motivators, the less the students are intrinsically motivated to learn. Although these policies get the students to learn enough to pass the course, they do not help the students become intrinsically motivated to learn.

When instructors use games they often subconsciously motivate students to learn intrinsically, as discussed in Box 5.6. The competition inherent in games is an intrinsic motivator for students to come to class better prepared.

Analysis of the Psych 101 Course for the Role of the Instructor

I described a general education psychology course in the Introduction to Part Two. If you identify the learner-centered to instructor-centered status of this course on the rubric for the Role of the Instructor before reading my analysis, you will gain a deeper understanding of the components of this practice. This activity will help you apply these ideas to your course.

Where would you place the Psych 101 course on the learner-centered to instructor-centered continuum for the Role of the Instructor? Use a copy of the rubric for the Role of the Instructor from Appendix B to indicate your ratings.

Here are my ratings and explanation for these ratings for the Psych 101 Course. (Table 5.4, which summarizes my ratings, appears after the individual component explanations.)

Component 1: Environment for Learning

Rating: Employs higher level of transitioning; the instructor creates a learning environment through use of one out of the two subcriteria.

- The instructor creates an environment that fosters student learning through the organization and use of materials:

  - She reinforces the material in the textbook in her lectures. She also gives copies of her lecture notes to the students.

  - She gives demonstrations on the concepts.

  - She gives a study guide outlining key concepts and questions for the students to learn.

  - The Intra-teach sessions foster student learning. During these sessions, the students review the material with each other and can ask questions on aspects of the material that they did not understand.

- The instructor does not attend to learning style differences.

Component 2: Alignment of the Course Components—Objectives, Teaching or Learning Methods, and Assessment Methods—for Consistency

Rating: Employs lower level of transitioning; the instructor *minimally* aligns objectives, teaching or learning methods, and assessment *or* aligns two out of the three course components.

The objectives state that the students will be able to recognize or describe both verbally and in the written mode basic knowledge of psychology. The learning activities used by the students are small-group discussions in which they describe this knowledge. The instructor uses short-answer and multiple-choice tests in the assessments; these tools require either recognition or description, thus showing alignment.

- The three objectives require the acquisition of three different types of knowledge, and that is the focus of the learning activities and assessments, thus showing alignment.

- The third objective, "Individual differences regarding cognition, affect, and behavior in organisms, especially the human species," could require the students to determine or analyze individual differences in novel situations. However, the instructor does not provide learning opportunities for this to happen, nor does the instructor assess the students on this. This is an area of nonalignment in this course.

- Although the students use the transdisciplinary skills, such as communication and teamwork, throughout the course, the instructor does not assess these skills. The instructor does not provide instruction or learning activities whereby the students can learn how to improve these skills. This is an area of nonalignment in this course.

Table 5.3 summarizes how the course is aligned.

Component 3: Teaching or Learning Methods Appropriate for Student Learning Goals

Rating: Employs higher level of transitioning; the instructor uses *some* teaching or learning methods that are appropriate for student learning goals.

- The instructor uses lectures, demonstrations, and reading assignments to help the students acquire the three types of knowledge listed in her objectives.

- The small group discussions in the Intra-teach sessions should help the students recognize and describe the knowledge listed in the learning goals.

- Although the students use the transdisciplinary skills, the instructor does not teach the students how to use these skills more effectively.

TABLE 5.3

Alignment of Levels of Objectives, Teaching or Learning Methods, and Assessment Methods in the Psych 101 Course.

What level is each of the following?	Aspect is not included in the course	Low level (knowledge or comprehension)	Medium level (application or analysis)	High level (synthesis or evaluation)
Objectives		Objectives 1 and 2, transdisciplinary skills	Objective 3	
Teaching or learning methods	Transdisciplinary skills	Small-group discussions		
Assessment methods	Transdisciplinary skills	Short-answer and multiple-choice examinations		

Component 4: Activities Involving Student, Instructor, Content Interactions

Rating: Employs lower level of transitioning; the instructor uses a *few* activities in which students actively interact with material, or instructor, or each other.

- The Intra-teach sessions allow the students to interact with the material and each other.

- The students do not interact with the instructor collaboratively during the course.

Figure 5.3 summarizes these interactions graphically.

Component 5: Articulation of SMART Objectives

Rating: Employs lower level of transitioning; the instructor articulates in the syllabus course objectives that do not have all five attributes of SMART objectives.

- The instructor does articulate course objectives in the syllabus, but does not refer to them in her teaching.

- The instructor does not employ SMART objectives:
  - The Psych 101 objectives are measurable, attainable, and relevant.
  - These objectives are not specific and not time oriented.

Component 6: Motivation of Students to Learn

Rating: Employs instructor-centered approaches; the instructor extensively uses extrinsic motivators to get students to earn grades.

- The instructor uses extrinsic motivators to get students to earn grades throughout the course:

FIGURE 5.3

Diagram of Interactions Among Students, Instructor, and Content in the Psych 101 Course.

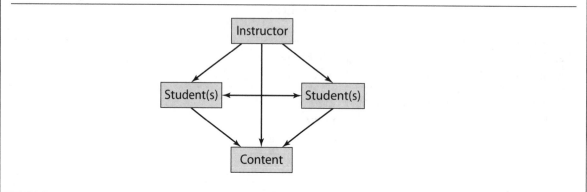

- All of the course policies, especially these relating to how the students earn their grades, reinforce the use of extrinsic motivation.

- The only reason students see for taking this course is that it meets a general education requirement.

- The only reason the students see for learning the content is to pass or get a good grade in the course.

- The instructor provides explicit study guides and examination outlines. Each study guide and examination outline tells the students exactly what they need to learn, but it does not explain why they need to learn this material.

In Table 5.4, the boldface cells indicate my ratings.

TABLE 5.4

Ratings for the Psych 101 Course on the Role of the Instructor Dimension.

The Role of the Instructor

Component	Employs *instructor-centered* approaches →	→ Transitioning to learner-centered approaches →		Employs *learner-centered* approaches
		Lower level of transitioning	**Higher level of transitioning**	
1. Creation of an environment for learning through (1) organization and (2) use of material that accommodates different learning styles	Instructor uses the same approach or approaches throughout the course even if the students are not learning.	Instructor does not focus on creating a learning environment, but students do learn.	**Instructor creates a learning environment through use of one out of the two subcriteria.**	Instructor creates a learning environment by using both subcriteria: through organization and use of material that accommodates different learning styles.
2. Alignment of the course components: objectives, teaching or learning methods, and assessment methods—for consistency	Instructor does *not* align objectives, teaching or learning methods, and assessment methods	**Instructor • *Minimally* aligns objectives, teaching or learning methods, and assessment methods *or* • Aligns two out of the three course components**	Instructor *somewhat* aligns objectives, teaching or learning methods, and assessment methods.	Instructor explicitly, coherently, and consistently aligns objectives, teaching or learning methods, and assessment methods.

(Continued)

TABLE 5.4

Ratings for the Psych 101 Course on the Role of the Instructor Dimension. (*Continued*)

The Role of the Instructor

Component	Employs *instructor-centered* approaches →	→ Transitioning to learner-centered approaches →		Employs *learner-centered* approaches
		Lower level of transitioning	Higher level of transitioning	
3. Teaching or learning methods appropriate for student learning goals	Instructor • Does *not* have specified learning goals *or* • Uses teaching and learning methods that conflict with learning goals	Instructor • Uses teaching and learning methods without regard for student learning goals *and/or* • Does not use active learning activities	**Instructor uses *some* teaching or learning methods that are appropriate for student learning goals.**	Instructor intentionally uses *various* teaching or learning methods that are appropriate for student learning goals.
4. Activities involving student, instructor, content interactions	Instructor uses no activities in which students actively interact with material, or instructor, or each other.	**Instructor uses a few activities in which students actively interact with material, or instructor, or each other.**	Instructor uses *some* activities in which • Students actively interact with material, or instructor, or each other *or* • There are some three-way interactions	Instructor *routinely* uses activities in which students actively interact with material, and instructor, and each other.
5. Articulation of SMART objectives: • **S**pecific • **M**easurable • **A**ttainable • **R**elevant • **T**ime oriented	Instructor • Articulates vague course objectives *and/or* • Does not articulate objectives in syllabus	**Instructor articulates in syllabus course objectives that do not have all five attributes of SMART objectives.**	Instructor articulates SMART objectives in syllabus but does not refer to them throughout the course.	Instructor articulates SMART objectives in syllabus and regularly refers to them throughout the course.
6. Motivation of students to learn (intrinsic drive to learn versus extrinsic reasons to earn grades)	**Instructor extensively uses extrinsic motivators to get students to earn grades.**	Instructor • Provides *limited* opportunities for students to become intrinsically motivated to learn • Uses extrinsic motivators to get students to earn grades	Instructor provides *some* opportunities for students to become intrinsically motivated to learn.	Instructor inspires and encourages students to become intrinsically motivated to learn.

Transforming the Psych 101 Course to Be More Learner-Centered

When the Psych 101 instructor reviewed how she rated her course in terms of the Role of the Instructor, she felt that she had to think about changing "Motivation of students to learn," because that was the only component on this dimension on which she rated her course as instructor-centered. Yet this is a general education course and many of the students are not intrinsically motivated to learn. Over the years, the students appreciated her extrinsic motivators, such as points for participating in the Intra-teach sessions. This instructor found that when she provided motivators that are more extrinsic, the students earned higher grades. This created a philosophical dilemma for her. Encouraging students to have intrinsic motivation for their own learning is quite different from what she has found works with the Psych 101 students in the past. She decided that the level most appropriate for general education courses would be the higher level of transitioning. Yet she was not comfortable that she could attain this level immediately. She completed the Planning for Transformation exercise for this component, as shown in Exhibit 5.1.

Chapter Summary

As a learner-centered instructor, you

- Create an environment for learning
- Align your curriculum
- Routinely use activities in which students interact with you, the material, and each other
- Articulate and refer to smart objectives
- Motivate and inspire your students to take responsibility for their own learning

When you engage in these learner-centered practices, you will use the students' time to foster their learning. Your assignments and the nature of your assignments further reinforce their learning. In the next chapter, you will focus on the students' developing abilities to take responsibility for learning. The instructors assist the students to be able to take this responsibility.

The application activity will help you to determine where your course is on the Role of the Instructor continuum and begin to help you think about transforming your course to be more learner-centered. First, answer the questions or complete the tables that relate to the components of the Role of Instructor rubric. Then copy and use the rubric for the Role of the Instructor

EXHIBIT 5.1

The Planning for Transformation Exercise 1 for the Role of the Instructor Component 2

Date: 3-25-07

A. Status of your course now

1. Dimension of learner-centered teaching: *The Role of the Instructor*

2. Component: 6. *Motivation of students to learn*

3. Current level:

    ☑ Instructor-centered

    ❏ Lower level of transitioning

    ❏ Higher level of transitioning

4. Briefly describe your current implementation (to document your baseline prior to transformation).

    I use extrinsic motivators, such as participation points to get the students to come to the Intra-teach sessions. I also take away points when they do not participate in these activities. Given the lack of enthusiasm I experience with these students, I doubt if anything I do in this course inspires them to learn intrinsically.

B. Desired changes:

1. Describe the desired changes you wish to make for this component in the near future.

    a. *I need to feel comfortable that general education students can use intrinsic motivators to learn. My current course supports my lack of faith in students to use intrinsic motivation. For example, my syllabus states the following objective: "Students should be able to describe fundamental concepts and theories that form the empirically supported knowledge base for cognition, affect, and behavior." Yet I do not explain why students should be motivated to learn this. Instead, I write expectations such as," Students are expected to read the textbook prior to the lecture. All students are encouraged to study regularly, not just before examinations, study actively, comparing, con-trasting, and organizing, and participate actively in class." I do not provide intrinsic reasons why the students should engage in these behaviors. Further, all of my policies reinforce extrinsic motivation to get a good grade.*

    b. *I need to develop a few opportunities that encourage students to become intrinsically motivated to learn, as a way to build my confidence in the students and as a way to begin to develop this type of motivation in the students. I need to change my policies away from extrinsic motivators to earn grades toward encouraging intrinsic motivation to learn.*

    c. *I think psychology is such a fascinating discipline that has so many applications to everyday life, yet I do not convey these intrinsic reasons to learn psychology to my students. I need to give the students real reasons why they should learn the material and not just to pass this course.*

(Continued)

2. What is the level you want to achieve with this/these changes?

   ❏ Instructor-centered

   ☑ Lower level of transitioning

   ❏ Higher level of transitioning

   ❏ Learner-centered

C. Tactical planning questions

   1. What do you need to do, decide, or learn about prior to making changes?

      a. *Explore how other instructors, especially those who teach general education courses, encourage their students to become intrinsically motivated to learn. Evaluate whether any of these strategies make sense for my course.*

      b. *Examine my policies and practices to see if I can change some of the extrinsic motivators to encourage students to become more intrinsically motivated.*

   2. What obstacles or challenges do you need to overcome to successfully implement this change? (Resistance may come from your philosophy of teaching, your chair, your peers, your students, or the culture of your institution.)

      I do not trust my students to become intrinsically motivated to learn.

      I need to develop some confidence that students will begin to change their motivation.

      These are big obstacles for me.

   3. Identify specific strategies (such as learning about successful implementations, trying a small pilot implementation, explaining to your students and other instructors why you are making these changes) for overcoming each obstacle or challenge.

      a. *I would like to hear that other instructors of these same general education students have been successful inspiring and encouraging students to become intrinsically motivated to learn.*

      b. *As a psychology instructor I can use learning and motivation principles (content that I cover in my course) to show how the students will learn more in the long term if they become intrinsically motivated to learn. I will apply the content of this course as a means to assist students to become intrinsically motivated to learn. I will talk about why intrinsic motivation is superior to extrinsic motivation and how such motivating forces will benefit them in their professional and personal lives.*

   4. What resources (such as time, money, student assistants, or computer software) would help you implement your change?

      I could consult with other instructors or the center for faculty development and teaching improvement, or I could read literature on learner-centered approaches.

   5. What do you need to do to get your students to accept this change? (Possibilities include repeated explanations for why you are doing what you are doing or having the activity count in the final grade.)

      I know that I will have to explain explicitly and repeatedly why I am encouraging the students to become intrinsically motivated to learn. I will have to be consistent in enforcing policies that encourage intrinsic motivation to learn and not fall back on my pattern of using extrinsic motivators.

      I can ask the students to reflect on their motivation for learning.

(Continued)

D. Outcomes of the change:

1. In what ways will implementing this change influence other aspects of your course to be more learner-centered? (For example, when you incorporate various teaching or learning methods that are consistent with your student learning goals [Component 3 of the Role of the Instructor dimension], most likely the students will more actively engage in the content [Component 2 of the Function of Content dimension].)

   Transitioning to more learner-centered approaches directly will effect the first component of the Responsibility for Learning dimension, "responsibility for learning." It will also influence the last component of the Balance of Power dimension, "opportunities to learn."

2. In what ways (such as increased learning) will your students benefit from this change? How will the students behave differently (such as increased participation in class or greater engagement with the content)?

   The students should engage more with the content and learn more. They will be motivated to learn the material and not just motivated to get good grades.

3. In what ways will you benefit from this change? (For example, more enjoyment of teaching, satisfaction that your students are learning more, anticipation of fewer student complaints.)

   I will be satisfied if my students learn more. I will gain more trust in my students.

   On the negative side, I anticipate more student complaints.

E. Possible future changes:

1. What is the optimal level for this component for this course?

   ❏ Lower level of transitioning

   ☑ Higher level of transitioning

   ❏ Learner-centered

2. In the long term, what additional changes, if any, might you make to further transform this component to reach this optimal level of the learner-centered approach?

   I will have to wait and see the results of my first attempts.

in Appendix B to evaluate the status of your course. After answering the questions, you should be able to complete the rubric easily. Your answers should also prepare you to select two or three components that you can transform.

Completing the Role of the Instructor Rubric for Your Course

Keep your answers to the questions in the application activity in mind as you complete the Role of the Instructor rubric, found in Appendix B, for your course.

- Read across each entire row before deciding which level is appropriate.

- For each specific component, circle or mark the appropriate level in the row.

- If you decide that the learner-centered level is not appropriate for your course on a component or subcomponent, think of a rationale or justification for that decision.

Planning for Transformation

After you complete the rubric, select two or three specific components that you might want to change. Then copy and complete a Planning for Transformation exercise, found in Appendix B, for each of those components.

APPLICATION ACTIVITY

Questions and Assessment Diagrams About the Role of the Instructor in Your Course

Component 1. Creation of an Environment for Learning
- What would be the ideal environment for learning through organization and use of material, and accommodating different learning styles in your course?

- To what extent are you incorporating this ideal learning environment in your course?
  - ❏ Not at all
  - ❏ Somewhat
  - ❏ Mostly
  - ❏ Completely
  - If you did not answer "Completely," how can you create a better environment for learning in your course?

Component 2. Alignment of the course components: objectives, teaching or learning methods and assessment methods for consistency
Think about the alignment of course components.

Complete a set of tables as presented in Table 5.5, one for each of your objectives for your course, by noting your objectives, teaching or learning methods, and assessment methods within the cell or cells for the appropriate level. If you do not have a teaching or learning method or an assessment for an objective, indicate that by checking "Aspect is not included in the course" in the second column.

- Next, draw a line or lines connecting these columns. If you drew a horizontal line within a row, your course uses more than one type of approach for this aspect. For example, you might use both low-level comprehension quizzes and a high-level synthesis project for assessment methods. Using more than one type of approach within a row can be appropriate. If you can draw a straight, vertical line connecting all three cells, you have an aligned course. You can have an aligned course at each of the three levels. If you drew a vertical and a diagonal line or two diagonal lines with two points in the same column, you have a mostly or partially aligned course.

To decide whether your course is at the higher level or the lower level of transitioning, refer to the wording in the rubric itself. A diagonal line means you have a nonaligned course. If you marked anything in the second column because you do not include this aspect in your objectives, teaching or learning methods, or assessment methods, you do not align this aspect of the course.

(Continued)

TABLE 5.5

Alignment of Levels of Objectives, Teaching or Learning Methods, and Assessment Methods of Your Course.

What level is each of the following?	Aspect is not included in the course	Low level (knowledge or comprehension)	Medium level (application or analysis)	High level (synthesis or evaluation)
Objective				
Teaching or learning methods				
Assessment methods				

- Your course is
  - ❏ Not aligned
  - ❏ Partially aligned
  - ❏ Mostly aligned
  - ❏ Aligned
- If you have a less than aligned course, how can you align your course more?

Component 3. Teaching or Learning Methods Appropriate for Student Learning Goals
- What are your student learning goals for this course?

Goal #1

Goal #2

Goal #3

- For goal #1, in an ideal learning environment, how would the students learn to reach this goal?

- For goal #2, in an ideal learning environment, how would the students learn to reach this goal?

- For goal #3, in an ideal learning environment, how would the students learn to reach this goal?

- Now compare your goals with these ideal teaching or learning methods. How many of these teaching or learning methods are you using now?
  - ❑ Few or none
  - ❑ Most
  - ❑ All

- How can you incorporate more of these teaching or learning methods into your course?

Component 4. Activities Involving Student, Instructor, Content Interactions

- In a classroom-style course, describe what you and the students typically do.

- In an online or distance course, describe how the students spend their time.

- Now diagram the interactions on the diamond configuration. Use arrows to show interactions.

(Continued)

```
                        ┌─────────────┐
                        │ Instructor  │
                        └─────────────┘


        ┌─────────────┐              ┌─────────────┐
        │  Student(s) │              │  Student(s) │
        └─────────────┘              └─────────────┘


                        ┌─────────────┐
                        │   Content   │
                        └─────────────┘
```

A single-headed arrow shows one-way communication, such as when an instructor is lecturing to the students. A double-headed arrow indicates two-way interactions among students, such as when the students are using content materials in a small group discussion. If no interaction occurs, do not place an arrow between them.

- If you do not foster interactions among the instructor, the students, and the content, how can you incorporate more of these interactions?

Component 5. Articulation of SMART objectives (SMART = Specific, Measurable, Attainable, Relevant, Time oriented)

- Do your objectives describe what change will result as a function of taking this course?
  ___Yes ___No

  (If yes, you employ the specific aspect of SMART objectives.)

- Do your objectives describe how much change will result as function of taking this course?
  ___Yes ___No

  (If yes, you employ the measurable aspect of SMART objectives.)

- Do your objectives describe who or what will change as a function of taking this course?
  ___Yes ___No

  (If yes, you employ the attainable aspect of SMART objectives.)

- Do your objectives describe how the changes are relevant as a function of taking this course?
  ___Yes ___No

  (If yes, you employ the relevant aspect of SMART objectives.)

- Do your objectives describe when the change will occur as function of taking this course?
  ___Yes ___No

  (If yes, you employ the timeframe aspect of SMART objectives.)

(Continued)

- How can you rewrite your objectives to be in a SMART format?

- How often and in what way do you refer to your objectives throughout your course?

- If you do not refer to your objectives consistently throughout the course, how could you do so more regularly?

Component 6. Motivation of Students to Learn

- In an ideal environment, how would an instructor inspire and encourage students to become intrinsically motivated to learn?

- How much do you explicitly inspire and encourage your students to become intrinsically motivated to learn?

  ❏ Not at all

  ❏ Somewhat

  ❏ Mostly

  ❏ Completely

- If you did not answer "Completely," how could you explicitly inspire and encourage your students to be more motivated to learn?

Chapter 6

The Responsibility for Learning

HISTORICALLY, IN THE eighteenth and nineteenth centuries, the highly motivated students who went to college most likely took responsibility for their own learning. However, as more people began going to college—particularly those with less motivation and more constraints on their time—fewer of them were autonomous, responsible learners on their own. As a result, by the second half of the twentieth century, instructors were taking more responsibility for the students' learning, perhaps without even thinking about it.

When instructors take responsibility for their students' learning, they define what will be learned, direct how it will be learned, and determine how well it is learned. Some people may accept these roles as appropriate for instructors. However, as a consequence of an instructor's assuming too much responsibility for student learning, the students remain passive and lack confidence in their abilities to learn on their own (Weimer, 2002). Today, because we do not explicitly teach college students the skills to become lifelong learners, many college graduates are not self-directed learners (Candy, 1991). Yet the ability to be a lifelong learner is an essential skill for success in one's career and personal life. Although this always was true, it is becoming much more relevant in today's fast-changing, globally connected world.

Needed: Proactive Development of Responsibility for Learning Skills

Many diverse internal and external drivers are pushing students toward taking greater responsibility for themselves, their learning, and the other components of this dimension. Thus self-direction is increasingly a goal for college students (Candy, 1991). The development of self-regulated learners (Pintrich, 2000) is another common goal of higher education. In addition, accreditation agencies now require students to have information literacy skills and to be more prepared to engage with their world through participation in democracy or civic engagement (Middle States Commission on Higher Education, 2003a and 2003b). Students who take responsibility for their own continued learning usually become citizens who are better informed on current issues (Association of American Colleges and Universities, 2002).

Many students fail to develop the responsibility for learning skills on their own. When the responsibility for learning shifts from the instructor to the students, the instructor supports students in their taking responsibility for their own learning and helps them acquire skills they can use to learn in the future. Students become proficient in independent learning and self-assessment skills only when they have numerous opportunities to practice these skills and consistently receive formative feedback to help them to improve. Therefore, as a learner-centered instructor you should be proactive to ensure this development by planning repeated and varied opportunities for all your students to practice them.

Components of the Responsibility for Learning

The rubric for the Responsibility for Learning dimension, Table 6.1, shows the continuum from instructor-centered to learner-centered approaches for six components.

Component 1: Responsibility for Learning

The key element in this component is who takes responsibility for learning to occur, along a continuum between the instructor taking full responsibility and the student taking increasing responsibility.

This component can be hard to accept, because we find that when we provide students with detailed and elaborate learning aids—such by as providing lecture notes, study questions, outlines from reading, or test reviews—they do better on our courses than if we did not provide them. Although these techniques get the students to meet the short-term objectives of the course, they do not help the students learn how to take responsibility for their own learning. When the instructor takes responsibility for the students' learning, it is unlikely that the students will learn how to do so. To become more learner-centered, instructors must overcome the tendency to do things for the students that take away their opportunities to assume responsibility for their own learning. However, before you help students to assume responsibility for their learning opportunities, *you* need

TABLE 6.1

The Rubric for the Responsibility for Learning Dimension of Learner-Centered Teaching.

The Responsibility for Learning

Component	Employs *instructor-centered* approaches →	→ Transitioning to learner-centered approaches →		Employs *learner-centered* approaches
		Lower level of transitioning	**Higher level of transitioning**	
1. Responsibility for learning	Instructor assumes *all* responsibility for student learning: • Provides content to memorize • Does not require students to create their own meaning of content • Tells students exactly what will be on examinations	Instructor assumes *most* responsibility for student learning: • Provides detailed notes of content to be learned • Reviews content to be examined while helping students learn the material and meet objectives	Instructor provides *some* opportunities for students to assume responsibility for their own learning.	Instructor provides *increasing* opportunities for students to assume responsibility for their own learning, leading to achievement of stated learning objectives.
2. Learning to learn skills for the present and the future—including, for example: • Time management • Self-monitoring • Goal setting • How to do independent reading • How to conduct original research	Instructor allows students to meet course objectives without developing further learning skills.	Instructor directs students to develop a *few* skills for further learning.	Instructor directs students to develop *some* skills for further learning.	Instructor facilitates students to develop *various and appropriate* skills for further learning.

(Continued)

TABLE 6.1

The Rubric for the Responsibility for Learning Dimension of Learner-Centered Teaching. (*Continued*)

The Responsibility for Learning

Component	Employs *instructor-centered* approaches →	→ Transitioning to learner-centered approaches →		Employs *learner-centered* approaches
		Lower level of transitioning	**Higher level of transitioning**	
3. Self-directed, lifelong learning skills—including, for example: • Determining a personal need to know more • Knowing who to ask or where to seek information • Determining when need is met *and* • Development of self-awareness of students' own learning abilities	Instructor does *not* consider: • Self-directed learning skills relevant *or* • Self-awareness of students' learning abilities relevant	The instructor does *not* assist students to become • Self-directed, lifelong learners *or* • Aware of their own learning and abilities to learn	Instructor assists students to become: • Self-directed, lifelong learners in a few areas *and* • Somewhat aware of their own learning, and abilities to learn	Instructor facilitates students to become: • Proficient, self-directed, lifelong learners *and* • Fully aware of their own learning and abilities to learn
4. Students' self-assessment of their learning	Instructor • Believes that instructors alone assess student learning *or* • Does not consider self-assessment of learning relevant	Instructor does not direct students to assess their own learning.	Instructor sometimes provides direction to help students assess their own learning.	Instructor motivates students to routinely and appropriately assess their own learning.
5. Students' self-assessment of their strengths and weaknesses	Instructor believes that only instructors should assess students' strengths and weaknesses.	Instructor does not direct students to practice self-assessments.	Instructor helps students practice some self-assessment skills.	Instructor encourages students to become proficient at self-assessment.

(Continued)

TABLE 6.1 (*Continued*)

The Responsibility for Learning

Component	Employs *instructor-centered* approaches →	→ Transitioning to learner-centered approaches →		Employs *learner-centered* approaches
		Lower level of transitioning	**Higher level of transitioning**	
6. Information literacy skills: (a) framing questions, (b) accessing sources, (c) evaluating sources, (d) evaluating content, (e) using information legally (as defined by the Association of College and Research Libraries)	Instructor does not help students acquire any information literacy skills.	Instructor helps students acquire two of the five information literacy skills.	Instructor helps students acquire four of the five information literacy skills.	Instructor facilitates students to become proficient in all five information literacy skills.

to accept philosophically the importance of students' taking responsibility for their own learning. The literature on improving college teaching has not emphasized the essential aspect of this acceptance enough. You need to believe that responsibility for learning should rest with the students.

With learner-centered approaches and the higher level of transitioning, the students take increasing—or at least some—responsibility for learning, under the guidance and support of the instructor. In the beginning, instructors give students more guidance and more structure. As the course progresses, instructors give students less guidance so that students will assume more responsibility for their own learning. For example, in the beginning of the course, the instructor might provide directed study questions and explain why these concepts are important. As the semester progresses, the instructor might help students to develop their own study questions. At the end of the semester, the students would develop their own study questions. Box 6.1 gives an example of how an instructor can help students take responsibility for their learning.

Box 6.1. Learner-Centered Example of Responsibility for Learning

Pamalyn Kearney and Paula Kramer (2007) provide increasing opportunities for their occupational therapy students to accept responsibility for learning. Throughout the semester, each student works with one client with a disability to develop accommodations that can help this person function better. The instructors provide different types of guiding questions for the students to answer in weekly, written reflections of their interactions with this client. These questions require the students to take increasing responsibility for the development of appropriate accommodations and reflect more deeply on their own learning. In addition, the instructors meet weekly with the students in small groups. In the beginning, they structure the discussion and model what the students should be considering. As the semester progresses, the instructors assist the students to take increasing leadership of the group discussions, and finally the students run the entire session, with the instructors offering guidance and professional insights.

Component 2: Learning-to-Learn Skills for the Present and Future

Good students use skills to make their learning time more efficient. Educators call these "learning-to-learn" skills (Candy, 1991). These include, for example, time management, self-monitoring, goal setting, how to do independent reading, and how to conduct original research. Students need to acquire further learning-to-learn skills as they progress through college. Unfortunately, many instructors either assume their students already have these skills or do not take the time to teach them. Learner-centered instructors explicitly teach students appropriate learning-to-learn skills throughout their careers in higher education:

- Instructors of beginning students often need to assist students to acquire and practice basic learning-to-learn skills, and many First Year Experience or College Success courses focus on the acquisition of these skills. Students in these courses plan how they want to spend their time to promote a balance among study, recreation, exercise, and sleep. They also learn different note-taking and study strategies and how to access resources (Kuh, Kinzie, Schuh, & Whitt, 2005).

- Upper-class students need guidance in time management when they are doing independent studies or conducting research.

- Faculty can also assist graduating students in the learning-to-learn skills of looking for full-time employment.

- Graduate students need to learn self-monitoring skills, such as knowing when they have done enough reading of previous literature to have a command of the content.

Component 3: Self-Directed, Lifelong Learning Skills

These skills include, for example, determining a personal need to know more, knowing who to ask or where to seek information, determining when a need is met, and development of self-awareness of one's own learning abilities. Lifelong learning patterns, such as the practices of reading the current professional literature and keeping up with the latest innovations in their field, do not develop naturally in all students. Instead, instructors often need to take a very active role in helping students develop self-directed learning skills so that learning continues after graduation.

Philip Candy (1991) defined three dimensions of self-directed learning: the processes of learning, learning strategies, and performance outcomes of self-directed learning. The *learning processes* include the ability to define what to learn, plan for, and conduct the learning through using effective time management strategies, and to evaluate the effectiveness of resources consulted and make an assessment of one's own learning. *Learning strategies* refer to how students study and process information. *Performance outcomes* include independent learning behaviors that persist beyond graduation.

Problem-based learning—a learner-centered approach widely used in health professions education—fosters the development of self-directed, lifelong learning. In problem-based learning, the iterative discussion of a problem is the essence of the teaching or learning method. Students discuss all material twice, once without prior preparation and then again after researching questions raised during the first discussion. The second time the students discuss a problem, they should synthesize all that they learned through an integrated discussion of the problem.

The following are some distinguishing features of problem-based learning that foster the development of self-directed learning:

- Students develop an intrinsic motivation to learn based on their own questions and their desire to solve the problems

- Students need to research the content on their own without the instructor giving it to them

- Peer pressure to come prepared to the second iteration of the problem

A review of the literature on problem-based learning programs concluded that these programs develop self-directed learning skills (Blumberg, 2000). Students in problem-based programs use information resources such as those found in libraries or in electronic databases in a self-directed fashion. They engage in learning for meaning so that they can apply what they have learned to solve the problems posed to them in their discussions. They also develop the learning process, self-directed learning skills, such as the ability to define what they need to learn and to self-assess if they have answered their own questions. Even after students finish their problem-based learning curriculum, they continue to use self-directed learning skills (Blumberg, 2000).

Component 4: Students' Self-Assessment of Their Learning

A key aspect of this component is self-awareness of learning and of one's abilities to learn. Students need to be able to assess their own learning and to determine how much mastery they have, independent of someone else telling them how much they have learned. Self-assessment of learning should focus on a combination of the learner, what students learned, and how they learned (Kramp & Humphries, 1995). Good students think about their learning and have insights into worthwhile learning experiences for themselves. They know how they prefer to learn. Many of these abilities are discipline-specific.

Box 6.2 describes how engineering students became aware of their abilities to learn through writing reflective journals on their learning.

Component 5: Students' Self-Assessment of Their Strengths and Weaknesses

In this component, students assess themselves on many different types of strengths and weaknesses including, but not limited to, interpersonal skills, organization, organizational abilities, mastery of skills including communication skills, and knowledge. Writing is a skill that can improve

---

Box 6.2. Learner-Centered Example of Students' Self-Assessment of Their Learning

Sati Maharaj and Larry Banta (2000) required engineering students to write at least one page per week in a journal or learning log throughout the semester. The directions for the entries changed during the semester, so they experienced writing different types of learning logs. Students wrote chapter summaries, analogies from the engineering principles to everyday life, explanations in their own words, and descriptions of how they solved word problems. They could also incorporate techniques used in previous weeks.

As would be expected, early in the semester these engineering students expressed skepticism and dislike of writing. However, by the end of the semester most students realized that these assignments had helped them to organize and retain the information better. End-of-semester interviews with the students and log inspections revealed that the students discovered which type of writing activity they preferred, and by the end of the semester they used their preferred writing activity in their logs, even when it was not required. They stated that the writing assignments helped them to see the relationships between the engineering concepts and real-world applications.

Box 6.3. Learner-Centered Example of Students' Self-Assessment of Their Strengths and Weaknesses

Rochelle Harris (2003) requires her students to include reflective letters in their composition portfolios. The students develop a portfolio documenting different types of writing they did during the course and showing examples of their most polished work. They hand in their portfolios at the midterm for feedback and again at the final for the summative grade. As an introduction to their portfolios, students submit a letter explaining what they included in their portfolio and reflecting on what they learned through the various components of the class activities, including their written responses to the reading, what they learned about revision, and about their own writing process and style. For the midterm reflective letter, the students need to define their learning goals and learning plans for the rest of the semester. They must quote their own writing to support their claims about what they are learning.

---

with reflection and self-critique, as shown in Box 6.3. The areas in which students employ self-assessment vary by course because of different student-learning outcomes.

Component 6: Information Literacy Skills

The Association of College and Research Libraries (2004) defined five essential information literacy skills: the ability to (a) frame researchable questions, (b) access sources, (c) evaluate sources, (d) evaluate content contained in these sources, and (e) use information legally and ethically. Access means the ability to obtain and use information acquired from print and electronic resources. In today's academic environment, students think they know how to find information because they use the Google search engine. However, there are many specialized databases for each discipline, and students need to learn how to use them to access information. Evaluation includes assessing the source of the information and the accuracy of the information itself. Legal and ethical use of information includes properly paraphrasing and citing, and not plagiarizing. Instructors, perhaps in conjunction with librarians, can teach these skills explicitly and assess their proper usage. Box 6.4 describes how a librarian teaches these skills.

Box 6.4. Learner-Centered Example of Information Literacy Skills

Leslie Ann Bowman (2007) teaches information literacy skills with an emphasis on finding and evaluating the sources, either in a one-credit course or incorporated in a course that concentrates on a discipline other than information science. She teaches students how to search effectively and efficiently common databases such as LexisNexis and specialized databases such as Facts & Comparisons. Although she explains how to evaluate any information source, she focuses on those found on the World Wide Web. She gives criteria for how to evaluate sites.

Professional and regional accreditation agencies now require that students demonstrate these information literacy skills (Middle States Commission on Higher Education, 2003b).

The Responsibility for Learning Analysis of the Psych 101 Course

Where would you place the Psych 101 course (described in the end of the Introduction to Part Two) on the learner-centered to instructor-centered rubric for the Responsibility for Learning? Use a copy of the rubric in Appendix B to indicate your ratings.

The following section details and explains my ratings for the Psych 101 Course. (Table 6.2, which summarizes my ratings, follows the individual component explanations.)

Component 1: Responsibility for Learning

Rating: Employs lower level of transitioning; the instructor assumes most responsibility for student learning.

- The instructor assumes most of the responsibility for learning because she

    - Gives the students copies of her lecture notes

    - Gives them all of the questions they need to prepare for the quizzes

    - Provides examination guides to help the students prepare for the examinations

The students have limited opportunities to take responsibility for their own learning when they come prepared for the Intra-teach sessions and use them as an effective review tool.

Component 2: Learning-to-Learn Skills for the Present and Future

Rating: Employs instructor-centered approach; the instructor allows students to meet course objectives without developing further learning skills.

- The instructor does not do anything to help the students develop learning skills even though this is a general education course.

- Although basic psychological principles, covered in the course, apply to some learning skills—such as the importance of goal setting and how to self-monitor or use time more effectively in distributed study sessions—the instructor does not help students to develop these skills through a discussion of them either during the relevant content or in class activities or assignments.

Component 3: Self-Directed, Lifelong Learning Skills *and* Development of Self-Awareness of Learning Abilities

Rating: Employs lower level of transitioning; the instructor does not assist students to become self-directed, lifelong learners *or* aware of their own learning and abilities to learn.

- Nothing in the course promotes the development of self-directed, lifelong learning. Instead, the instructor directs how the students learn.

- We do not know if the instructor considers self-directed, lifelong learning skills relevant or if she considers self-awareness of students' learning abilities relevant. The instructor-level could also be the appropriate rating.

Component 4: Students' Self-Assessment of Their Learning

Rating: Employs lower level of transitioning; the instructor does not direct students to assess their own learning.

- The instructor does not direct the students to assess their own learning, although there are many opportunities to do so. Instead, the instructor assesses students learning alone.

- We do not know whether the instructor believes that students' assessment of their own learning is relevant. The instructor-centered level could also be the appropriate rating.

Component 5: Students' Self-Assessment of Their Strengths and Weaknesses

Rating: Employs lower level of transitioning; instructor does not direct students to practice self-assessments.

The instructor does not assess students' strengths and weaknesses beyond knowledge of the content. She may not have considered it. She certainly neither directs nor helps students to do these self-assessments.

Component 6: Information Literacy Skills

Rating: Employs instructor-centered approach; the instructor does not help students acquire any information literacy skills.

The students do not acquire information literacy skills, as they receive all information from either the instructor or the textbook.

In Table 6.2, the boldface cells indicate my ratings.

TABLE 6.2

Ratings for the Psych 101 Course on the Responsibility for Learning Dimension of Learner-Centered Teaching.

The Responsibility for Learning

Component	Employs *instructor-centered* approaches →	→ Transitioning to learner-centered approaches →		Employs *learner-centered* approaches
		Lower level of transitioning	**Higher level of transitioning**	
1. Responsibility for learning	Instructor assumes *all* responsibility for student learning: • Provides content to memorize • Does not require students to create their own meaning of content • Tells students exactly what will be on examinations	**Instructor assumes *most* responsibility for student learning:** **• Provides detailed notes of content to be learned** **• Reviews content to be examined while helping students learn the material and meet objectives**	Instructor provides *some* opportunities for students to assume responsibility for their own learning.	Instructor provides *increasing* opportunities for students to assume responsibility for their own learning, leading to achievement of stated learning.
2. Learning to learn skills for the present and the future—including, for example: • Time management • Self-monitoring • Goal setting • How to do independent reading • How to conduct original research	**Instructor allows students to meet course objectives without developing further learning skills.**	Instructor directs students to develop a *few* skills for further learning.	Instructor directs students to develop *some* skills for further learning.	Instructor facilitates students to develop *various and appropriate* skills for further learning.

(Continued)

TABLE 6.2 (*Continued*)

The Responsibility for Learning

Component	Employs *instructor-centered* approaches →	→ Transitioning to learner-centered approaches →		Employs *learner-centered* approaches
		Lower level of transitioning	Higher level of transitioning	
3. Self-directed, lifelong learning skills—including, for example: • Determining a personal need to know more • Knowing who to ask or where to seek information • Determining when need is met *and* Development of self-awareness of students' own learning abilities	Instructor does *not consider:* • Self-directed learning skills relevant *or* • Self-awareness of students' learning abilities relevant	**The instructor does *not* assist students to become** • **Self-directed, lifelong learners** *or* • **Aware of their own learning and abilities to learn**	Instructor assists students to become: • Self-directed, lifelong learners in a few areas *and* • Somewhat aware of their own learning, and abilities to learn	Instructor facilitates students to become: • Proficient, self-directed, lifelong learners *and* • Fully aware of their own learning and abilities to learn
4. Students' self-assessment of their learning	Instructor • Believes that instructors alone assess student learning *or* • Does not consider self-assessment of learning relevant	Instructor does not direct students to assess their own learning.	**Instructor sometimes provides direction to help students assess their own learning.**	Instructor motivates students to routinely and appropriately assess their own learning.
5. Students' self-assessment of their strengths and weaknesses	Instructor believes that only instructors should assess students' strengths and weaknesses.	**Instructor does not direct students to practice self-assessments.**	Instructor helps students practice some self-assessment skills.	Instructor encourages students to become proficient at self-assessment.

(Continued)

TABLE 6.2

Ratings for the Psych 101 Course on the Responsibility for Learning Dimension of Learner-Centered Teaching. (*Continued*)

The Responsibility for Learning

Component	Employs *instructor-centered* approaches →	→ Transitioning to learner-centered approaches →		Employs *learner-centered* approaches
		Lower level of transitioning	**Higher level of transitioning**	
6. Information literacy skills: (a) framing questions, (b) accessing sources, (c) evaluating sources, (d) evaluating content, (e) using information legally (as defined by the Association of College and Research Libraries)	**Instructor does not help students acquire any information literacy skills.**	Instructor helps students acquire two of the five information literacy skills.	Instructor helps students acquire four of the five information literacy skills.	Instructor facilitates students to become proficient in all five information literacy skills.

Transforming the Psych 101 Course to Be More Learner-Centered

Given that this is a general education course, the instructor felt that components 1, "Responsibility for learning," 2, "Learning-to-learn skills or skills for future learning," and 4, "Students' self-assessment of their learning" were the most appropriate ones to begin to transform. They are also the most consistent with the objectives of the course and the content of general psychology. In addition to broadening knowledge and perspective, one of the purposes of general education is to develop students' ability to learn at a college level. The instructor's completion of the Planning for Transformation exercises on these components appears in Exhibits 6.1, 6.2, and 6.3.

EXHIBIT 6.1

The Planning for Transformation Exercise 1 for the Responsibility for Learning Component 1

A. Status of your course now   Date: 3-25-07

   1. Dimension of learner-centered teaching: *The Responsibility for Learning*

   2. Component: 1. *Responsibility for learning*

   3. Current level:

   ❑ Instructor-centered

   ☑ Lower level of transitioning

   ❑ Higher level of transitioning

   ❑ Learner-centered

   4. Briefly describe your current implementation (to document your baseline prior to transformation).

   I assume most of the responsibility for learning because I give the students copies of my lecture notes, give them all of the questions they need to prepare for the quizzes, and provide examination guides to help the students prepare for the examinations. The students take responsibility for their own learning when they come prepared for the Intra-teach sessions and use them as an effective review tool.

B. Desired changes:

   1. Describe the desired changes you wish to make for this component in the near future.

   My experience teaching general education students led me to assume greater responsibility for their learning. I need to encourage students to take responsibility for their own learning.

   I will see how other instructors of general education courses get students to assume responsibility for learning.

   2. What is the level you want to achieve with this/these changes?

   ❑ Instructor-centered

   ❑ Lower level of transitioning

   ☑ Higher level of transitioning

   ❑ Learner-centered

C. Tactical planning questions:

   1. What do you need to do, decide, or learn about prior to making changes?

   Explore how other instructors, especially those who teach general education courses, give their students opportunities to assume responsibility for their own learning. Evaluate if any of these strategies make sense for my course.

   As I explored what other instructors did within the Role of the Instructor, I believe that many of the techniques described in that chapter, taken together, should also help students to take responsibility for learning. Once I realized this, I knew that I had several ways to assist students to take responsibility for their own learning without compromising my course. Here are examples of the techniques that others are using that I could implement:

   • *Just-in-Time Teaching (JiTT) (Novak, Patterson, Gavrin, & Christian, 1999) is a technique that might help the students to take responsibility for their own learning. [Author's note: See Box 5.4 for more on JiTT.]*

(Continued)

- *I already ask a few questions in most lectures. Currently I get a response from one student. I could ask the same questions in a multiple-choice format and by using an audience response systems (clickers), I could get answers from all of the students at once even in a large lecture class.*

- *Further, if I implement the extra-credit bingo card assignment, students might assume greater responsibility for their own learning.* [Author's note: See Box 5.2.] *Students would do different types of extra work on the bingo cells. All of these assignments would reinforce the content of the course.*

2. What obstacles or challenges do you need to overcome to successfully implement this change? (Resistance may come from your philosophy of teaching, your chair, your peers, your students, or the culture of your institution.)

    I need to find the time to develop the JiTT questions and the bingo card assignment.

    Unlike the physics instructor who uses the audience response system, I am a little hesitant to incorporate more technology, which might fail, into my class. I could use a low-technology way of students showing their answers by holding up different colored cards. For example, students would hold up a blue card if they chose alternative a and green card if they chose alternative b.

3. Identify specific strategies (such as learning about successful implementations, trying a small pilot implementation, explaining to your students and other instructors why you are making these changes) for overcoming each obstacle or challenge.

    I will seek assistance from other instructors who use these techniques to help me as I implement these techniques.

    I will also ask the IT technician to work with me and my students to use the audience response system effectively.

4. What resources (such as time, money, student assistants, or computer software) would help you implement your change?

    Make time to implement these changes.

5. What do you need to do to get your students to accept this change? (Possibilities include repeated explanations for why you are doing what you are doing or having the activity count in the final grade.)

    Because the JiTT and the bingo card assignment will be part of their grade, I think the students will accept these changes easily. It should relieve some of the pressure to do well on the examinations.

D. Outcomes of the change:

1. In what ways will implementing this change influence other aspects of your course to be more learner-centered? (For example, when you incorporate various teaching or learning methods that are consistent with your student learning goals [Component 3 of the Role of the Instructor dimension], most likely the students will more actively engage in the content [Component 2 of the Function of Content dimension].)

    If I continue to use Intra-teach, and I incorporate JiTT, use of clickers in the lectures, and assign the extra-credit bingo card, I would achieve the level of learner-centered for Component 3 of the Role of the Instructor dimension, "Teaching or learning methods appropriate for student learning goals."

    The bingo card assignment would allow me to accommodate different learning styles, thus moving my course to the level of learner-centered for Component 1 of the Role of the Instructor dimension, "Creation of an environment for learning."

(Continued)

The use of JiTT and the clickers in the lectures would increase the interaction between students and myself. I would achieve the level of higher level of transitioning for Component 4 of the Role of the Instructor dimension, "Activities involving student, instructor, and content interactions."

These changes also influence Component 6 of the Balance of Power dimension, "Opportunities to learn."

The students should engage more with the material, per Component 2 of the Function of Content dimension, "Level to which students engage in content."

2. In what ways (such as increased learning) will your students benefit from this change? How will the students behave differently (such as increased participation in class or greater engagement with the content)?

The students should engage more with the content and learn more.

3. In what ways will you benefit from this change? (For example, more enjoyment of teaching, satisfaction that your students are learning more, anticipation of fewer student complaints.)

After exploring these possibilities, I feel encouraged about giving students greater responsibility for their own learning as well as transforming other components. These strategies are appropriate for large general education courses.

E. Possible future changes:

1. What is the optimal level for this component for this course?

   ❑ Instructor-centered

   ❑ Lower level of transitioning

   ❑ Higher level of transitioning

   ☑ Learner-centered

2. In the long term, what additional changes, if any, might you make to further transform this component to reach this optimal level of the learner-centered approach?

After incorporating these changes, I might change my philosophy of content coverage. I could incorporate the learner-centered approach used by Paula Kramer in her course. [Author's note: Box 6.5 describes the learner-centered approach of Paula Kramer.]

Box 6.5. Learner-Centered Example of Responsibility for Learning

Paula Kramer (2007) makes it very explicit that she expects the students to come to class prepared to discuss the material. Throughout the first weeks of classes, she spends time in class discussing this expectation and explaining how she will conduct classes. In addition, she tells them that if she feels the majority of students are not prepared to discuss the material, she will give the students two options: either they can adjourn for thirty minutes to read the material and convene again when they are prepared, or she will cancel class and reschedule the class later in the week. She tells them she will not cover all of the material in the assigned reading. However, she will explain whatever they have tried to understand on their own, provided they ask questions that show they have read the material. When the students do not have questions in class, she asks questions. Early in the semester, she assists the students to learn how to read the required assignments by giving them guiding questions.

In the beginning of the semester, few students believe that their instructor will actually do what she says she will do. Usually many students do not come to class prepared. The few students who dc come prepared often ask and answer all the questions. Within a month, most or all of the students understand that they must come prepared to discuss the material. Kramer says it can be very frustrating during this first month of class—and easy to assume responsibility by lecturing. However, she has learned to trust her students and the teaching method she uses. She has only had to exercise the option of a thirty-minute break for reading or rescheduling class once per class, at most. Kramer stresses that consistently reinforcing her expectations is the most important aspect to getting the students to assume responsibility for their own learning.

EXHIBIT 6.2

The Planning for Transformation Exercise 2 for the Responsibility for Learning Component 2

A. Status of your course now
Date: 3-27-07

1. Dimension of learner-centered teaching: *The Responsibility for Learning*

2. Component: 2. *Learning-to-learn skills for the present and the future*

3. Current level:

☑ Instructor-centered

❑ Lower level of transitioning

❑ Higher level of transitioning

❑ Learner-centered

4. Briefly describe your current implementation (to document your baseline prior to transformation).

Although this is a general education course, I do not assist the students to develop learning skills; instead, they meet objectives without developing further learning skills. I never thought about doing this in this course.

B. Desired changes:

1. Describe the desired changes you wish to make for this component in the near future.

The learning-to-learn skills I want to develop include note taking, talking to the instructor to get help, and learning from peers.

I notice that many students come to the Intra-tech sessions without notes. I think they may be unprepared for these sessions in one of two ways: they did not prepare for the class, or they did not know how to prepare by taking appropriate notes. Yet note taking is an important learning skill for students to acquire.

- *To be more proactive to get the students take notes, I decided to explain the kind of notes I expect students to prepare for the Intra-teach sessions prior to the first of these sessions.*

- *I will go around the room looking at the students' notes during the first few Intra-teach sessions. I will encourage students who did not have any notes, or those with very incomplete notes, to meet with me during my office hours. In small groups, we will develop a small section of notes to learn how to prepare for these sessions.*

- *I will also pay more attention to peer discussions during the Intra-teach sessions and encourage students to learn more from their peers.*

2. What is the level you want to achieve with this/these changes?

❑ Instructor-centered

❑ Lower level of transitioning

☑ Higher level of transitioning

❑ Learner-centered

(Continued)

C. Tactical planning questions:

1. What do you need to do, decide, or learn about prior to making changes?

   Develop model notes for a few questions in the beginning of the study guide.

   Although my giving my detailed lecture notes to students because they do not take notes during class is popular with the students, I am questioning this practice. In the future, I may want students to develop their own note-taking skills from my lectures as a further way to see if they can synthesize the material. I am considering giving an outline of my lectures to the students in advance to help the students take notes from my lectures.

2. What obstacles or challenges do you need to overcome to successfully implement this change? (Resistance may come from your philosophy of teaching, your chair, your peers, your students, or the culture of your institution.)

   Probably the hardest thing will be to get students to come to my office to learn how to develop appropriate notes. I need to make this nonthreatening to the students and promote a supportive atmosphere as I check the student notes.

   The students will resist the change from getting detailed lecture notes to outlines.

3. Identify specific strategies (such as learning about successful implementations, trying a small pilot implementation, explaining to your students and other instructors why you are making these changes) for overcoming each obstacle or challenge.

   I will encourage all students to come for office hours throughout the course. This is a way for me to get to know the students better as this is a large class.

   I will make my lecture notes less detailed over time, evolving to an outline, so students will not notice the change if they get the notes from a friend who took the course recently.

4. What resources (such as time, money, student assistants, or computer software) would help you implement your change?

   None.

5. What do you need to do to get your students to accept this change? (Possibilities include repeated explanations for why you are doing what you are doing or having the activity count in the final grade.)

   I will tell students when they have good notes and appear to be learning well from each other.

   I will be supportive of students when they come to my office.

D. Outcomes of the change:

1. In what ways will implementing this change influence other aspects of your course to be more learner-centered? (For example, when you incorporate various teaching or learning methods that are consistent with your student learning goals [Component 3 of the Role of the Instructor dimension], most likely the students will more actively engage in the content [Component 2 of the Function of Content dimension].)

(Continued)

These changes should also give students more opportunities for them to assume responsibility for their own learning, Component 1 in the Responsibility for Learning dimension, "Responsibility for learning." If I meet with students in small groups during my office hours, I will be more learner-centered in terms of Component 4 of the Role of the Instructor dimension, "Activities involving student, instructor, and content interactions."

2. In what ways (such as increased learning) will your students benefit from this change? How will the students behave differently (such as increased participation in class or greater engagement with the content)?

The students will come prepared with good notes. The discussions should improve during the Intra-teach sessions and the subsequent student grades on the quizzes should improve. Further, more students should earn the maximum number of effectiveness points if they are better prepared. The bottom line is that students will learn more.

3. In what ways will you benefit from this change? (For example, more enjoyment of teaching, satisfaction that your students are learning more, anticipation of fewer student complaints.)

I hope to enjoy teaching this course more.

E. Possible future changes:

1. What is the optimal level for this component for this course?

   ❑ Instructor-centered

   ❑ Lower level of transitioning

   ☑ Higher level of transitioning

   ❑ Learner-centered

2. In the long term, what additional changes, if any, might you make to further transform this component to reach this optimal level of the learner-centered approach?

   This level is probably appropriate for general education courses.

Box 6.6 explains how one instructor uses note taking as a way to help students analyze the material better.

Box 6.6. Learner-Centered Example of Learning-to-Learn Skills

When students ask Thomas Berg (2006) how they can do better in class, he asks them to come to his office individually with their notes from the lectures and from the assigned readings. He has found that by inspecting their notes he can see whether they are taking effective notes, including enough details, and synthesizing the important information appropriately. He can also teach them how to take notes on their reading or his lectures. This instructor gives the students feedback on how to take notes that are more effective. He invites his students to show him their notes again in the future.

EXHIBIT 6.3

The Planning for Transformation Exercise 3 for the Responsibility for Learning Component 4

A. Status of your course now   Date: 3-27-07

   1. Dimension of learner-centered teaching: *The Responsibility for Learning*

   2. Component: 4. *Students' self-assessment of their learning*

   3. Current level:

      ❏ Instructor-centered

      ☑ Lower level of transitioning

      ❏ Higher level of transitioning

      ❏ Learner-centered

   4. Briefly describe your current implementation (to document your baseline prior to transformation).

      I never ask students to assess their own learning, although I have many potential opportunities to do so.

B. Desired changes:

   1. Describe the desired changes you wish to make for this component in the near future.

      Once I realized that self-assessment of learning is an important skill for students to practice, I thought of a simple way to do this immediately. I decided that I could ask the students to complete a very brief survey asking them to rate how prepared they were for the Intra-teach sessions and examinations.

      I believe that the students will not be good at determining how prepared they are. They might have unrealistic beliefs about their comprehension of the material. In addition, even if they identify areas in which they are not competent, they may not know how to remediate their identified weaknesses. Therefore, I decided to give the students self-assessment activities that do not count, to help students prepare for the examinations.

      I especially liked the idea of using online quizzes that students can take on their own. [Author's note: An example is described in Box 6.7.] I decided to develop a few online self-assessment activities for the beginning of the course. In addition to giving the correct answer, I will cite references to the pages in the textbook that explain this concept.

   2. What is the level you want to achieve with this/these changes?

      ❏ Instructor-centered

      ❏ Lower level of transitioning

      ☑ Higher level of transitioning

      ❏ Learner-centered

C. Tactical planning questions:

   1. What do you need to do, decide, or learn about prior to making changes?

      a. I need to develop the self-assessment quizzes and place these quizzes online for the students to be able to use them. I can take many questions from the instructor's manual and resource material provided by the publisher of the textbook. I also need to find the pages in the textbook that discuss the concepts referred to in the questions.

      b. I need to develop the self-assessment of preparation survey.

(Continued)

2. What obstacles or challenges do you need to overcome to successfully implement this change? (Resistance may come from your philosophy of teaching, your chair, your peers, your students, or the culture of your institution.)

   Although this should not be a difficult task, it will be time consuming. I need to find the time to develop these self-assessment quizzes.

3. Identify specific strategies (such as learning about successful implementations, trying a small pilot implementation, explaining to your students and other instructors why you are making these changes) for overcoming each obstacle or challenge.

   I should plan to make the time, or I could assign these tasks to my current teaching assistant.

4. What resources (such as time, money, student assistants, or computer software) would help you implement your change?

   I will ask my teaching assistant to select the questions from the instructor's manual and other resources. I will also ask this teaching assistant to find the relevant pages. Then I will only have to review what he does.

5. What do you need to do to get your students to accept this change? (Possibilities include repeated explanations for why you are doing what you are doing or having the activity count in the final grade.)

   I need to convince my students why it is a good idea to take these self-assessment quizzes as a review. The more motivated students will immediately understand this concept. The lazy students may not want to do extra work. Because I can track who does the self-assessments and correlate this activity to grades, I can show future students that doing these self-assessment quizzes leads to better grades.

D. Outcomes of the change:

1. In what ways will implementing this change influence other aspects of your course to be more learner-centered? (For example, when you incorporate various teaching or learning methods that are consistent with your student learning goals [Component 3 of the Role of the Instructor dimension], most likely the students will more actively engage in the content [Component 2 of the Function of Content dimension].)

   Self-assessment skills influence four components of the Purposes and Processes of Assessment dimension: components 1, "Assessment within the learning process," 2, "Formative assessment," 3, "Peer and self-assessment," and 4, "Demonstration of mastery and ability to learn from mistakes."

   By providing these self-assessment quizzes, I made the course more learner-centered on Component 6 of the Balance of Power dimension, "Opportunities to learn."

   Therefore, by giving students self-assessments I can greatly transform my course to be more learner-centered.

2. In what ways (such as increased learning) will your students benefit from this change? How will the students behave differently (such as increased participation in class or greater engagement with the content)?

   If students take the self-assessment quizzes seriously, their grades in the course should go up. They should also learn more.

(Continued)

3.   In what ways will you benefit from this change? (For example, more enjoyment of teaching, satisfaction that your students are learning more, anticipation of fewer student complaints.)

I anticipate fewer student complaints, and I will be satisfied that the students learn more.

E.   Possible future changes:

1.   What is the optimal level for this component for this course?

❑ Instructor-centered

❑ Lower level of transitioning

❑ Higher level of transitioning

☑ Learner-centered

2.   In the long term, what additional changes, if any, might you make to further transform this component to reach this optimal level of the learner-centered approach?

Because the online course management system this course uses tracks how many students open and use the documents, I will be able to determine the actual student usage. If the students use them, I will feel confident that I have transformed the course to the learner-centered level in which students can and do assess their own learning.

Although this activity will be time consuming, I realize it will have great payoff in terms of transforming the course to be more learner-centered, and at the same time it should help the students to learn and do well in the course.

Box 6.7 presents an example of an instructor providing online quizzes that students can take on their own.

Box 6.7. Learner-Centered Example of Students' Self-Assessment of Their Learning

Cathy Poon (2006) helps her students to realize what they do not know, and then she helps them remedy their deficiencies. She posts online a series of self-assessment exercises that she calls "good faith activities." In addition to providing the correct answers, Poon provides links to resources the students can refer to that further explain the material. Students complete these activities, get feedback on the accuracy of their answers, and can learn the material more completely, all within these good faith activities. Sometimes, to motivate students to use the good faith activities, she gives a point for each one completed, regardless of how well they did on the questions. Poon considers the process of self-assessment and reading about the content to be more important than the accuracy of their answers.

As these completed Planning for Transformation exercises show, incremental changes in one component lead to changes in other components both within and across dimensions. The implication is that instructors can make small incremental changes that can have a large impact on implementing learner-centered teaching. This makes the task of becoming a learner-centered instructor far less daunting and easier to achieve.

Chapter Summary

This chapter focuses on the skills that students need to develop to assume responsibility for their own learning:

- Taking responsibility for one's own learning

- Developing learning-to-learn skills for the present and the future

- Gaining self-directed, lifelong learning skills (such as determining a personal need to know more, knowing who to ask or where to look for information, determining when a need is met)

- Assessing their own learning

- Assessing their own strengths and weaknesses

- Acquiring information literacy skills

Although most of these skills transcend disciplines, they do not develop naturally in all students. Therefore, as a learner-centered instructor you should provide opportunities for the students to practice these skills in a supportive environment. Once you give students opportunities for self-assessment, many other aspects of your course will become more learner-centered.

The following application activity will help you determine where your course is on the Responsibility for Learning continuum and begin transforming your course to be more learner-centered. First, answer the following questions that relate to the components of the Responsibility for Learning rubric. Then copy and use the rubric for the Responsibility for Learning in Appendix B to evaluate the status of your course. After answering the questions, you should be able to complete the rubric easily. Your answers should also prepare you to select two or three components that you can transform.

Completing the Responsibility for Learning Rubric for Your Course

Keep your answers to the preceding questions in mind as you complete the Responsibility for Learning rubric, found in Appendix B, for your course.

- Read across each entire row before deciding which level is appropriate.

- For each specific component, circle or mark the appropriate level within the row.

- If you decide that the learner-centered level is not appropriate for your course on a component or subcomponent, think of a rationale or justification for that decision.

Planning for Transformation

After you complete the rubric, select two or three specific components that you might want to change. Then copy and complete a Planning for Transformation exercise, found in Appendix B, for each of those components.

APPLICATION ACTIVITY

Questions About the Responsibility for Learning in Your Course

Component 1: Responsibility for Learning

- How much do you value students accepting responsibility for their own learning?

    ❏ Not at all

    ❏ Somewhat

    ❏ Mostly

    ❏ Completely

- In an ideal learning environment, how can the instructor provide increasing opportunities for students to assume responsibility for their own learning?

- What opportunities do you provide for the students to assume responsibility for their own learning?

- How do you increase the opportunities for student to assume responsibility for their own learning throughout the course?

Component 2: Learning-to-Learn Skills for the Present and the Future

- What learning skills for further learning are appropriate for this course and the level of your students?

    Skill 1 _____

    Skill 2 _____

    Skill 3 _____

    Skill 4 _____

- What do you do now explicitly to develop these learning skills?

    Develop learning skill 1 _____

    Develop learning skill 2 _____

    Develop learning skill 3 _____

    Develop learning skill 4 _____

- What else could you do to develop these learning skills?

    Further develop learning skill 1 _____

    Further develop learning skill 2 _____

    Further develop learning skill 3 _____

    Further develop learning skill 4 _____

(Continued)

Component 3: Self-Directed, Lifelong Learning Skills

- How would you characterize a self-directed, lifelong learner in your discipline?

- What do you do to promote self-directed, lifelong learning in your course?

- What can you do in your course to promote self-directed, lifelong learning that is similar to what the professionals or practitioners do as lifelong learners?

Component 4: Students' Self-Assessment of Their Learning

- What aspects of self-assessment of learning would be appropriate for your course?

- How often do you ask students to assess their own learning?
  - ❏ None of the time
  - ❏ Rarely
  - ❏ Some of the time
  - ❏ Frequently
- How do you increase the opportunities for students to practice assessing their own learning?

Component 5: Students' self-assessment of their strengths and weaknesses

- What strengths and weaknesses would be appropriate for your students to self-assess in this course?

- How often do you ask students to self-assess these strengths and weaknesses?
  - ❏ None of the time
  - ❏ Rarely
  - ❏ Some of the time
  - ❏ Frequently
- How do you increase the opportunities for students to practice assessing their own strengths and weaknesses?

(Continued)

Component 6. Information Literacy Skills

- What information literacy skills are appropriate for your students to develop and or to use in your course?

Skill #1 _____

_____

Skill #2 _____

_____

Skill #3 _____

_____

Skill #4 _____

_____

Skill #5 _____

_____

_____

- What do you do to develop these skills?

Skill #1 _____

_____

Skill #2 _____

_____

Skill #3 _____

_____

Skill #4 _____

_____

Skill #5 _____

_____

- What more could you do to develop these skills?

Further development of skill #1 _____

_____

Further development of skill #2 _____

_____

Further development of skill #3 _____

_____

Further development of skill #4 _____

_____

Further development of skill #5 _____

_____

Chapter 7

The Purposes and Processes of Assessment

WHY DO YOU assess students? This question seems straightforward. Generally, instructors assume assessment means evaluating student performance on tests or essays or their mastery of skills, then determining a final grade for the course. Most instructors believe it is *their* responsibility to do the assessments. However, when you transition to learner-centered teaching, the questions of why and how you assess students become more complex.

In a typical instructor-centered course, the instructor assesses students' abilities or skills to determine what grades to give them. Educators call this process *summative assessment*. Many instructors see assessment, although necessary, as taking time away from learning.

In contrast, the learner-centered instructor integrates assessment into the learning process. Learner-centered assessments take on a different quality. They occur earlier and more often, to integrate learning and assessment and to allow students opportunities to improve. The instructor includes both summative assessments and formative assessments, which include giving feedback to help the students to improve. As a learner-centered instructor, you will incorporate students' perspectives into the assessment process by routinely including peer and self-assessments, encouraging students to justify their answers, and including them in the timeframe for providing feedback. Thus students take a more empowered role in the assessment process. You will provide opportunities for your students to learn from their mistakes and then demonstrate mastery of the material. Learner-centered assessments are usually projects that mimic what practitioners do, rather than multiple-choice or short-answer tests.

Although Weimer (2002) used the term *evaluation*, I use *assessment* because assessment more accurately conveys the intended meaning. Evaluation often connotes judgment and implies that instructors own this process. Many of the instructor-centered approaches described in this dimension imply evaluation or making judgments without providing feedback. In contrast, assessment relies on using evidence to guide decisions, and it is more ongoing. Assessment is more concerned with learning (Suskie, 2004).

This dimension is a good one to start changing if your course is very instructor-centered. When you begin to transform both your rationale for assessment and the way in which you assess students, you may not have to change the overall organization of the course, nor how you teach. As most educators realize, assessment is the driver for learning. Therefore, changes to your assessment will influence the rest of the course and especially the students' behavior in the course. Once you begin to use a more learner-centered approach to assessment, you will begin to see how you can change in the other dimensions also.

The Components of the Purposes and Processes of Assessment

Table 7.1 shows the rubric for the Purposes and Processes of Assessment dimension, including the seven main components and the four levels of transitioning from instructor-centered to learner-centered approaches.

Component 1: Assessment Within the Learning Process

As a learner-centered instructor, you will integrate assessment within the learning process. You can integrate assessment within the learning process by including opportunities for student learning during assessment activities or by learning activities that incorporate assessments components. The Readiness Assessment Test, described in Box 7.1, and Immediate Feedback Assessment Technique, described in Box 7.2, illustrate ways that instructors can integrate assessment and learning.

Component 2: Formative Assessment

The purpose of formative assessment is to give feedback and to foster improvement. Therefore, you should provide continuous formative assessments throughout a course. In contrast, summative assessment means to make decisions to assign grades without trying to foster improvement. Here are a few ways instructors can give formative feedback:

- They can use formative assessments such as those suggested in *Classroom Assessment Techniques* (Angelo & Cross, 1993). As the instructor is interested in trends or general understanding, students may complete them without putting their names on them. Instructors do not have to grade them, only read them over quickly.

- Instructors can ask students to show them drafts on paper for formative feedback before they hand in the final copy.

TABLE 7.1

The Rubric for the Purposes and Processes of Assessment Dimension of Learner-Centered Teaching.

The Purposes and Processes of Assessment

Component	Employs *instructor-centered* approaches →	→ Transitioning to learner-centered approaches →		Employs *learner-centered* approaches
		Lower level of transitioning	**Higher level of transitioning**	
1. Assessment within the learning process	Instructor • Sees assessment as less important than teaching *and* • Does not integrate assessment within the learning process	Instructor *minimally* integrates assessment within the learning process.	Instructor *somewhat* integrates assessment within the learning process.	Instructor *mostly* integrates assessment within the learning process.
2. Formative assessment (giving feedback to foster improvement)	Instructor • Uses only summative assessment (to make decisions to assign grades) *and* • Provides students with no constructive feedback	Instructor • Uses *a little* formative assessment *and/or* • Provides students with limited constructive feedback	Instructor gives students *some* • Formative assessment *and* • Constructive feedback following assessments	*Consistently* throughout the learning process, instructor integrates • Formative assessment *and* • Constructive feedback
3. Peer and self-assessment	Instructor does not • Consider peer and self-assessments relevant *and/or* • Factor these assessments into final grade	Instructor *rarely* requires students to use peer and self-assessments.	Instructor requires students to use *some* peer and self-assessments.	Instructor *routinely* encourages students to use peer and self-assessments.
4. Demonstration of mastery and ability to learn from mistakes	Instructor does *not* provide any opportunities for students to demonstrate that they have learned from mistakes and then show mastery.	Instructor provides a *few* opportunities for students to demonstrate that they have learned from mistakes.	Instructor provides *some* opportunities for students to demonstrate mastery after making mistakes.	Instructor offers students *many* opportunities to learn from their mistakes and then demonstrate mastery.

(Continued)

TABLE 7.1

The Rubric for the Purposes and Processes of Assessment Dimension of Learner-Centered Teaching. (*Continued*)

The Purposes and Processes of Assessment

Component	Employs *instructor-centered* approaches →	→ Transitioning to learner-centered approaches →		Employs *learner-centered* approaches
		Lower level of transitioning	Higher level of transitioning	
5. Justification of the accuracy of answers	Instructor • Determines accuracy of answers *and* • Does not allow students to ask why they got answers wrong	Instructor allows students to ask why they got answers wrong.	Instructor allows students to justify their answers when they do not agree with those of instructor.	Instructor encourages students to justify their answers when they do not agree with those of instructor.
6. Timeframe for feedback	Instructor does • Not provide a timeframe for feedback. *or* • Not return tests or does not grade assignments.	Instructor • Provides a timeframe for feedback, without seeking students' input *and* • Usually follows the timeframe for providing feedback.	Instructor • Provides a timeframe for feedback, with students' input *and* • Usually follows the timeframe for providing feedback.	Instructor and students: • Mutually agree on a timeframe for feedback *and* • Always follows the timeframe for providing feedback.
7. Authentic assessment (what practitioners and professionals do)	Instructor *rarely or never* uses authentic assessment.	Instructor uses a few assessments that have authentic elements.	Instructor uses some authentic assessments or assessments that have authentic elements.	Instructor uses authentic assessment throughout the course.

- Instructors can post answers and explanations online and let the students determine how well they did.

- Peers can also give each other feedback, using a grading rubric that the instructor develops.

Angelo and Cross (1993) describe hundreds of different formative assessment techniques that can be used quickly during classes. Probably the most commonly used classroom assessment technique is called the

---

Box 7.1. Learner-Centered Example 1 of Assessment Within the Learning Process: The Readiness Assessment Test

The Readiness Assessment Test (Michaelsen, Knight, & Fink, 2004) is a learner-centered example of the integration of learning and assessment. At the beginning of the unit, students come to class prepared to take a short quiz assessing their understanding of the key concepts covered in their assigned reading. They first take this multiple-choice quiz individually and turn in their answer sheets. Immediately following the individual tests, the students take the same quiz again in small groups. Each small group of students must agree upon every answer. The discussion required to reach agreement serves as a review of the content covered in the reading. The students can use Immediate Feedback Assessment Technique answer sheets (as discussed in Box 7.2) on the group quiz). Students can also get immediate feedback on computer-generated tests.

Box 7.2. Learner-Centered Example 2 of Assessment Within the Learning Process: The Immediate Feedback Assessment Technique

Another way to integrate assessment within the learning process is to use Immediate Feedback Assessment Technique (IF-AT) answer sheets (Epstein, Lazarus, Calvano, Matthews, Hendel, & Epstein, 2002), which provide immediate feedback on the accuracy of selected answers. These answer sheets indicate the correct answer once it has been selected. Students can continue to select alternatives by scratching off the covering on the answer sheets until they get the correct answer, receiving less partial credit for each additional selection.

"muddiest point." At the end of a class, instructors, using this technique, ask students to each write on a piece of paper, that the instructor will collect, what was the most confusing concept discussed in class that day. When the instructors read what the students wrote, they get immediate feedback on what the students did and did not understand. Instructors should review the topics that are confusing to many students during the next class. Classroom assessment techniques can assess factual knowledge or higher-order learning such as problem solving or assessment. For example, in problem recognition tasks, instructors give students a few scenarios of common types of problems. The students need to recognize and identify the type of problem each example illustrates (Angelo & Cross, 1993).

Box 7.3. describes two variations on the classroom assessment technique of problem recognition tasks that requires the students to make judgments or assessments.

As Box 7.3 example of determining diagnoses indicates, when students need to develop complex skills, such as laboratory skills or effective presentations, they need repeated opportunities to practice these skills, with feedback provided. Instructors need to plan for these opportunities to occur and for the students to receive formative feedback throughout.

Box 7.3. Learner-Centered Examples of Formative Assessment

Preprofessional clinical students often have difficulty identifying a list of differential diagnoses and then selecting the main problem. To help students acquire these skills, a counseling professor gave students short cases and asked them to identify the main problem, such as family conflict or depression, in each scenario. They had to support their diagnosis with a sentence or two of evidence from the case. This instructor assigned this problem recognition task every three weeks during the semester to assess the development of this diagnostic skill (Angelo & Cross, 1993).

Students taking statistics courses need to determine the best statistical procedure—such as chi-square, linear regression, or ANOVA—to use with a problem or data set. Yet this is often a difficult job for students. A statistics instructor gave his students five different types of problems. The students identified what kind of statistical procedure would best solve the problem. The students justified their choices and talked about the assumptions for use with each statistical procedure (Angelo & Cross, 1993).

Component 3: Peer and Self-Assessment

Giving and receiving feedback are essential skills for personal and professional success, so students benefit from opportunities to practice giving and receiving feedback.

The combination of peer, self-assessment, and instructor assessments leads to triangulation of data, thus creating data that are more complete and ultimately a more valid assessment. In assessment, triangulation of data means the collecting of data from different sources or over time and avoiding dependence on the validity of only one source of information. Greater support for the finding comes when different sources agree (Scriven, 1991). Thus, peer and self-assessments are useful for obtaining rich assessment data.

Many educators resist the idea of students as legitimate assessors, for many reasons. At first students feel uncomfortable giving each other anything but positive, even superficial feedback. Therefore, if instructors ask students to assess each other once a semester, they may be disappointed with the quality of the information. Many people think that peers will just assess each other equally well without offering real feedback. Others believe that students will be either too hard or too easy on themselves, without sharing insights into their abilities. However, students can overcome all of these shortcomings through instructors' offering training and repeated opportunities to give feedback, being specific about expectations, and providing guidance in what to assess. Instructors find that when they give students an assessment form containing specific assessment criteria, students often give feedback that is more constructive than when the students receive less structure in which to frame their feedback.

Box 7.4. Learner-Centered Example of Peer and Self-Assessment

Carol Maritz and Robin Zappin (2007) modeled how to give professional patient education presentations prior to their assigning a similar presentation to health professions students. They analyzed their own presentation and discussed various aspects of an effective presentation. While the students were preparing their own presentations, they also, together with their instructors, discussed the pros and cons of the organization of the planned presentation and the students' choice of the information they plan to convey and the words they will use. Next, the students presented their patient education presentation to their classmates and instructors as practice for a formal presentation to others. The audience gave them oral and written feedback on their presentation style, the clarity of presentation, content covered, and their ability to engage the participants. Some students gave their presentation again after they received feedback on the first presentation. Prior to the formal presentation, the students met with the instructors to discuss the feedback they received and to ensure that the students incorporated the suggested changes into their presentations. Next, the students gave their presentations to an audience of university employees and students in a formal patient education seminar.

Although training students to do assessments improves their ability to assess themselves and their peers, it also is instructive in that it shows students the level of performance expected (Blumberg, 2005). Instructors can model how to give specific and concrete feedback that is helpful for promoting changes. Box 7.4 shows the way in which instructors modeled how to give professional presentations and how students can give each other feedback. These instructors offered students opportunities to give and get formative feedback.

Peer and self-feedback are most useful for formative assessments, as students can offer excellent insights for improvement (Blumberg, 2005). As Table 7.2 shows, students have legitimate perspectives about their own and their peers' performances, such as showing respect for others, functioning in small groups, and making clear presentations or written statements. However, students are not appropriate assessors for determining the accuracy and mastery of knowledge and skills. Students should not make summative decisions, nor assign grades. Instructors, of course, have the final authority in summative assessment.

The emphasis on learning and improvement explains why two of the components of the Responsibility for Learning dimension, as well as one component in this dimension, involve self-assessment. Although it may seem repetitious, there are differences in purposes, as the names of the dimensions imply. People who are responsible for their own learning continuously assess both their learning and their strengths and weaknesses to further their own learning. The self-assessments in the Responsibility for Learning dimension are personal. On the other hand, within the Purposes

TABLE 7.2

Examples of Types of Activities for Which Peer and Self-Assessments Are Appropriate.

Type of Activity	Appropriate use of peer assessment	Appropriate use of self-assessment	Comment
Making clear written statements or documents	X		Students should not comment on accuracy of information, nor on the adequacy of content mastery.
Presenting clearly	X		Students should not comment on accuracy of information, nor on the adequacy of content mastery.
Learning to learn skills		X	Students often have excellent insight into their abilities to become a self-directed learner.
Developing respect for others, especially people with different perspectives, those coming from different cultures	X	X	Peers offer perspectives on student behaviors that the faculty may not observe. For example, a student might always show respect publicly, but may be discourteous to a certain student member of the group such as a female or a minority student outside of class.
Functioning in small groups, including taking responsibility for group tasks, participation, flexibility in roles	X	X	When instructors assign grades for group projects, they can add or subtract points for individuals depending on how their peers assessed their group functioning.
Engaging in the content to make their own meaning out of it		X	Self-report questionnaires or journals can determine whether the students are making the material meaningful.

TABLE 7.2 (*Continued*)

Type of Activity	Appropriate use of peer assessment	Appropriate use of self-assessment	Comment
Collaborating on problem-solving activities by providing knowledge or insights or integrating ideas	X		Students can comment on how helpful peers were to their own problem solving or to the collaborative efforts. They should not comment on the accuracy of the problem-solving process.
Developing information literacy skills	X	X	Peers can comment on who assisted them to formulate better information-searching strategies.

Source: Adapted from Blumberg (2006).

and Processes of Assessment dimension, students use self-assessments along with peer and instructor assessments to create a rich database for assessment.

Self-assessment has so many learner-centered implications that implementing changes in this component alone can result in a more learner-centered course. When students engage in self-assessment, they are likely to:

- Engage with the content more

- Take more responsibility for their own learning

- Develop the learning skill of self-monitoring

- Become aware of their own learning and their abilities to learn

- Assess their own learning

- Eventually become proficient at self-assessment

- Integrate assessment within the learning process

- Take advantage of opportunities to learn

Component 4: Demonstration of Mastery and Ability to Learn from Mistakes

In a learner-centered approach, the students have more than one opportunity to show that they have mastered the material. For example, students might hand in drafts of papers to receive feedback but not a grade.

Box 7.5. Learner-Centered Example of Demonstration of Mastery and Ability to Learn from Mistakes

Kevin Lee (2003) developed a large bank of online exam questions to allow his large class multiple opportunities to practice and receive individual feedback on their performance. Each week they were required to take a short online exercise consisting of about ten questions. They could take these exercises as many times as they wanted to, and only the highest grade counted. These exercises counted for 15 percent of the grade. In addition, the students took three online exams during the course that counted 60 percent of the grade. For each exam, the students were encouraged to take two online practice exams that were similar to the real exam. They obtained immediate feedback on their performance on these practice exams. Students could take the real online examination only once. There was a strong correlation between the amount of practice and the students' grades for the course. In addition, after the instructor developed the online examination pool more students received excellent grades in this course, compared with before he made it available to his students.

The graded product incorporates the changes made because of feedback. Allowing students several opportunities to demonstrate mastery is a learner-centered principle for several reasons:

- After students receive feedback that they did not master something well enough, they can learn the material or master the skill better. Thus they can show that they learned from their mistakes.

- Some students take longer to master content or skills; therefore instructors can spread out these opportunities to demonstrate mastery over time.

- If students can get feedback on drafts or improve their grade on tests through additional work, they are likely to learn more and earn higher grades.

When learner-centered instructors give tests, they allow students more than one opportunity to show that they have learned the material. Box 7.5 describes how an instructor of general astronomy wanted to reward those students who worked hard by allowing them to master the material.

Component 5: Justification of the Accuracy of Answers

When students justify their answers, they engage more with the content by stating the concept in their own words or checking the material in the textbook. On examinations, there can be alternative perspectives that might be right, although the instructor did not realize it before he gave the test. For example, two alternatives could be right on a multiple-choice item, but when the instructor created the test he thought that only one of them was correct. When students can justify their answers logically and even cite references to support their argument, they show that they understand the material. They can do this exercise for the items marked wrong after the instructor has returned the graded examinations test but has not gone over the answers. (The explanation following Table 2.5 in Chapter Two describes the levels of this component.)

Component 6: Timeframe for Feedback

Students like to know how long it will take before they get their grades on their tests, projects, or papers. Students expect to get their papers graded immediately and can become impatient when instructors take more than a day or two to return papers. In addition to grading, as a learner-centered instructor you will provide constructive feedback on their performance and offer suggestions on how to improve. Instructors should give feedback as soon as possible to help the students to incorporate this feedback, but sometimes this is not possible. At the beginning of the semester or as students are handing in their work for corrections or grading, you and the students can agree on a timeframe for feedback. You develop your perspective on this timeframe based on knowledge of how long it takes you to complete the grading for this type of assessment and how many you have to grade. Knowing that it may be a week or longer before instructors grade essays, the students can concentrate on learning other material and not contact you about their grades.

You need to involve your students in this timeframe decision because students should receive feedback on earlier performance before they work on further assignments. They can incorporate these suggestions for improvement only if they get them in time to use them. Further, when students have a large project divided into several smaller assignments that build on each other, they need to know how they did on the earlier assignments before they can work on the later ones. For example, early in a semester students might turn in their selected references that they plan to use in a large paper or the outline. They cannot begin to work on the next steps of the paper until they receive feedback from you on these earlier assignments. Asking students to turn in parts of larger assignments throughout the semester often leads to a better final product, as the students tend to spend more time on the project; this also reduces the amount of plagiarism from available completed papers. (The explanation following Table 2.9 in Chapter Two describes the levels of this component.)

Box 7.6. Learner-Centered Example of Authentic Assessment

John Hertel (Hertel & Millis, 2002) uses either one extended simulation or a series of smaller simulations consistently throughout a law course for future military leaders. At the beginning of the course, the instructors tell their students that all their decisions and actions during all of the simulations will count as part of their grade. Thus assessments are embedded within the simulation activities; there are no separate tests or assignments. Students also submit a weekly written report of their activities relating to the simulation. In these reports, students summarize all of their activities, responses, or actions to tasks assigned them during the simulation, their plans for future work, problems they encountered, and their thoughts about the simulation scenario. Students also attach copies of documents they developed. The instructors also grade the students on how well they interact with the other students in the course.

This course employs a learner-centered approach for the authentic assessment component, as all of the assessments in this course reflect how military leaders need to use and interact with the law.

Component 7: Authentic Assessment (What Practitioners and Professionals Do)

Educators call assessments that require the students to do real-world tasks *authentic assessments*. Authentic assessments mimic reality using simplified real-world situations—for example, analyzing case studies using real data or conducting realistic laboratory experiments (Suskie, 2004). When designing authentic assessments, the instructor selects only the elements that are relevant to the learning objectives for the course. For example, clinical instructors can use scenarios in which the patient has only one disease rather than many problems. They can also present the material in a more straightforward manner than might be the case in actual practice. These representations of reality become simulations and can involve both a learning component and assessment at the same time. Box 7.6 describes an entire course revolving around simulations.

Analysis of the Psych 101 Course for the Purposes and Processes of Assessment

Where would you place the Psych 101 course (described in the end of the Introduction to Part Two) on the learner-centered to instructor-centered rubric for the Purposes and Processes of Assessment? Use a copy of the rubric for this dimension in Appendix B to indicate your ratings.

This section details and explains my ratings for the Psych 101 course. (Table 7.3, which summarizes my ratings, follows the individual component explanations.)

Component 1: Assessment Within the Learning Process

Rating: Employs lower level of transitioning; the instructor minimally integrates assessment within the learning process.

- The Intra-teach sessions could incorporate assessment within the learning process, because students can assess themselves informally on how well they understood the material while they are reviewing the questions. However, some students may not take advantage of these assessment opportunities, because the instructor does not explicitly discuss how assessment can be part of this learning process. Further, neither the students nor the instructor assess the quality of the Intra-teach discussions themselves.

- For the most part, the instructor separates the assessments (that is, the quizzes and examinations) from the learning process.

- The participation points are not assessments of the quality of participation; just coming to the session gives students these participation points.

- Effectiveness points reflect how well students did on the quiz; they do not assess how effective the Intra-teach sessions are. The instructor assumes that if both students in an Intra-teach dyad did well on the quiz immediately following the Intra-teach session, they reviewed the material during the session.

Component 2: Formative Assessment (Giving Feedback to Foster Improvement)

Rating: Employs lower level of transitioning; the instructor uses *little* formative assessment *and/or* provides students with limited constructive feedback.

- During the Intra-teach sessions, the students can give each other feedback on the accuracy of their answers.

- The instructor does not give the students feedback on how they can use the Intra-teach sessions more effectively.

- The instructor does not discuss why the answers are correct or incorrect on the quizzes and examinations. She does not show them how to do better on examinations in the future.

Component 3: Peer and Self-Assessment

Rating: Employs instructor-centered approach; the instructor does not consider peer and self-assessments relevant *and/or* factor these assessments into final grade.

The Psych 101 course does not use any peer and self-assessments. Because they are not used, they cannot factor into student grades.

Component 4: Demonstration of Mastery and Ability to Learn from Mistakes

Rating: Employs learner-centered approach; the instructor offers students many opportunities to learn from their mistakes and then demonstrate mastery.

- There are eight Intra-teach sessions. All of these sessions are opportunities for students to learn from their mistakes.

- Opportunities to learn from mistakes do not have to be formal assessments.

- After the Intra-teach sessions, the students can demonstrate mastery through the quizzes.

Component 5: Justification of the Accuracy of Answers

Rating: Employs instructor-centered approach; the instructor determines accuracy of answers *and* does not allow students to ask why they got answers wrong.

- The instructor does not go over the answers on the quizzes or examinations.

- Students do not have the option of asking the instructor why their answer is wrong.

Component 6: Timeframe for Feedback

Rating: Employs instructor-centered approach; the instructor does not provide a timeframe for feedback.

- The instructor does not discuss when or how soon she will grade and return quizzes and examinations.

- There does not appear to be a planned timeframe for feedback. Because the examinations are multiple-choice questions, the instructor posts these grades quickly.

Component 7: Authentic Assessment (What Practitioners and Professionals Do)

Rating: Employs instructor-centered approach; the instructor rarely or never uses authentic assessment.

All of the assessments are short-answer or multiple-choice tests. These formats do not reflect what psychologists actually do.

In Table 7.3, the boldface cells indicate my ratings.

TABLE 7.3

Ratings for the Psych 101 Course on the Purposes and Processes of Assessment Dimension.

The Purposes and Processes of Assessment

Component	Employs *instructor-centered* approaches →	→ Transitioning to learner-centered approaches →		Employs *learner-centered* approaches
		Lower level of transitioning	Higher level of transitioning	
1. Assessment within the learning process	Instructor • Sees assessment as less important than teaching *and* • Does not integrate assessment within the learning process	**Instructor *minimally* integrates assessment within the learning process.**	Instructor *somewhat* integrates assessment within the learning process.	Instructor *mostly* integrates assessment within the learning process.
2. Formative assessment (giving feedback to foster improvement)	Instructor • Uses only summative assessment (to make decisions to assign grades) *and* • Provides students with no constructive feedback	**Instructor** **• Uses a *little* formative assessment** ***and/or*** **• Provides students with limited constructive feedback**	Instructor gives students *some* • Formative assessment *and* • Constructive feedback following assessments	*Consistently* throughout the learning process, instructor integrates • Formative assessment *and* • Constructive feedback
3. Peer and self-assessment	**Instructor does not** **• Consider peer and self assessments relevant** ***and/or*** **• Factor these assessments into final grade**	Instructor *rarely* requires students to use peer and self assessments.	Instructor requires students to use *some* peer and self assessments.	Instructor *routinely* encourages students to use peer and self assessments.

(*Continued*)

TABLE 7.3

Ratings for the Psych 101 Course on the Purposes and Processes of Assessment Dimension. (*Continued*)

The Purposes and Processes of Assessment

Component	Employs *instructor-centered* approaches →	Transitioning to learner-centered approaches →		Employs *learner-centered* approaches
		Lower level of transitioning	**Higher level of transitioning**	
4. Demonstration of mastery and ability to learn from mistakes	Instructor does *not* provide any opportunities for students to demonstrate that they have learned from mistakes and then show mastery.	Instructor provides a *few* opportunities for students to demonstrate that they have learned from mistakes.	Instructor provides *some* opportunities for students to demonstrate mastery after making mistakes.	**Instructor offers students *many* opportunities to learn from their mistakes and then demonstrate mastery.**
5. Justification of the accuracy of answers	**Instructor** **• Determines accuracy of answers** ***and*** **• Does not allow students to ask why they got answers wrong**	Instructor allows students to ask why they got answers wrong.	Instructor allows students to justify their answers when they do not agree with those of instructor.	Instructor encourages students to justify their answers when they do not agree with those of instructor.
6. Timeframe for feedback	**Instructor does** **• Not provide a timeframe for feedback.** *or* • Not return tests or does not grade assignments	Instructor • Provides a timeframe for feedback, without seeking students' input *and* • Usually follows the timeframe for providing feedback	Instructor • Provides a timeframe for feedback, with students' input *and* • Usually follows the timeframe for providing feedback	Instructor and students: • Mutually agree on a timeframe for feedback *and* • Always follows the timeframe for providing feedback
7. Authentic assessment (what practitioners and professionals do)	**Instructor *rarely or never* uses authentic assessment.**	Instructor uses a few assessments that have authentic elements.	Instructor uses some authentic assessments or assessments that have authentic elements.	Instructor uses authentic assessment throughout the course.

Transforming the Psych 101 Course to Be More Learner-Centered

As the instructor completed the rubrics for this dimension, she expanded her conception of the Purposes and Processes of Assessment. In Chapter Six, the instructor determined that she should be able to incorporate self-assessment easily. Next she realized that she can include peer assessment. She also thought of several easy-to-implement techniques that will move her course toward more learner-centered approaches to assessment. Therefore, she decided that she can modify her course to be more learner-centered on both Component 1, "Assessment within the learning process" and Component 2, "Formative assessment," by incorporating formative feedback in a more structured way. She completed the Planning for Transformation exercise for these components, shown in Exhibit 7.1. Without completing a Planning for Transformation exercise, she knew how to incorporate peer and self-assessment, Component 3 of this dimension. Exhibit 7.2 shows the Planning for Transformation exercise for Component 5, "Justification of the accuracy of answers." All of these proposed changes are appropriate for large general education classes.

EXHIBIT 7.1

The Planning for Transformation Exercise 1 for the Purposes and Processes of Assessment Components 1 and 2

A. Status of your course now   Date: 3-29-07

1. Dimension of learner-centered teaching: *The Purposes and Processes of Assessment*

2. Component: 1. *Assessment within the learning process,* and 2. *Formative feedback*

3. Current level:

    ❏ Instructor-centered

    ☑ Lower level of transitioning

    ❏ Higher level of transitioning

4. Briefly describe your current implementation (to document your baseline prior to transformation).

    For the most part, I separate assessment from the learning process. I do not use the examinations as learning opportunities. The Intra-teach sessions allow the students opportunities for formative assessments, but they may not realize it and may not take advantage of these opportunities.

B. Desired changes:

1. Describe the desired changes you wish to make for this component in the near future.

    1. *I can talk about how and why groups can give each other feedback on preparedness and cooperation.*

    2. *Prior to the Intra-teach session, the students can assess themselves on how prepared they are for the discussion. I can give the students an easy-to-rate survey of one or two questions to assess their perceptions of their preparedness. Peers will share how prepared they are. This might motivate them to come more prepared. These self-assessments, validated by their peers, might enter into the participation points.*

    3. *I will discuss how they should review the questions so that they might learn more. Students will reflect on the quality of their interactions during the Intra-teach sessions to make it more of a learning experience.*

    4. *Each group will rate the quality of their discussions during the Intra-teach sessions. I will have to monitor that the students are taking their assessments seriously. I will factor these ratings into the participation and effectiveness points.*

    5. *The Intra-teach sessions can end with a brief feedback session on how prepared the students were, how effective their review session was, and how they can improve their Intra-teach discussions in the future.*

(Continued)

2. What is the level you want to achieve with this/these changes?

❏ Instructor-centered

❏ Lower level of transitioning

☑ Higher level of transitioning

❏ Learner-centered

C. Tactical planning questions:

1. What do you need to do, decide, or learn about prior to making changes?

   Plan how to model the assessment of the quality of the interactions during the Intra-teach sessions.

   Develop simple assessment tools for the students to assess their preparedness and quality of interactions.

   Decide how to count and how much to count the student assessments of their degree of preparedness and effectiveness of the Intra-teach sessions into the participation and effectiveness scores.

   Because students are doing additional tasks during the Intra-teach sessions, I will have to monitor their time more closely to ensure they are getting everything done.

2. What obstacles or challenges do you need to overcome to successfully implement this change? (Resistance may come from your philosophy of teaching, your chair, your peers, your students, or the culture of your institution.)

   Convincing the students to take these self- and peer assessments seriously and honestly will be the hardest part of implementing this change. I will have to monitor groups and their assessments to ensure that this happens. I will have to develop a system that subtracts points for individuals or groups that do not assess themselves and others honestly.

3. Identify specific strategies (such as learning about successful implementations, trying a small pilot implementation, explaining to your students and other instructors why you are making these changes) for overcoming each obstacle or challenge.

   Throughout the course, I need to explain and reinforce the importance of honest and appropriate assessments of preparedness and quality of interactions during the Intra-teach sessions.

   I will have to model how to do it, and I will need to observe students in their discussions and assessments.

   I will have to talk to students who are not taking these assessments seriously.

   I will have to develop a system to penalize students who routinely assess themselves and others as prepared and functioning well in the Intra-teach sessions and yet do poorly on the quizzes.

4. What resources (such as time, money, student assistants, or computer software) would help you implement your change?

   None.

(Continued)

5. What do you need to do to get your students to accept this change? (Possibilities include repeated explanations for why you are doing what you are doing or having the activity count in the final grade.)

    As discussed previously, I need to consistently reinforce the importance of honest and appropriate assessments.

    If I design a good system of rewards and penalties associated with these assessments, students might accept the change or at least comply in their behaviors and assessments. I realize this may take some tinkering, and the first time I implement these assessments and the reward and penalty system, I may not achieve the right balance.

D. Outcomes of the change:

1. **In what ways will implementing this change influence other aspects of your course to be more learner-centered?** (For example, when you incorporate various teaching or learning methods that are consistent with your student learning goals [Component 3 of the Role of the Instructor dimension], most likely the students will more actively engage in the content [Component 2 of the Function of Content dimension].)

    When I demonstrate how to assess themselves and their peers in the Intra-teach sessions and how to give each other feedback, I will be helping the students to improve in the trans-disciplinary skill of teamwork. This will bring this aspect of the course into greater alignment, which is Component 2 of the Role of the Instructor dimension, "Alignment of course components." This teaching should also help the students to develop self-monitoring skills, thus moving the course toward being more learner-centered on Component 2 of the Responsibility for Learning dimension, "Learning-to-learn skills or skills for future learning."

    When students assess themselves and receive feedback from their peers and from their performance on the quizzes throughout the course, they should become more proficient at assessing their own learning, Component 4 of the Responsibility for Learning dimension, "Students' self-assessment of their learning."

2. In what ways (such as increased learning) will your students benefit from this change? How will the students behave differently (such as increased participation in class or greater engagement with the content)?

    Students will come prepared for the Intra-teach sessions and admit to their peers when they are not prepared.

    Students will take the Intra-teach sessions seriously and have a good review of the material.

    Students will give each other honest and appropriate feedback on the quality of their interactions during the Intra-teach sessions.

    Students will improve in their interactions in the Intra-teach sessions during the course.

    All of this should lead to improved learning.

3. **In what ways will you benefit from this change?** (For example, more enjoyment of teaching, satisfaction that your students are learning more, anticipation of fewer student complaints.)

    I will be satisfied that the students are learning more.

    I will know that I am achieving one of the transdisciplinary objectives of general education better.

(Continued)

E. Possible future changes:

1. What is the optimal level for this component for this course?

   ❏ Instructor-centered

   ❏ Lower level of transitioning

   ☑ Higher level of transitioning

   ❏ Learner-centered

2. In the long term, what additional changes, if any, might you make to further transform this component to reach this optimal level of the learner-centered approach?

   1. *I could reevaluate the impact of these changes to see further ways to integrate assessment with learning. Perhaps I will change the Intra-teach sessions so that students do not just recall answers to questions that the students prepared in advance.*

   2. *I could add classroom assessment techniques (Angel & Cross, 1993) throughout my lectures. Many of these formative assessment tools are easy to implement and quick to use in a class without having to make significant changes to plan for the lecture. Students get feedback on their adequacy of comprehension, and I determine immediately if the students learned the material.*

   3. *Psych 101 Instructor's Note on peer and self-assessment: Without having to go through the planning questions, I already identified ways to incorporate peer and self-assessment in my course. The obstacles and strategies for overcoming these obstacles remain the same as for integrating assessment within the learning process. There are other ways to use peer and self-assessments, in addition to asking the students to assess themselves and their peers on their preparedness and to assess their peers on the quality of their interactions during the Intra-teach sessions. The students can evaluate each other on their functioning within these small groups, including taking responsibility for group tasks and their flexibility in roles, demonstrating respect for each other, and the clarity of their explanations of the concepts. Separate from the Intra-teach sessions, students can assess themselves on their development of appropriate learning-to-learn skills and their engagement with the content to make their own meaning out of it.*

EXHIBIT 7.2

The Planning for Transformation Exercise 2 for the Purposes and Processes of Assessment Component 5

A. Status of your course now   Date: 3-29-07

1. Dimension of learner-centered teaching: *The Purposes and Processes of Assessment*

2. Component: 5. *Justification of the accuracy of answers*

3. Current level:

☑ Instructor-centered

❏ Lower level of transitioning

❏ Higher level of transitioning

❏ Learner-centered

4. Briefly describe your current implementation (to document your baseline prior to transformation).

I do not go over the answers on the quizzes or examinations. Students do not have the option of asking me why their answer is wrong.

B. Desired changes:

1. Describe the desired changes you wish to make for this component in the near future.

1. *Return the graded midterm examination without going over the answers. Then I can encourage my students to look up the answers to questions they got wrong. If they can write justifications for some of the answers they got wrong, citing the textbook, they can hand in their justifications before the next class. If I agree with the student's justification, I will give them credit for the answer. They will learn more as they go through this process.*

2. *Give the students a blank piece of paper to use in conjunction with their final examination. Explain that the students can write their justifications for some of their answers on the blank piece of paper (with the item number clearly indicated by their explanation). If the student selects an answer different from the one I chose as correct, I will read the student's explanation and determine whether the justification is reasonable; if so, I will give that student credit for the item.*

2. What is the level you want to achieve with this/these changes?

❏ Instructor-centered

❏ Lower level of transitioning

❏ Higher level of transitioning

☑ Learner-centered

C. Tactical planning questions:

1. What do you need to do, decide, or learn about prior to making changes?

Nothing beyond what I have already described.

2. What obstacles or challenges do you need to overcome to successfully implement this change? (Resistance may come from your philosophy of teaching, your chair, your peers, your students, or the culture of your institution.)

I do not foresee any obstacles to making these changes.

3. Identify specific strategies (such as learning about successful implementations, trying a small pilot implementation, explaining to your students and other instructors why you are making these changes) for overcoming each obstacle or challenge.

NA.

(Continued)

4. What resources (such as time, money, student assistants, or computer software) would help you implement your change?

Allow more time to grade or regrade the examinations.

5. What do you need to do to get your students to accept this change? (Possibilities include repeated explanations for why you are doing what you are doing or having the activity count in the final grade.)

Because justifying answers is a voluntary activity, it should be easy to get the students to accept this change. If they do not accept it, they would not write their justifications.

D. Outcomes of the change:

1. **In what ways will implementing this change influence other aspects of your course to be more learner-centered?** (For example, when you incorporate various teaching or learning methods that are consistent with your student learning goals [Component 3 of the Role of the Instructor dimension], most likely the students will more actively engage in the content [Component 2 of the Function of Content dimension].)

The strategy for giving credit for alternative interpretations on the midterm examination should help students to engage in the content—Component 2 of the Function of Content dimension, "Level to which students are engaged in content." This strategy should also transform the course to be more learner-centered on Component 2 of the Balance of Power dimension, "Expression of alternative perspectives."

The strategy used for the final exam will also move the course to be more learner-centered, Component 2 of the Balance of Power dimension, "Expression of alternative perspectives."

2. In what ways (such as increased learning) will your students benefit from this change? How will the students behave differently (such as increased participation in class or greater engagement with the content)?

Students should learn more.

3. **In what ways will you benefit from this change?** (For example, more enjoyment of teaching, satisfaction that your students are learning more, anticipation of fewer student complaints.)

I anticipate fewer student complaints about grades. I will enjoy fielding fewer complaints, as I find these encounters very stressful.

E. Possible future changes

1. What is the optimal level for this component for this course?

❏ Instructor-centered

❏ Lower level of transitioning

❏ Higher level of transitioning

☑ Learner-centered

2. In the long term, what additional changes, if any, might you make to further transform this component to reach this optimal level of the learner-centered approach?

NA

Psych 101 Instructor's Note: This exercise gave me many new ideas on how I can use assessment in my course. I am pleased that I can transform the course to be more learner-centered by making simple-to-implement changes. I realize that the students may have a hard time accepting their roles as assessors and that their initial attempts or their lack of honesty may discourage me from continued use of students as assessors.

Chapter Summary

As a learner-centered instructor, you will

- Integrate assessment within the learning process

- Use frequent assessments for the purposes of providing constructive feedback for improvement

- Not have to grade all of these assessments

- Ask your students to create products that are similar to what practitioners in your field do, instead of giving multiple-choice tests

Students will become partners in the assessment process, as they will

- Reflect on their own performance or learning.

- Have opportunities to show that they learned from their mistakes or earlier attempts

- Offer feedback to themselves and to their peers to help each other to improve

When you implement learner-centered approaches, students take more empowered roles in the assessment process. Examples of student empowerment in the assessment process include

- The use of students as assessors

- Students justification of their answers

- Students' being part of the decision-making process in which they will receive feedback

These empowered roles lead to a greater balance of power—the dimension we focus on in the next chapter.

This application activity will help you determine where your course is on the Purposes and Processes of Assessment continuum and begin planning your transformations of your course to be more learner-centered. First, answer the following questions that relate to the components of the rubric for the Purposes and Processes of Assessment. Then copy and use the rubric for the Purposes and Processes of Assessment in Appendix B to determine the status of your course. After answering the questions, you should be able to complete the rubric easily. Your answers should also prepare you to select two or three components that you can transform.

APPLICATION ACTIVITY

Questions About the Purposes and Processes of Assessment in Your Course

Component 1: Assessment Within the Learning Process

- In an ideal learning environment, how would you integrate assessment within the learning process?

- To what extent do you integrate assessment within the learning process in your course?

  ❑ Not at all

  ❑ Somewhat

  ❑ Mostly

  ❑ Completely

- How could you further integrate assessment into the learning process for your students?

Component 2: Formative Assessment

- In an ideal learning environment, how would you integrate formative assessment within the learning process?

- To what extent do you integrate formative assessment within the learning process in your course?

  ❑ Not at all

  ❑ Somewhat

  ❑ Mostly

  ❑ Completely

- How could you further integrate formative assessment into the learning process for your students?

(Continued)

Component 3: Peer and Self-Assessment

- In an ideal learning environment, how would students use self-assessments?

- How often do you ask your students to assess themselves?
  - ❑ None of the time
  - ❑ Rarely
  - ❑ Sometimes
  - ❑ Frequently
- How do your students assess themselves?

- How could you further integrate self-assessments into your course?

- In an ideal learning environment, how would students give and receive feedback from their peers?

- How often do you ask students to assess their peers?
  - ❑ None of the time
  - ❑ Rarely
  - ❑ Sometimes
  - ❑ Frequently
- How do your students assess their peers?

- How could you further integrate peer assessments into your course?

Component 4: Demonstration of Mastery and Ability to Learn from Mistakes

- Within your discipline, how do people learn from their mistakes or less than perfect attempts?

- Within your discipline, how do people demonstrate mastery?

- How often can students in your course learn from their mistakes and then demonstrate mastery?
  - ❑ None of the time
  - ❑ Rarely
  - ❑ Sometimes
  - ❑ Frequently
- How could you further integrate demonstration of mastery and the ability to learn from mistakes into your course?

Component 5. Justification of the accuracy of answers

- How can students justify the accuracy of their answers in your discipline?

- Where would you place your course on the following continuum about student justification of answers?

Resists   Tolerates   Allows   Encourages student justification

|_____|_____|_____|

- How can you encourage students to justify their answers more?

Component 6: Timeframe for Feedback

- How often do you discuss a timeframe for feedback?

  ❏ None of the time

  ❏ Rarely

  ❏ Sometimes

  ❏ Frequently

- Do you and your students agree upon a timeframe for providing feedback?
  Yes_____ No_____

- How often do you follow the timeframe discussed and agreed upon?

  ❏ None of the time

  ❏ Rarely

  ❏ Sometimes

  ❏ Frequently

Component 7: Authentic Assessments

- Describe authentic assessments in your discipline.

- How often do you incorporate authentic assessments in your course?

  ❏ None of the time

  ❏ Rarely

  ❏ Sometimes

  ❏ Frequently

- How could you further incorporate authentic assessments in your course?

Completing the Purposes and Processes of Assessment Rubric for Your Course

Keep your answers to the preceding questions in mind as you complete the Purposes and Processes of Assessment rubric (Appendix B) for your course.

- Read across the entire row before deciding which level is appropriate.

- For each specific component, circle or mark the appropriate level in the row.

- If you decide that the learner-centered level is not appropriate for your course on a component or subcomponent, think of a rationale or justification for that decision.

Planning for Transformation

After you complete the rubric, select two to three specific components that you might want to change. Then copy and complete a Planning for Transformation exercise (Appendix B) for each of those components.

Chapter 8

The Balance of Power

WHO CONTROLS THE power in your course? Some instructors think that is appropriate for them to have most of the power. Others have never even thought about this issue.

When instructors first hear about this practice, they often express fear that if students have too much power, there will be chaos, that no learning will take place, or that all students will receive unearned A's. I am not promoting this kind of student power. Rather, learner-centered approaches empower students to be responsible and to share in the decisions for some of the policies and methods of learning and assessment.

In a typical instructor-centered course, the instructor determines everything that will transpire in the course, including all of the content, how it is learned, the perspectives expressed, the assessment methods, deadlines, and all of the course policies. There is no discussion with the students over these decisions; they are just mandated.

In contrast, the learner-centered instructor seeks student input on course governance and allows students grading options. As a learner-centered instructor, you will encourage your students to express alternative perspectives whenever appropriate and you will create open-ended assignments that allow students to take different paths to completion. Learner-centered instructors share control of the course with the students. The amount of power sharing varies with the type of course and the level of the students. For example, certain disciplines lend themselves to alternative perspectives more than others. Learner-centered instructors encourage and guide students to take responsibility for aspects of the course. When you make the balance of power more equitable, your students will take advantage of opportunities to learn and will understand the consequences of not taking such opportunities.

As you begin to transform your course toward more learner-centered approaches in the other dimensions, the balance of power naturally will begin to shift. You will also have more confidence and trust in your students and therefore be more willing to give up some control. Once students begin to gain some control, they will engage more in the course and will learn more (Weimer, 2002).

Perhaps to a greater degree in this dimension than in the others, instructors may want to transition to a more learner-centered approach in an incremental way. The amount of power you give your students depends on their maturity, their motivation, and your own comfort with this redistribution of power.

The Components of the Balance of Power Dimension

Table 8.1 presents the rubric for the Balance of Power, including the six components and the four levels of transitioning from instructor-centered to learner-centered approaches.

Component 1: Determination of Course Content

As content experts, instructors need to determine the majority of the content the students will learn. When courses are prerequisites for other courses, the instructors teaching both the basic and the more advanced courses should collaboratively determine the content coverage. In some cases, professional

---

TABLE 8.1

The Rubric for the Balance of Power Dimension of Learner-Centered Teaching.

The Balance of Power

Component	Employs *instructor-centered* approaches →	→ Transitioning to learner-centered approaches →		Employs *learner-centered* approaches
		Lower level of transitioning	**Higher level of transitioning**	
1. Determination of course content	• Instructor entirely determines course content *and* • Does not seek feedback on the content	• Instructor determines course content *and* • Allows students to offer insights or feedback on content after course is over	• Instructor determines course content *and* • Allows students to choose some assignment topics (with permission)	• Instructor largely determines course content *and* • Encourages students to explore additional content independently or through projects
2. Expression of alternative perspectives	Instructor expresses all of the perspectives.	Instructor infrequently allows students to express alternative perspectives, even when appropriate.	Instructor allows students to express alternative perspectives when appropriate.	Instructor encourages students to express alternative perspectives when appropriate.

(Continued)

TABLE 8.1 (*Continued*)

The Balance of Power

Component	Employs *instructor-centered* approaches →	→ Transitioning to learner-centered approaches →		Employs *learner-centered* approaches
		Lower level of transitioning	**Higher level of transitioning**	
3. Determination of how students earn grades	All performance and assignments count toward students' grades.	Instructor allows students to drop one assessment but provides no alternative opportunities for them to demonstrate mastery.	Instructor allows students to resubmit assignments or other assessments for regrading	Instructor uses either mastery (students may retake exam until reaching acceptable performance standard) *or* contract grading (students contract for their grade based upon how much acceptable work they do) to determine what grade students will earn.
4. Use of open-ended assignments	Even when appropriate, instructor does *not* use • Assignments that are open-ended or allow alternative paths *and/or* • Test questions that allow for more than one right answer	When appropriate, instructor uses *a few* • Assignments that are open-ended or allow alternative paths *and/or* • Test questions that allow for more than one right answer	When appropriate, instructor *sometimes* uses • Assignments that are open-ended or allow alternative paths *and/or* • Test questions that allow for more than one right answer	If appropriate, instructor *routinely* uses • Assignments that are open-ended or allow alternative paths *and/or* • Test questions that allow for more than one right answer
5. Flexibility of course policies, assessment methods, learning methods, and deadlines	Instructor mandates all policies and deadlines *or* Instructor does not adhere to policies.	Instructor is flexible on *a few* • Course policies • Assessment methods • Learning methods • Deadlines *and* Infrequently adheres to these flexible decisions.	Instructor is flexible on *some* • Course policies • Assessment methods • Learning methods • Deadlines *and* Somewhat adheres to what they agreed upon.	Instructor is flexible on *most* • Course policies • Assessment methods • Learning methods • Deadlines *and* Always adheres to what instructor has agreed to with the students.

(Continued)

TABLE 8.1

The Rubric for the Balance of Power Dimension of Learner-Centered Teaching. (*Continued*)

The Balance of Power

Component	Employs *instructor-centered* approaches →	→ Transitioning to learner-centered approaches →		Employs *learner-centered* approaches
		Lower level of transitioning	**Higher level of transitioning**	
6. Opportunities to learn	Instructor mandates that students attend all classes even when they are not expected to be active learners.	Instructor provides consequences for • Not attending classes *and/or* • Not participating in active learning experiences	Instructor provides • attendance options for some classes so students may miss a few classes without penalty *and/or* • Participation options for some activities	• Instructor helps students to take advantage of opportunities to learn *and* • Fosters understanding of consequences of not taking advantage of such learning opportunities, like missing class

licensing examinations or accreditation agencies specify what the students need to learn. However, even in these prescribed content courses there still can be room for selection of some additional content, depending on the students' interests. If instructors know of their student's career interests, learner-centered instructors encourage their students to try to relate what they are learning toward their preferences, even in required courses. Of course, the instructor needs to know the students' interests to be able to accommodate them. Assigned, independent projects or papers often allow the students to explore additional content. Box 8.1 describes how an archaeology instructor requires his advanced undergraduate or beginning graduate students to research a topic of interest to them.

Component 2: Expression of Alternative Perspectives

Disciplines vary in how much they encourage students to express alternative perspectives. Instructors of some disciplines, especially in the humanities, naturally encourage students to express alternative perspectives on a topic. In these disciplines, instructors believe that students develop a

---

**Box 8.1. Learner-Centered Example of
Determination of Course Content**

Paul Demers (2006) requires each of his students to select a theoretical, methodological, or material-oriented archaeological topic that interests them. The students have to do an in-depth review of the literature, synthesize the opposing views of the topic, and develop their own perspective on the topic. They then develop an annotated bibliography on the topic and present their synthesis of the literature and their perspectives in a twenty-minute presentation to the class. These culminating products, based on this individual exploration of a topic of interest to the students, count for more than one-third of the final grade. Demers sees this project as a basis for the beginning of independent research because it helps students to see how previous researchers have answered questions.

**Box 8.2. Learner-Centered Example of
Expression of Alternative Perspectives**

Each week Lloyd Ambrosius (2006) requires his students to read between six and twelve short essays or speeches written during the historical period they are studying. He and his students discuss these essays in the weekly recitations. To prepare for the recitation discussions, the students prepare a short (one- to two-page) essay comparing the perspectives raised by two of the historical essay or speech authors. In their essays the students respond to the same open-ended questions each week, which encourage the students to develop their own perspectives on these historical figures. In addition to comparing the views of the historical authors, the students contrast these views with those held in contemporary America. The readings, student-generated essays, and recitation discussions require the students to develop their own unique historical interpretations.

---

critical view by expressing alternative perspectives. Box 8.2 describes how a history instructor encourages general education students to express alternative perspectives of historical essays they are required to read. Instructors in the sciences, mathematics, and engineering probably elicit less expression of alternative perspectives, especially in beginning courses. However, instructors of all courses can encourage students to take different perspectives from that of the instructor or of the author of an assignment, when appropriate.

Although researchers often take opposing views to promote an understanding of a scientific topic, this is not as common in early undergraduate courses. This may be because many science instructors who teach undergraduate courses believe that the students have to learn so many facts that there is little room for alternative perspectives. Yet controversial or current topics in science lend themselves to the students' looking at different points of view. For example, students in an astronomy course might debate the evidence that there once was life on Mars.

Component 3: Determination of How Students Earn Grades

In instructor-centered courses, where the instructor exerts complete control over how grades are determined, students cannot demonstrate mastery through alternative methods, and have only one attempt to demonstrate mastery. In learner-centered courses, instructors give students some control over how the earn their grades. When students perceive that they have some control over the grades they earn, they are likely to learn more and earn higher grades (Weimer, 2002).

Instructors can give students some control over their grades by using different methods such as mastery or contract grading.

Mastery grading. The instructor determines a minimum acceptable level (usually a high standard) that the students need to reach to pass the course. Students either receive full credit for attaining the acceptable level of performance or do not receive any credit for their attempt because it was below the acceptable level—they do not receive partial points. Many instructors allow multiple attempts to reach this acceptable level. For example, instructors in the health sciences often use mastery grading to determine whether students can perform clinical skills at an acceptable level.

Contract grading. Students contract for the grade they are seeking based on how many assignments they complete and how much the assignments count. They do not receive the grade unless they complete assignments well. In contract grading, in contrast to mastery grading, the instructor assigns full or partial points based on the quality of work submitted. The management course described in Chapter One uses contract grading. Box 8.3 describes another use of contract grading.

Box 8.3. Learner-Centered Example of Determination of How Students Earn Grades

Tammy Hiller and Amy Hietapelto (2001) use contract grading in their undergraduate and graduate management courses. These instructors require students to complete some assignments; however, each student chooses how much weight these assignments are worth for them individually. Other assignments in these management courses are optional. Students choose which ones and how many they do. They also choose the weights of these assignments. Students could choose to do fewer assignments or for the assignments to be worth fewer points and therefore contract to earn a grade less than an A. The instructors determine the students' final grade depending on the total number of assignments the students did in a satisfactory manner according to the individual weights each student selected for these assignments. Hiller and Hietapelto reported that more students earned higher grades when they use contract grading and their students liked that they had more control over what grade they received.

Component 4: Use of Open-Ended Assignments

Assignments can be open-ended in terms of the content, the methods of achievement, alternative paths to completion, or consideration of more than one right answer. Students find their own resources in open-ended assignments. When assignments have alternative paths, students may have a choice in the type of product they develop, such as written report or an interactive webpage. The process of development and the product of open-ended assignments will be unique for each student.

Like Component 2, "Expression of alternative perspectives," Component 4 probably varies by discipline. Here too the humanities probably use more open-ended assignments than the sciences or mathematics. In most of the later courses, instructors assume that there is a preferred path to a solution. Yet even in mathematics courses, instructors can give students open-ended assignments, as discussed in Box 8.4.

Component 5: Flexibility of Course Policies, Assessment Methods, Learning Methods, and Deadlines

Probably more than any other component in this dimension, this component empowers students to take responsibility within a course. This leads to the students' being more motivated to work harder and having greater engagement in their learning (Weimer, 2002). Students generally like involvement in the decisions relating to the governance, deadlines, and learning and assessment methods used in their courses. When students have a say in these decisions, they are more satisfied with the course and offer more constructive comments on how to improve the course in the

---

Box 8.4. Learner-Centered Example of Use of Open-Ended Assignments

Salar Alsardary (Alsardary & Blumberg, 2009) requires his students in his Discrete Mathematics course to do a presentation on a topic of student interest that is relevant to the content. Most of the students in this upper-level mathematics course are majoring in the biological or physical sciences. In consultation with the instructor, the students select a topic in discrete mathematics that they can use in their major or a topic that the instructor does not cover in the course. Examples of topics chosen include probability and its applications in Mendel's laws of inheritance, graph theory in evolutionary biology, RNA chains, and graph theory applications in bioinformatics. Students research the topic and develop a short (eight- to ten-minute) presentation on the topic. The format and style of the presentation is open-ended, although most students do the standard Microsoft PowerPoint podium presentation common at scientific meetings. After presenting to the class and receiving feedback on the presentation, the students formally deliver their presentation at a regional meeting of the Mathematical Association of America.

future (Weimer, 2002). When students participate in determining the policies for a class, they often develop the same rules that instructors usually impose, such as coming on time and being prepared. When the students and instructor mutually develop these rules, students more readily accept them. In a democratic, orderly, and efficient way, instructors and students can agree on certain policies, deadlines, and methods used in the course.

Yet instructors often resist using learner-centered approaches relating to sharing governance and determination of deadlines and assessment methods or weights, for many reasons. Instructors are afraid to give up this much power because we think we impose these rules for the good of the students or because we do not think the students can determine policies themselves.

Many instructors feel the students could never agree or it would take too long. Others think this component is difficult to achieve, especially in large classes.

In the syllabus to her general education speech communications course, Weimer (2002) gives a detailed example of how she allows students to determine the assignments they will do. She reprinted this syllabus as an appendix in her book, *Learner-Centered Teaching* (Weimer, 2002). She gives students choices of earning their grades through a large variety of types of activities. Although allowing the students to select their own assessment methods seems like granting a huge amount of freedom, Weimer sets clear rules and expectations. For example, students cannot hand in work past the due date, and they must commit to certain types of assignments early in the semester and must do them consistently.

The team-based learning method (Michaelsen, Knight, & Fink, 2004) employs another learner-centered approach, in which the students determine how much individual and team performance on tests count and how much team functioning counts in the final grade. Box 8.5 describes this decision-making process to determine grades. Although the team-based learning method started with management students, instructors in many other disciplines and levels of courses use it successfully. This method works in large classes.

Briefly, the team-based learning approach follows an instructional activity sequence for each instructional unit, consisting of preclass preparation, readiness assessment, and a team application of course concepts. The preapplication assessment uses a Readiness Assessment Test. (Box 7.1 in Chapter Seven describes the Readiness Assessment Test. With Readiness Assessments Tests, students come to class prepared to take a quiz on the reading. They take the quiz individually and then as a small group.) During

Box 8.5. Learner-Centered Example 1 of Flexibility of Course Policies, Assessment Methods, Learning Methods, and Deadlines: Group Determination of Weights for Grading

Early in a team-based learning (Michaelsen, Knight, & Fink, 2004) course, but after the teams have formed, students determine the percentage of the grade they would like to allocate for individual performance, for group performance, and for team functioning. The individual scores on the Readiness Assessment Tests and the final examination constitute the individual performance component. The instructor gives ranges for how much individual performances can count. There are several graded, group problem-solving exercises in addition to the group performance on the Readiness Assessment Tests. The students also determine how much peer assessment of group functioning will count in the final grade. Students make these decisions in a grade-weight-setting exercise that also builds the team process. In the first step of this grade-weight-setting exercise, individual teams decide the percentage of the grade for each of the components just listed and select a representative from each team to be part of a task force. The task force members need to agree on the final grade weights for the entire class. Task force representatives deliberate while the rest of the students listen. These representatives confer with their team members throughout the task force meeting. Each time the representatives reach a consensus on one component, the instructor confirms that all representatives agree with the decision. When the representatives reach a consensus on all components and on the final weights, the students have established the grading system for the course. This entire exercise usually takes less than one hour to complete. If the class has more than sixty students, the instructor can divide them into two sets of teams and form two separate task forces. These two task forces develop separate grade weights within the same course.

the "Application of course concepts" component of team-based learning, teams work on progressively more complex problems. Each instructional unit ends with a graded group problem-solving exercise. The students take a final examination individually at the end of the course.

Component 6: Opportunities to Learn

Instead of mandating what students should do to achieve the course learning objectives, instructors can help students understand that they have different types of opportunities to learn through in- and out-of-class activities. In learner-centered approaches, there are few instructor-mandated attendance, lateness, and participation rules. With learner-centered approaches, students should recognize and accept that there are consequences for not taking advantage of opportunities to learn. Instructor-centered instructors may have a hard time believing that students willingly take advantage of their learning opportunities without rules and penalties. However, I have seen it work with my learner-centered classes. For example, once when I was teaching using problem-based learning (described in Chapter Six in the description of Component 3: Self-Directed, Lifelong Learning Skills),

---

Box 8.6. Learner-Centered Example of Opportunities to Learn

Judith Miller (Groccia & Miller, 1996, and Miller, DiBiasio, Minasian, & Catterall, 2001) teaches a biotechnology course in a group problem-solving format. Small groups of students meet once a week in a conference, together with an undergraduate teaching assistant, to plan their research and problem-solving strategies. The instructor encourages her students to work together at other times also. Almost two-thirds of the final grade is a group grade based on group performance in solving problems and group projects such as writing reports or making presentations. The instructor can modify the group grade because of peer assessment of the relative efforts of the members of the group.

Even the quizzes have an optional group component. For each quiz, everyone takes the quiz individually first. Those students who wish to participate and who have passed the individual quiz may then retake the quiz collaboratively within their small group. Students who take the quiz as part of the group will receive a score that is the average of their individual scores and the group score.

Miller has evidence that most of her students learned to take advantage of group learning activities. For example, she found that students who take advantage of the group quiz option generally increase their quiz grades. She also found that students who actively participate in all aspects of the course—especially the group problem solving—learn more and do better in subsequent courses compared with students who took the course in a more traditional lecture format. Students who participated in the group activities report they gain confidence in their abilities to handle difficult open-ended questions and to give oral presentations.

---

one of my students injured herself in a soccer game. While she was in traction in a hospital room, she arranged for her small group and me to come to her hospital room so that she could participate in the problem-based learning discussions. She knew that she learned from these discussions and did not want to miss these opportunities.

When instructors provide small-group activities, they expect students to work together and learn from each other. If students divide group projects into individual assignments without developing a collaborative project, they have missed an important opportunity to learn from each other. However, with learner-centered teaching, students understand why they need to work together and how it benefits them. Box 8.6 describes a general education biotechnology course that emphasizes the importance of learning through small-group problem solving.

Analysis of the Psych 101 Course for the Balance of Power

Where would you place the Psych 101 course (described in the end of the Introduction to Part Two) on the learner-centered to instructor-centered continuum for the Balance of Power? Use a copy of the rubric for this dimension in Appendix B to indicate your ratings.

The following section describes and explains my ratings for the Psych 101 Course. (Table 8.2, which summarizes my ratings, follows the individual component explanations.)

Component 1: Determination of Course Content

Rating: Employs instructor-centered approach; the instructor entirely determines course content *and* does not seek feedback on the content.

- The instructor determines all of the content the students will learn.

- The instructor does not require the students to complete any papers or projects. Therefore they do not get to select any additional content.

- The instructor does not seek input into the content after the completion of the course.

Component 2: Expression of Alternative Perspectives

Rating: Employs lower level of transitioning; the instructor infrequently allows students to express alternative perspectives, even when appropriate.

- The study guide contains some thought questions, such as, "Why, do you suppose, psychologists have an interest in human biology?" These thought questions allow students to express alternative perspectives.

- There are few of these types of questions compared with many factual questions.

- Some of these questions for which students can express alternative perspectives appear on the quizzes.

- The examinations are multiple-choice questions and do not allow alternative perspectives.

Component 3: Determination of How Students Earn Grades

Rating: Employs instructor-centered approach; all performance and assignments count toward students' grades.

- The syllabus of this course states,

  Final grades are determined using the following formula: Final Grade = (0.24 × score on the midterm examination) + (0.28 × score on the final examination) + (0.48 × Average quiz scores) + Effectiveness Points +/− Participation Points

  This means that all performance counts.

- Not only do all performances count, but there is also an additional penalty of the loss of one point for missing a quiz, beyond getting a zero on the quiz.

Component 4: Use of Open-Ended Assignments

Rating: Employs instructor-centered approaches; even when appropriate, the instructor does not use assignments that are open-ended or allow alternative paths, *and* test questions that allow for more than one right answer.

- None of the assignments are open-ended.

- The students receive a study guide telling them what to prepare.

- The instructor uses test questions that allow for only one answer.

Component 5: Flexibility of Course Policies, Assessment Methods, Learning Methods, and Deadlines

Rating: Employs instructor-centered approaches; the instructor mandates all policies and deadlines *or* the instructor does not adhere to policies.

- The syllabus, given to students on the first day of class, mandates all policies and deadlines.

- The syllabus states the following expectations: "Students are expected to read the textbook prior to the lecture. All students can encouraged to study regularly, not just before examinations, study actively, comparing, contrasting, and organizing and participate actively in class." The instructor does not adhere to this policy because she does not give students opportunities to participate actively in class except on the Intra-teach sessions. Although the instructor put the expectation in her syllabus that students should read the textbook prior to the lecture, they soon learn that she does not enforce this policy, as the students do not actively use any of the material in lectures themselves.

Component 6: Opportunities to Learn

Rating: Employs lower level of transitioning; the instructor provides consequences for not attending classes *and/or* not participating in active learning experiences.

- The language used in the syllabus, stated previously, sets the expectation for learner-centered opportunities to learn, but the activities in the course itself are not consistent with these expectations. It probably does not matter whether the students read the textbook prior to lectures, study regularly and actively, or participate in the majority of the classes, as most are lectures.

- Course policies, listed in the syllabus, state that "students must attend class regularly." However, the instructor does not take attendance at the lectures. Therefore students may miss lectures without penalty.

- Students need to attend the eight Intra-teach sessions and take the quizzes that follow these sessions. There are no makeups for these sessions. There are consequences for missing Intra-teach sessions and the quizzes that follow the discussion.

In Table 8.2, the cells that appear in boldface indicate my ratings.

Transforming the Psych 101 Course to Be More Learner-Centered

The Psych 101 instructor does not want to make the kind of large-scale changes to her course that would be required to implement the types of courses described in most of the boxes in this chapter. Further, she does not have much confidence in her students' acting responsibly if she gives them more control of the course. Many students come unprepared for the

---

TABLE 8.2

Ratings for the Psych 101 Course on the Balance of Power.

The Balance of Power

| Component | Employs *instructor-centered* approaches → | → Transitioning to learner-centered approaches → | | Employs *learner-centered* approaches |
		Lower level of transitioning	Higher level of transitioning	
1. Determination of course content	• **Instructor entirely determines course content** *and* • **Does not seek feedback on the content**	• Instructor determines course content *and* • Allows students to offer insights or feedback on content after course is over	• Instructor determines course content *and* • Allows students to choose some assignment topics (with permission)	• Instructor largely determines course content *and* • Encourages students to explore additional content independently or through projects

(Continued)

TABLE 8.2

Ratings for the Psych 101 Course on the Balance of Power. (*Continued*)

The Balance of Power

Component	Employs *instructor-centered* approaches →	→ Transitioning to learner-centered approaches →		Employs *learner-centered* approaches
		Lower level of transitioning	**Higher level of transitioning**	
2. Expression of alternative perspectives	Instructor expresses all of the perspectives.	**Instructor infrequently allows students to express alternative perspectives, even when appropriate.**	Instructor allows students to express alternative perspectives when appropriate.	Instructor encourages students to express alternative perspectives when appropriate.
3. Determination of how students earn grades	**All performance and assignments count toward students' grades.**	Instructor allows students to drop one assessment but provides no alternative opportunities for them to demonstrate mastery.	Instructor allows students to resubmit assignments or other assessments for regrading.	Instructor uses either mastery (students may retake exam until reaching acceptable performance standard) *or* contract grading (students contract for their grade based upon how much acceptable work they do) to determine what grade students will earn.
4. Use of open-ended assignments	**Even when appropriate, instructor does *not* use** • **Assignments that are open-ended or allow alternative paths** ***and/or*** • **Test questions that allow for more than one right answer**	When appropriate, instructor uses *a few:* • Assignments that are open-ended or allow alternative paths *and/or* • Test questions that allow for more than one right answer	When appropriate, instructor *sometimes* uses • Assignments that are open-ended or allow alternative paths *and/or* • Test questions that allow for more than one right answer	If appropriate, instructor *routinely* uses: • Assignments that are open-ended or allow alternative paths *and/or* • Test questions that allow for more than one right answer

(Continued)

TABLE 8.2 (*Continued*)

The Balance of Power

Component	Employs *instructor-centered* approaches →	→ Transitioning to learner-centered approaches →		Employs *learner-centered* approaches
		Lower level of transitioning	Higher level of transitioning	
5. Flexibility of course policies, assessment methods, learning methods, and deadlines	**Instructor mandates all policies and deadlines** *or* **Instructor does not adhere to policies.**	Instructor is flexible on *a few* • Course policies • Assessment methods • Learning methods • Deadlines *and* Instructor infrequently adheres to these flexible decisions.	Instructor is flexible on *some* • Course policies • Assessment methods • Learning methods • Deadlines *and* Instructor somewhat adheres to what they agreed upon.	Instructor is flexible on *most* • Course policies • Assessment methods • Learning methods • Deadlines *and* Instructor always adheres to what instructor has agreed to with the students.
6. Opportunities to learn	Instructor mandates that students attend all classes even when they are not expected to be active learners.	**Instructor provides consequences for** • **Not attending classes** *and/or* • **Not participating in active learning experiences**	Instructor provides • Attendance options for some classes so students may miss a few classes without penalty • Participation options for some activities	Instructor • Helps students to take advantage of opportunities to learn *and* • Fosters understanding of consequences of not taking advantage of such learning opportunities, like missing class

Intra-teach sessions and do not do well on the quizzes that follow them. Therefore, she has decided that she only wants to change two components of this dimension ultimately to the higher level of transitioning. These components are 3, "Determination of how students earn grades" and 5, "Flexibility of course policies, assessment methods, learning methods, and deadlines." Both of these proposed changes are consistent with the maturity of the students and how much commitment they make to most general education courses.

EXHIBIT 8.1

The Planning for Transformation Exercise 1 for the Balance of Power Component 3

A. Status of your course now   Date: 3-30-07

  1. Dimension of learner-centered teaching: *The Balance of Power*

  2. Component: 3. *Determination of how students earn grades*

  3. Current level:

   ☑ Instructor-centered

   ❏ Lower level of transitioning

   ❏ Higher level of transitioning

   ❏ Learner-centered

  4. Briefly describe your current implementation (to document your baseline prior to transformation).

   All performance counts. Not only do all performances count, but also there is an additional penalty for missing a quiz.

B. Desired changes:

  1. Describe the desired changes you wish to make for this component in the near future.

   There are eight quizzes during the course. I could allow the students to drop the lowest quiz grade and take the average of the other seven quizzes as the score of the eighth quiz, provided the students took all eight quizzes. I will not drop a zero grade because the student did not take the quiz or got none of the answers right.

  2. What is the level you want to achieve with this/these changes?

   ❏ Instructor-centered

   ☑ Lower level of transitioning

   ❏ Higher level of transitioning

   ❏ Learner-centered

C. Tactical planning questions:

  1. What do you need to do, decide, or learn about prior to making changes?

   This psychology course has only two examinations, so I did not want to allow the students to drop one out of two of them.

  2. What obstacles or challenges do you need to overcome to successfully implement this change? (Resistance may come from your philosophy of teaching, your chair, your peers, your students, or the culture of your institution.)

   None. Once I decided this is appropriate, there are no other obstacles.

  3. Identify specific strategies (such as learning about successful implementations, trying a small pilot implementation, explaining to your students and other instructors why you are making these changes) for overcoming each obstacle or challenge.

   NA.

(Continued)

4. What resources (such as time, money, student assistants, or computer software) would help you implement your change?

    None.

5. What do you need to do to get your students to accept this change? (Possibilities include repeated explanations for why you are doing what you are doing or having the activity count in the final grade.)

    The students will probably like this change.

D. Outcomes of the change:

1. **In what ways will implementing this change influence other aspects of your course to be more learner-centered?** (For example, when you incorporate various teaching or learning methods that are consistent with your student learning goals [Component 3 of the Role of the Instructor dimension], most likely the students will more actively engage in the content [Component 2 of the Function of Content dimension].)

    This change may move the course a little toward being in the lower level of transitioning for Component 5 of this dimension, "Flexibility of course policies, assessment methods, learning methods, and deadlines." Compared with many of the other suggested changes, this one has limited impact on other practices.

2. In what ways (such as increased learning) will your students benefit from this change? How will the students behave differently (such as increased participation in class or greater engagement with the content)?

    Students might not prepare for one Intra-teach session or may not take one quiz seriously. The further transformation described shortly will remedy this problem of students deciding not to study one unit. Students will probably like this change.

3. **In what ways will you benefit from this change?** (For example, more enjoyment of teaching, satisfaction that your students are learning more, anticipation of fewer student complaints.)

    I anticipate fewer student complaints.

E. Possible future changes:

1. What is the optimal level for this component for this course?

    ❏ Instructor-centered

    ❏ Lower level of transitioning

    ☑ Higher level of transitioning

    ❏ Learner-centered

2. In the long term, what additional changes, if any, might you make to transform further this component to reach this optimal level of the learner-centered approach?

    The students could elect to drop their quiz grades below 80 percent correct and then do a makeup assignment covering this same content. As a makeup, I would require the students to find the correct information to answers the questions they got wrong and write their new answer as well as an explanation for the answer, including the page in the textbook indicating where they found the content. Although this creates more work for the students and for me, it will allow students

(Continued)

to demonstrate that they learned material that they got wrong originally. Students will realize that this is not an easy makeup for quizzes for which they did not adequately prepare. [Author's note: This makeup system is consistent with the modification this instructor suggested regarding Component 5 of the Purposes and Processes of Assessment dimension, "Justification of the accuracy of answers," in Chapter Seven.]

If I allow students to demonstrate mastery of the content covered in a quiz by researching the correct answer, writing their revised answers and the explanations, and citing the textbook page, the students will be justifying their answers and demonstrating mastery and that they learned from their mistakes. By allowing students the opportunity to make up their low quiz grades in this manner, the course can become more learner-centered on two components of the Purposes and Processes of Assessment dimension—Component 4, "Demonstration of mastery and ability to learn from mistakes," and Component 5, "Justification of the accuracy of answers." This change will also move this course toward more learner-centered approaches on Component 5 of the Balance of Power dimension, "Flexibility of course policies, assessment methods, learning methods, and deadlines the flexibility of policies." Now this change has greater impact on the learner-centered status of the course.

EXHIBIT 8.2

The Planning for Transformation Exercise 2 for the Balance of Power Component 5

A. Status of your course now   Date: 3-30-07

   1. Dimension of learner-centered teaching: *The Balance of Power*

   2. Component: 5. *Flexibility of course policies, assessment methods, learning methods, and deadlines*

   3. Current level:

      ☑ Instructor-centered

      ❏ Lower level of transitioning

      ❏ Higher level of transitioning

      ❏ Learner-centered

   4. Briefly describe your current implementation (to document your baseline prior to transformation).

      The syllabus, given to students on the first day of class, mandates all policies and deadlines. However, I do not always enforce my own policies.

B. Desired changes:

   1. Describe the desired changes you wish to make for this component in the near future.

      On the first day of class:

      1. *I will announce that I will allow the class to determine the dates for Intra-teach sessions and the midterm examination. I will give the students three choices for each one. The students will vote on their choices at the end of the first week of classes, once they know when all of their other assessments take place. The dates receiving the most votes will be the dates these activities and assessments will take place.*

      2. *I will ask the students to answer questions about what they think I should be responsible for and how I should behave, and similar questions about their own responsibilities and behaviors. The results of this survey will allow the students to determine some of the course expectations, especially those relating to civility and respect.* [Author's note: Box 8.7 explains the procedure she uses.]

   2. What is the level you want to achieve with this/these changes?

      ❏ Instructor-centered

      ❏ Lower level of transitioning

      ☑ Higher level of transitioning

      ❏ Learner-centered

C. Tactical planning questions:

   1. What do you need to do, decide, or learn about prior to making changes?

      • *Look at a calendar and the plan for the course, and select three alternative dates that would work for these activities and assessment.*

      • *Create a ballot giving the students the possible dates and let them vote for each one.*

      • *Create a survey asking students what my and their responsibilities to the class should be.*

(Continued)

All of these are quick and easy to do.

2. What obstacles or challenges do you need to overcome to successfully implement this change? (Resistance may come from your philosophy of teaching, your chair, your peers, your students, or the culture of your institution.)

   None.

3. Identify specific strategies (such as learning about successful implementations, trying a small pilot implementation, explaining to your students and other instructors why you are making these changes) for overcoming each obstacle or challenge.

   NA.

4. What resources (such as time, money, student assistants, or computer software) would help you implement your change?

   None.

5. What do you need to do to get your students to accept this change? (Possibilities include repeated explanations for why you are doing what you are doing or having the activity count in the final grade.)

   - *I will explain the choices and how the voting procedure works. Once the students vote, the dates are final. Students who voted for another date will have to take the assessments on the date selected by the majority of the students. I think the students will accept this change easily.*

   - *I will explain why I am asking the students to complete the expectations of individual's survey. I will create a behavioral contract with the students. I think they will accept this survey and contract.*

D. Outcomes of the change:

1. **In what ways will implementing this change influence other aspects of your course to be more learner-centered?** (For example, when you incorporate various teaching or learning methods that are consistent with your student learning goals [Component 3 of the Role of the Instructor dimension], most likely the students will more actively engage in the content [Component 2 of the Function of Content dimension].)

   Allowing students to choose when they will have to come to class prepared and when they will have assessments may increase the likelihood of students' taking responsibility for learning, which is Component 1 of the Responsibility for Learning dimension, "Responsibility for learning."

2. In what ways (such as increased learning) will your students benefit from this change? How will the students behave differently (such as increased participation in class or greater engagement with the content)?

   The students will select their preferred dates for the Intra-teach sessions and the midterm examination. They will not be able to complain that they have too many assessments on one day. I hope that, because they will have distributed their workload a little, they will come better prepared for these activities.

3. **In what ways will you benefit from this change?** (For example, more enjoyment of teaching, satisfaction that your students are learning more, anticipation of fewer student complaints.)

(Continued)

I anticipate fewer student complaints.

Because of the more distributed workload, and the fact that they had some say in course expectations, students may take my course a little more seriously, and perhaps do a little better.

E. Possible future changes:

1. What is the optimal level for this component for this course?

    ❏ Instructor-centered

    ❏ Lower level of transitioning

    ☑ Higher level of transitioning

    ❏ Learner-centered

2. In the long term, what additional changes, if any, might you make to further transform this component to reach this optimal level of the learner-centered approach?

    None at this time.

    Psych 101 Instructor's Note: Although I was initially hesitant to give my students more control, I am comfortable making these changes. I feel that the students will be able to handle these shifts in the balance of power. Most likely, they will even like these changes. Because this is a general education course, the students are probably not yet ready for to take more control over their courses.

> ## Box 8.7. Learner-Centered Example 2 of Flexibility of Course Policies, Assessment Methods, Learning Methods, and Deadlines: Contract of Student and Instructor Responsibilities
>
> One way to get students to develop the rules of the course is develop a contract of student and instructor responsibilities (Byrnes, 2001). To develop a responsibility contract, the students answer questions about what they think the instructor is responsible for and how the instructor should behave and similar questions about their own responsibilities and behaviors. Once the students and the instructor agree on the policies, the instructor makes a contract listing the students' and the instructor's responsibilities and all parties sign these contracts. At the end of the course, students assess whether they honored their contract by abiding by the expectations for student conduct. When these responsibility contracts are in place, instructors find that there is greater civility in the classroom. Further, students take more responsibility for their own contributions to the class and the grades they earn (Byrnes, 2001). (This is not the same as a grading contract.)

Review of All Suggested Changes to the Psych 101 Course

Throughout this part of the book, I suggest two to three components per dimension that the Psych 101 instructor could implement to make her course more learner-centered. I am not suggesting that she should make all of these changes. However, a review of the suggestions leads to the realization that making a change in one component influences other components also. Two clusters of suggested changes emerge. The first is low-risk changes; the second, those potentially having the greater impact on learning and on transforming the course to be more learner-centered.

Six of these suggested changes are low risk because they are easy to implement and most likely to be popular with the students:

- Using extra credit bingo cards for additional assignments

- Asking multiple-choice questions during lectures and using an audience response system (clickers) for students to answer the questions

- Incorporating classroom assessment techniques (Angelo & Cross, 1993) throughout the lectures

- Encouraging students to justify their answers on examinations or find the correct answers after they got a question wrong

- Incorporating flexibility on dates for Intra-teach and examinations

- Developing a behavior contract with the students that describes the expected behaviors of the students and the instructor

Table 8.3 lists these low-risk changes along with the components they would influence. The instructor could implement these techniques immediately without rethinking the entire course structure.

The other cluster relates to having the potential for great impact on student learning and making the course more learner-centered. These changes are not as easy to implement, and the students may not like some of them. They require more planning and implementation of larger changes beyond just adding a few techniques. However, for the long term they are worth

TABLE 8.3

Summary of Low-Risk Changes Along with the Components They Would Influence.

Suggested change/Technique	Dimensions this change would address	Components this change would address
Using extra credit bingo cards for additional assignments	The Function of Content *and* the Role of the Instructor *and* the Responsibility for Learning	2. Level to which students are engaged in content *and* 1. Creation of an environment for learning *and* 1. Responsibility for learning
Asking multiple-choice questions during lectures and using an audience response system (clickers) for students to answer the questions	The Function of Content *and* the Role of the Instructor *and* the Purposes and Processes of Assessment *and* the Balance of Power	2. Level to which students are engaged in content *and* 3. Teaching or learning methods appropriate for student learning goals 4. Activities involving student, instructor, content interactions *and* 1. Assessment within the learning process 2. Formative assessment *and* 4. Use of open-ended assignments 6. Opportunities to learn

(Continued)

TABLE 8.3

Summary of Low-Risk Changes Along with the Components They Would Influence. (*Continued*)

Suggested change/Technique	Dimensions this change would address	Components this change would address
Incorporating Classroom Assessment Techniques (Angelo & Cross, 1993) throughout the lectures	The Function of Content *and* The Role of the Instructor *and* The Responsibility for Learning *and* the Purposes and Processes of Assessment *and* The Balance of Power	2. Level to which students are engaged in content *and* 1. Creation of an environment for learning 3. Teaching or learning methods appropriate for student learning goals 4. Activities involving student, instructor, content interactions *and* 1. Responsibility for learning *and* 1. Assessment within the learning process 2. Formative assessment 3. Peer and self-assessment 4. Demonstration of mastery and ability to learn from mistakes *and* 6. Opportunities to learn
Encouraging students to justify their answers on examinations or find the correct answers after they got a question wrong	The Function of Content *and* The Responsibility for Learning *and* The Purposes and Processes of Assessment *and* The Balance of Power	2. Level to which students are engaged in content *and* 1. The responsibility for learning *and* 1. Assessment within the learning process 5. Justification of the accuracy of answers *and* 2. Expression of alternative perspectives 5. Flexibility of course policies, assessment methods, learning methods, and deadlines

(*Continued*)

TABLE 8.3 (*Continued*)

Suggested change/Technique	Dimensions this change would address	Components this change would address
Incorporating flexibility on dates for Intra-teach and examinations	The Responsibility for Learning *and* The Balance of Power	1. Responsibility for learning *and* 5. Flexibility of course policies, assessment methods, learning methods, and deadlines
Developing a behavior contract with the students that describes the expected behaviors of the students and the instructor	The Responsibility for Learning *and* The Balance of Power	1. Responsibility for learning 2. Learning to learn skills for the present and the future *and* 5. Flexibility of course policies, assessment methods, learning methods, and deadlines 6. Opportunities to learn

considering. As listed in Table 8.4, the changes that have the potential for great impact on student learning and result in a more learner-centered course are

- Incorporating organizing schemes into how the course is taught
- Using different types of self and peer assessments, including
  - Self-assessment of adequacy of learning through online quizzes, with feedback provided
  - Self-assessment on how prepared students are for Intra-teach sessions and reporting this assessment to students' study peer(s) (the other students in their Intra-teach groups)
  - Incorporating self- and peer assessments into the participation and effectiveness grades by assessing performance in groups
  - Incorporating classroom assessment techniques (Angelo & Cross, 1993) throughout the lectures that allow the students to informally assess themselves

For example, if the instructor were to incorporate the use of organizing schemes throughout the course, she might reorganize what she lectures on and how she lectures. These schemes might help students to better see the larger picture.

TABLE 8.4

Suggested Changes with Potential for Great Impact on Student Learning and the Learner-Centeredness of the Psych 101 Course.

Suggested change	Dimensions this change would address	Components this change would address
Incorporating organizing schemes into how the course is taught	The Function of Content	1. Varied uses of content: • Know why they need to learn content • Use inquiry or ways of thinking in the discipline 3. Use of organizing schemes 4. Use of content to facilitate future learning
	and	*and*
	The Role of the Instructor	1. Creation of an environment for learning
Using different types of self- and peer assessments, including the combination of: • Self-assessment of adequacy of learning through online quizzes with feedback provided • Reporting this self-assessment on how prepared students are for Intra-teach sessions to their study peer(s) • Incorporating self- and peer assessments into the participation and effectiveness grades by assessing performance in groups • Incorporating classroom assessment techniques throughout the lectures that allow the students to informally assess themselves	The Function of Content	2. Level to which students are engaged in content
	and	*and*
	The Role of the Instructor	1. Creation of an environment for learning 3. Teaching or learning methods appropriate for student learning goals 4. Activities involving student, instructor, content interactions 6. Motivation of students to learn
	and	*and*
	The Responsibility for Learning	1. Responsibility for learning 2. Learning to learn skills for the present and the future 4. Students' self-assessment of their learning
	and	*and*
	The Purposes and Processes of Assessment	1. Assessment within the learning process 2. Formative assessment 3. Peer and self-assessment 4. Demonstration of mastery and ability to learn from mistakes 7. Authentic assessment
	and	*and*
	The Balance of Power	6. Opportunities to learn

When students assess themselves and their peers, there is a significant effect on how much the course changes to become more learner-centered. However, many students do not feel comfortable doing self- and peer assessments and are not good at doing them. Therefore, the instructor needs to spend more time explaining why and how students should do these assessments. She needs to model how students will do these assessments. The instructor needs to develop forms listing the criteria the students will use in their peer and self-assessments. She needs to monitor how seriously the students are doing these assessments. Yet the effort is probably worth it, because by using different types of self-assessments, the instructor can transform many different components to be more learner-centered.

Chapter Summary

As a learner-centered instructor, you will

- Allow students some latitude in selecting content they will learn, perhaps on their own

- Encourage your students to express alternative perspectives when appropriate

- Create open-ended assignments or assignments that the students can follow alternative paths to complete

- Include the students in some of this decision making, instead of mandating classroom policies, methods of assessment and learning, and deadlines or due dates

- Determine what grade they will earn by your using mastery or contract grading while also considering the quality and quantity of their work

- Not require attendance nor assign points for participation

When you have distributed the balance of power more equitably, your students will

- Take advantage of opportunities to learn

- Take responsibility for their behavior in the course

- Take responsibility for their learning

Although some learner-centered instructors design courses in which the students have a great deal of control over their courses, it is possible to shift the balance of power toward more learner-centered approaches by making small changes, as I have illustrated with the Psych 101 course. Small transitions in the Balance of Power dimension can be liberating for the students and the instructor.

This chapter also reviewed all of the suggested changes for the Psych 101 courses for all of the dimensions. It suggested a cluster of easy-to-implement, low-risk changes and a cluster of changes that have the potential for great influence on student learning and for the course to become more learner-centered.

This application exercise will help you to determine where your course is on the Balance of Power continuum and begin to transform your course to be more learner-centered. First, you will answer questions that relate to each component of the Balance of Power dimension. Then copy and use the rubric for the Balance of Power in Appendix B to determine the status of your course. After you answer these questions, you should be able to complete the rubric easily. The answers to these questions should also prepare you to select two or three components that you can transform.

APPLICATION ACTIVITY

Questions About the Balance of Power in Your Course

Component 1: Determination of Course Content

- In an ideal environment, how could an instructor allow students more latitude in determining the course content?

- How much latitude do the students have in selecting paper or project topics?
  - ❏ Not at all
  - ❏ Somewhat
  - ❏ Mostly
  - ❏ Completely

(Continued)

- How much do you let the students select additional content?
  - ❏ Not at all
  - ❏ Somewhat
  - ❏ Mostly
  - ❏ Completely
- How could you allow students more latitude in determining the course content?

Component 2: Expression of Alternative Perspectives

- Within your discipline, how do experts express alternative perspectives?

- Within your discipline, what are the commonly expressed types of alternative perspectives?

- How can an instructor inform students about these alternative perspectives?

- How often do you encourage students to express alternative perspectives?
  - ❏ None of the time
  - ❏ Rarely
  - ❏ Sometimes
  - ❏ Frequently

(Continued)

• How could you allow students more latitude to express alternative perspectives?

Component 3: Determination of How Students Earn Grades

• How often can your students make mistakes and then demonstrate mastery?

❑ None of the time

❑ Rarely

❑ Sometimes

❑ Frequently

• How often do you allow students to take practice examinations or get feedback on drafts before they complete an assignment that counts for a grade?

❑ None of the time

❑ Rarely

❑ Sometimes

❑ Frequently

• If you are not currently using mastery grading or contract grading, how could you adapt your present grading system to use mastery or contract grading?

• How could you allow students more latitude in determining their grades?

Component 4: Use of open-ended assignments

• In an ideal environment, how would instructors provide open-ended assignments in your course?

(Continued)

- How often do you use open-ended assignments in your course?

  ❏ None of the time

  ❏ Rarely

  ❏ Sometimes

  ❏ Frequently

- In an ideal environment, how would instructors provide alternative paths in assignments in your course?

- How often do you use assignments that allow alternative paths in your course?

  ❏ None of the time

  ❏ Rarely

  ❏ Sometimes

  ❏ Frequently

- In an ideal environment, how would instructors provide assignments that have more than one right answer in your course?

- How often do you use assignments that have more than one right answer in your course?

  ❏ None of the time

  ❏ Rarely

  ❏ Sometimes

  ❏ Frequently

- How could you provide assignments that are more open-ended?

(*Continued*)

Component 5: Flexibility of Course Policies, Assessment Methods, Learning Methods, and Deadlines

Complete the following table to determine your status on the flexibility considerations.

Category	List the Category Elements for Your Course
Classroom management policies	1. 2. 3. 4.
Assessment methods	1. 2. 3. 4.
Teaching or learning methods	1. 2. 3. 4.
Deadlines for assignments, dates for tests	1. 2. 3. 4.

- Circle each of the elements you listed in the table that you could negotiate with your students.
- What percentage of the total number you listed do you currently negotiate with your students?

- How could you allow students more latitude in determining policies, methods, and deadlines?

(Continued)

Component 6: Opportunities to Learn

- In an ideal learning environment, how would students show that they take advantage of opportunities to learn?

- What is your attendance policy?

- How can you make your attendance policy more learner-centered, if it is not already?

- What happens when students do not take advantage of learning opportunities?

Students realize that they have lost an opportunity to learn	Neutral or no real consequence	You have a punitive policy; students receive a lower grade
❏	❏	❏

- How could you allow students more latitude in taking advantage of opportunities to learn?

Completing the Balance of Power Rubric for Your Course

Keep your answers to the preceding questions in mind as you complete the Balance of Power rubric in Appendix B for your course.

- Read across each entire row before deciding which level is appropriate.

- For each specific component, circle or mark the appropriate level within the row.

- If you decide that the learner-centered level is not appropriate for your course on a component or subcomponent, think of a rationale or justification for that decision.

Planning for Transformation

After you complete the rubric, select two to three specific components that you might want to change. Then copy and complete a Planning for Transformation exercise in Appendix B for each of those components.

Part Three

Discussion and Conclusion

Chapter 9

Can All Courses Be Learner-Centered?

THIS CHAPTER DISCUSSES factors to consider when determining whether a learner-centered approach is appropriate for a particular course.

All courses can have learner-centered components. Although achieving the learner-centered standard for every component of all five dimensions is not realistic for most courses, it should be your goal to transition your course to be as learner-centered as possible.

Even the most learner-centered courses have some components that are not learner-centered. For example, Andrew Peterson, the instructor of the learner-centered Pharmacy Management Systems course discussed in Chapter One, does not use organizing schemes (Component 3 of the Function of Content dimension) in his teaching to help his students understand the material, and he does not use SMART objectives (Component 5 of the Role of the Instructor dimension). Further, he does not facilitate students to become proficient, self-directed, lifelong learners (Component 3 for the Responsibility for Learning dimension).

This chapter will help you decide which of the components of the five dimensions may be appropriate to transform for your course. The chapter presents two models. The first model considers the relationship between course characteristics and all of the specific learner-centered components. (The Function of Content has four major components, with Component 1 further divided into four subcomponents. The Role of the Instructor, the Responsibility for Learning, and the Balance of Power each have six components, and the Purposes and Processes of Assessment has seven components.) The second model takes a developmental or program-wide approach to becoming learner-centered.

Model One: The Relationship Between Course Characteristics and Specific Learner-Centered Components

Six characteristics can influence whether a course can be learner-centered on a specific component. These characteristics and their relevant subcategories are

1. The type of students
   - Motivation and maturity of the students enrolled in the course
   - Nontraditional or older students, as they may have unique needs
2. The level of the course
   - Lower-level courses that are intended as developmental courses designed to prepare students for college-level work or general education
   - Upper-level courses that are intended for advanced undergraduate or graduate or professional students
3. A large number of students enrolled in the class (I did not consider small enrollments, because most instructors think it is easier to implement learner-centered approaches in small classes)
4. The content of the course
   - Perceived relevancy of the course
   - Unique characteristics of the content as it relates to the component
5. Your own personal philosophy of teaching and your trust of the students
6. The culture or philosophy of the campus, your department, or the educational program

The first four are course characteristics. These four characteristics are often associated with the common myths about learner-centered teaching listed in Box 9.1 (Blumberg & Everett, 2005). I consider these "myths" because courses with these characteristics *can* have learner-centered components. Learner-centered instructors certainly should consider these characteristics when they develop their courses. It may take a more deliberate

---

Box 9.1. Myths About Learner-Centered Teaching

- It requires small classes, because instructors cannot use active learning activities or assign group projects in large classes.

- It requires upper-level or graduate classes, because students in lower-level courses would not be able to succeed in learner-centered courses.

- It reduces the content covered, because instructors cover less material when they use active learning activities or when they need to create an environment that supports learning.

- It reduces the rigor of the courses, because

  - When instructors use learner-centered techniques, there is grade inflation.

  - When students engage in active learning, they learn less content.

effort by the instructors to implement these practices with large-enrollment, or content-rich, or lower-level courses than with small-enrollment, upper-level, or seminar courses. I will discuss these deliberate efforts as they relate to categories of these course characteristics in the next sections of this chapter.

The last two characteristics are different from the course characteristics because they relate to you and your department. I will explore these characteristics in more detail in Chapter Ten when I discuss overcoming obstacles and challenges, because your philosophy of teaching can be a huge obstacle to overcome. The culture or philosophy characteristic also relates to overcoming resistance to becoming a learner-centered instructor, so I discuss this characteristic in the next chapter as well. Finally, please note that of all six characteristics, the most important is the fifth: your own personal philosophy of teaching and your trust of the students.

Relationships Among Course Characteristics and Implementing Learner-Centered Approaches

I determined whether a course with these specific characteristics could be learner-centered by analyzing the relationship between each of the subcategories of the four course characteristics and each of the learner-centered components. I determined individually how much, if any, each course characteristic interacts with each of the learner-centered components. These are value judgments.

There are many components that apply equally well to all course characteristics. In addition, many learner-centered components either are irrelevant to these course characteristics or have no relationship to the course characteristic. Thus learner-centered instructors could use these components with courses with these characteristics without special consideration of this course characteristic. For example, all courses should be aligned (Component 2 of the Role of the Instructor) regardless of the type of student, the level of the course, or the size of the enrollment. If I do not list a component on the following lists and tables, it means you do not have to pay special attention to this component in a course with this characteristic.

I emphasize that when the course characteristic matters to the component, in every case the course characteristic does *not* rule out the possibility of being learner-centered on this component. A relationship between the course characteristics and the learner-centered component simply means instructors need to consider this characteristic in their teaching, as the following discussion illustrates. If there is a relationship, I have determined the nature of the relationship; for example, "this course characteristic becomes a special consideration when using this learner-centered component." Special considerations include paying extra attention to how you plan or implement your course, emphasizing to your students why these components are relevant and important, and explicitly teaching how to do or how to use this component when your course has these course characteristics. A unique relationship exists between some course characteristics and some learner-centered components. The rest of this section gives examples of each of these relationships.

The Type of Students

Less mature, less motivated students. Less mature or less motivated students may want instructor-centered approaches because those are what they are used to or comfortable with. Open-ended situations or situations lacking structure may frighten less mature or less motivated students. Some of these students are also leery of working in groups. However, one of the purposes of education is to push students beyond their comfort range.

As a learner-centered instructor, you will consider the maturity and motivation of your students and teach differently. In fact, using many of these learner-centered approaches should help them to succeed more than using instructor-centered approaches. The maturity or motivation level of the students is an important consideration for many learner-centered components, as Tables 9.1 and 9.2 show. Here are some specific examples:

- When you have less mature and less motivated students, you may pay special attention to how you plan or implement your course. Table 9.1 lists the relevant learner-centered components.

  - Some teaching or learning methods are more appropriate for less mature, less motivated students than other methods. Many classroom assessment techniques that quickly monitor the student's mastery of factual knowledge are helpful for unmotivated or immature students. These interactions relate to Component 1, "Creation of an environment for learning," and Component 3, "Teaching or learning methods appropriate for student learning goals," both within the Role of the Instructor dimension.

  - Contract grading can motivate less motivated students. Contract grading is a learner-centered approach of Component 3 of the Balance of Power dimension, "Determination of how students earn grades."

  - When instructors use contract grading, the students feel that they have some control over the grades they earn. This control can be empowering and motivating to students. Unmotivated students may not be able to blame the instructor for poor grades that they earn through contract grading.

- You could model how to do or use some of these components with less mature and less motivated students, as listed in Table 9.2; for example:

  - Less motivated students may need more guidance in selecting additional content, referring to Component 1 of the Balance of Power dimension, "Determination of course content."

  - Less mature and less motivated students may require more help with less structured or more open-ended assignments. This interaction relates to two components of the Role of the Instructor dimension: Component 1, "Creation of an environment for learning," and Component 3, "Teaching or learning methods appropriate for student learning goals."

Components to Emphasize as Relevant and Important with Less Mature or Less Motivated Students

- The Function of Content

  1. Varied uses of content

     Know why they need to learn content

  4. Use of content to facilitate future learning

- The Role of the Instructor

  4. Activities involving student, instructor, content interactions

- The Responsibility for Learning

  1. Responsibility for learning

  2. Learning-to-learn skills for the present and the future

  3. Self-directed, lifelong learning skills

  4. Students' self-assessment of their learning

  5. Students' self-assessment of their strengths and weaknesses

  6. Information literacy skills

- The Purposes and Processes of Assessment

  3. Peer and self-assessment

  7. Authentic assessment

Nontraditional or older students. Older, nontraditional students are a very heterogeneous group. Some are very motivated and career-directed, whereas other returning students are less familiar with alternative learning environments and are less flexible. Of course, all nontraditional students benefit from learner-centered approaches, just as "traditional" students do. I describe characteristics that are true of all nontraditional students. These students may need special considerations on some of the learner-centered components. Here are some examples:

- These students may require special consideration when the instructor assigns students to groups. It may be better to put two older students together when forming groups of four or five rather than having each be the only older student in such a working group. This consideration relates to Component 1 of the Role of the Instructor dimension, "Creation of an environment for learning."

- These students may be less flexible with their time due to many competing demands. They may not have time to interact outside of class. Instructors might need to allow these interactions to occur in class or help them to use online or other electronic interactions. This relates to Component 4 of the Role of the Instructor, "Activities that involve student, teacher, content interactions."

- Nontraditional students may prefer authentic assessments more than standard types of testing. They can use their real-world experiences on these authentic assessments.

- For older, nontraditional students you may need to address some components in two ways:

  - Some nontraditional students may have well-developed information literacy skills that they learned through their careers or life experiences. Other nontraditional students may lack the basic computer skills needed to access resources. This relates to Component 6 of the Responsibility for Learning dimension, "Information literacy."

  - Some nontraditional students may have a very clear sense of what they want or need to learn. Others just want their instructors to tell them what to do and have no interest in selecting additional content to learn. This relates to Component 1 of the Balance of Power dimension, "Determination of course content."

For reference purposes, Tables 9.1 and 9.2 give complete lists of the components that I think are relevant for these two types of students. Throughout the discussion of this model, I identify the components by

TABLE 9.1

Components Relevant to Course Planning or Implementation Considerations with Less Motivated, Less Mature, and Nontraditional Students.

Less Mature or Less Motivated Students	Nontraditional or Older Students
The Function of Content	
2. Level to which students engage in content	2. Level to which students engage in content
The Role of the Instructor	
1. Creation of an environment for learning	1. Creation of an environment for learning
3. Teaching or learning methods appropriate for student learning goals	
	4. Activities involving student, instructor, content interactions
6. Motivation of students to learn	
The Responsibility for Learning	
1. Responsibility for learning	1. Responsibility for learning
	2. Learning-to-learn skills for the present and the future
	3. Self-directed lifelong learning skills
	4. Students' self-assessment of their learning
	5. Students' self-assessment of their strengths and weaknesses
The Purposes and Processes of Assessment	
	7. Authentic assessment
The Balance of Power	
3. Determination of how students earn grades	
4. Use of open-ended assignments	

dimension and number them as they appear on the rubrics. Table 9.1 lists the components by dimensions that are relevant for course planning or implementation with both less mature or less motivated students and older, nontraditional students. Table 9.2 lists the components by dimensions that learner-centered instructors will explicitly teach how to do or use with less mature or less motivated students and nontraditional or older students.

TABLE 9.2

Learner-Centered Instructors Will Explicitly Teach How to Use These Components to Less Motivated, Less Mature, and Nontraditional Students.

Less Mature or Less Motivated Students	Nontraditional or Older Students
The Function of Content	
1. Varied uses of content	1. Varied uses of content
Acquire discipline-specific learning methodologies	Acquire discipline-specific learning methodologies
Use inquiry or ways of thinking	
Learn to solve real-world problems	
3. Use of organizing schemes	
4. Use of content to facilitate future learning	
The Responsibility for Learning	
2. Learning-to-learn skills for the present and the future	2. Learning-to-learn skills for the present and the future
3. Self-directed, lifelong learning skills	3. Self-directed, lifelong learning skills
4. Students' self-assessment of their learning	4. Students' self-assessment of their learning
5. Students' self-assessment of their strengths and weaknesses	5. Students' self-assessment of their strengths and weaknesses
6. Information literacy skills	6. Information literacy skills
The Purposes and Processes of Assessment	
3. Peer and self-assessment	
The Balance of Power	
1. Determination of course content	
2. Expression of alternative perspectives	
4. Use of open-ended assignments	
6. Opportunities to learn	

Level of the Course

Lower-level courses. In many ways, the relationship between lower-level courses and learner-centered components is similar to that of less mature, less motivated students. There are a few subtle differences. For example, on Component 4 of the Role of the Instructor dimension, "Activities involving student, instructor, content interactions," learner-centered instructors will emphasize the relevance of these activities with less motivated, less mature students regardless of the level of the course. Moreover, learner-centered instructors will explicitly teach students how to interact with each other or with the instructor in appropriate ways in lower-level courses. Instructors might explain the importance of talking to peers or the instructor when students do not understand the material in lower-level classes. Obviously, the level of motivation relates to Component 6 of the Role of the Instructor dimension, "Motivation of students to learn." However, this component does not have a special relationship with lower-level classes, as there can be students who are motivated to learn in lower-level courses.

Here are some examples of how the lower level of courses interact with the learner-centered components:

- I have found that beginning college students do not understand the aspect of contract grading that they have to decide what assignments they want to do early in the semester. They do not understand that they will not get credit for an assignment that they have not contracted to do. Perhaps it was the way I explained it in the beginning of the semester. These same students had no trouble with contract grading in a more advanced course. (This is Component 3 of the Balance of Power dimension, "Determination of how students earn grades.")

- Beginning students, like less mature ones, may not know how to complete assignments that are more open-ended. (This is Component 4 of the Balance of Power dimension, "Use of open-ended assignments.") They may need more guidance and more structure to understand what instructors expect them to do.

- For students in lower-level courses, instructors could teach how to use proper citations and how to paraphrase as opposed to plagiarizing. This consideration is part of Component 6 of the Responsibility for Learning dimension, "Information literacy skills."

- Instructors might focus on the development of all of the skills described in Components 2, 3, 4, 5, and 6 of the Responsibility for Learning dimension. Instructors would emphasize the relevance of these skills as well as explicitly teach them in lower-level courses.

- Instructors might teach students in lower-level classes that they read different types of material in different ways. For example, students should read textbooks differently than they would novels and editorials. Instructors might also teach how to read the tables and figures in textbooks.

Upper-level or professional courses. With upper-level or advanced courses, the learner-centered instructor could plan the course to ensure that the students practice how to continue learning and be able to function after graduation. Upper-level courses may provide increasing opportunities to achieve the relevant components. Examples include:

- Instructors could consider giving students opportunities to demonstrate mastery of all of the skills described in the Responsibility for Learning dimension. These components would be relevant planning considerations for instructors of advanced, graduate, or professional level courses.

- Instructors might teach upper-level students advanced skills such as how to read primary literature or conduct independent research, part of Component 1 of the Function of Content dimension, "Varied uses of content: Acquire discipline-specific learning methodologies."

- Instructors might use authentic assessment extensively in upper-level courses as the students are getting ready to graduate. Authentic assessment is Component 7 of the Purposes and Processes of Assessment dimension.

For reference purposes, Tables 9.3 and 9.4 present complete lists of the components that I think are relevant for these two levels of courses. Table 9.3 lists the components that are relevant for course planning or implementation with both lower-level courses and advanced courses. Table 9.4 lists the components that learner-centered instructors will explicitly teach in lower-level and more advanced courses.

Large Enrollment in the Course

Whenever large enrollment is relevant to the learner-centered components, it relates to course planning or implementation considerations. Large enrollments make certain components more complex to plan or implement, but do not rule them out. As summarized in the following list, courses with large enrollments of students might require additional

TABLE 9.3

Components Relevant to Course Planning or Implementation Considerations with Different Levels of Courses.

Lower-Level Course	Advanced Undergraduate, Graduate, or Professional-Level Course
The Function of Content	
2. Level to which students engage in content	
The Role of the Instructor	
1. Creation of an environment for learning	
3. Teaching or learning methods appropriate for student learning goals	
The Responsibility for Learning	
	1. Responsibility for learning
	2. Learning-to-learn skills for the present and the future
	3. Self-directed lifelong learning skills
	4. Students' self-assessment of their learning
	5. Students' self-assessment of their strengths and weaknesses
The Purposes and Processes of Assessment	
	3. Peer and self-assessment
7. Authentic assessment	7. Authentic assessment
The Balance of Power	
3. Determination of how students earn grades	
4. Use of open-ended assignments	

resources on this component. These resources could be teaching assistants, graders, or technological aids. For example, large classes might require more structure to achieve Component 5 of the Balance of Power dimension, "Flexibility of course policies, assessment methods, learning methods, and deadlines."

TABLE 9.4

Components That Learner-Centered Instructors Will Explicitly Teach How to Use in Different Levels of Courses.

Lower-Level Course	Advanced Undergraduate, Graduate, or Professional-Level Course
The Function of Content	

1. Varied uses of content
  • Acquire discipline-specific methodologies
  • Use inquiry or ways of thinking
  • Learn to solve real-world problems
	1. Varied uses of content
	  • Acquire discipline-specific methodologies
	  • Use inquiry or ways of thinking
	  • Learn to solve real-world problems

3. Use of organizing schemes	
4. Use of content to facilitate future learning	
The Role of the Instructor	
4. Activities involving student, instructor, content interactions	
The Responsibility for Learning	
1. Responsibility for learning	
2. Learning-to-learn skills for the present and the future	
3. Self-directed lifelong learning skills	
4. Students' self-assessment of their learning	
5. Students' self-assessment of their strengths and weaknesses	
6. Information literacy skills	6. Information literacy skills
The Purposes and Processes of Assessment	
3. Peer and self-assessment	
The Balance of Power	
2. Expression of alternative perspectives	
4. Use of open-ended assignments	
6. Opportunities to learn	

Instructors can employ learner-centered assessment tools without grading all of students' papers individually by using self- and peer assessments, providing feedback to the students online, or using some of the other tools discussed in Chapter Seven. Therefore, the size of the class does not rule out various components in the Purposes and Processes of Assessment.

Components Relevant to Course Planning or Implementation Considerations with Large-Enrollment Courses

- The Role of the Instructor
  1. Creation of an environment for learning
  3. Teaching or learning methods appropriate for student learning goals
  4. Activities involving student, instructor, content interactions
- The Purposes and Processes of Assessment
  1. Assessment within the learning process
  2. Formative assessment
  4. Demonstration of mastery and ability to learn from mistakes
  5. Justification of the accuracy of answers
  6. Timeframe for feedback
  7. Authentic assessment
- The Balance of Power
  1. Determination of course content
  2. Expression of alternative perspectives
  3. Determination of how students earn grades
  4. Use of open-ended assignments
  5. Flexibility of course policies, assessment methods, learning methods, and deadlines

Components That Learner-Centered Instructors Will Emphasize Are Relevant and Important in Lower-Level Courses
- The Function of Content
  1. Varied uses of content
     Know why they need to learn content
  4. Use of content to facilitate future learning

- The Role of the Instructor

    4. Activities involving student, instructor, content interactions

- The Responsibility for Learning

    1. Responsibility for learning

    2. Learning-to-learn skills for the present and the future

    3. Self-directed, lifelong learning skills

    4. Students' self-assessment of their learning

    5. Students' self-assessment of their strengths and weaknesses

    6. Information literacy skills

- The Purposes and Processes of Assessment

    3. Peer and self-assessment

- The Balance of Power

    6. Opportunities to learn

Course Content

The relationship between content and the learner-centered components. Obviously, content relates to all of the components of the Function of Content. Some components in the remaining four dimensions have a unique relationship with content. These relationships are especially relevant to consider with content-rich courses. Table 9.5 lists these components and their explanations.

Perceived lack of relevancy of the course content. When the content of the course seems less relevant to the students or to their careers, the instructor can plan ways to make the components in the following list more relevant. These considerations apply to many developmental or general education courses.

Relevant Components for Course Planning or Implementation Considerations When Students Perceive a Lack of Relevancy in Course Content

- The Function of Content

    1. Varied uses of content

    2. Level to which students engage in content

    3. Uses of organizing schemes

    4. Use of content to facilitate future learning

- The Role of the Instructor

    1. Creation of an environment for learning

    6. Motivation of students to learn

TABLE 9.5

The Unique Relationships Among Components and Content.

Dimension	Component	Comment
The Role of the Instructor	3. Teaching or learning methods appropriate for student learning goals	The content of the course should dictate the teaching or learning methods appropriate for student learning goals.
The Responsibility for Learning	5. Students' self-assessment of their strengths and weaknesses	The content of the course should help to determine what skills the students should assess.
	6. Information literacy skills	The content of the course may help to determine what information literacy skills the students should practice.
The Purposes and Processes of Assessment	7. Authentic assessment	With some content, instructors may have a very hard time using authentic assessment.
The Balance of Power	1. Determination of course content	In an elective course, instructors may feel that students can have more latitude in determining some of the course content. If a course is a prerequisite for more advanced courses, instructors may feel they can give the students less latitude in determining some of the course content.
	2. Expression of alternative perspectives	Some disciplines encourage the expression of the alternative perspectives more than others.
	4. Open-ended assignments	The ease of giving open-ended assignments varies by discipline.

- The Responsibility for Learning
  1. Responsibility for learning
- The Purposes and Processes of Assessment
  6. Authentic assessment
- The Balance of Power
  1. Determination of course content

Summary of Comparisons Between the Course Characteristics and the Learner-Centered Components

The comparison of the influence of these four types of course characteristics gives further evidence for why the myths about learner-centered teaching are not true:

- Contrary to popular beliefs (Blumberg & Everett, 2005), the number of students in a class has less influence on whether it can be learner-centered than does the maturity of the students or the level of the course.

- The content of the course does not influence many components beyond the Function of Content dimension. Content-rich courses can still have many learner-centered approaches without sacrificing the rigor of the course. In fact, using learner-centered approaches may allow the students to learn more content and learn better.

- Instructors of lower-level courses or classes with many less-mature or less-motivated students can use many learner-centered approaches. When these instructors model how to do these approaches with these types of students, their students can succeed in these learner-centered courses.

Model Two: A Developmental, Curriculum-Wide Approach to Becoming Learner-Centered

Another way to consider how much learner-centered teaching is appropriate for a particular course is to take a planned developmental approach across a curriculum or program. This model has two different manifestations. The first integrated approach involves planning when courses will stress the development of specific learner-centered skills. Instructors would focus on developing some skills that relate to being learner-centered in some courses and focus on other skills in other courses. The development of information literacy skills discussed in Table 2.7 in Chapter Two is an example of this planned focus on specific skills.

The second integrated approach expects courses to have more learner-centered components as the students progress through the curriculum. Early courses can be less learner-centered and more advanced courses more learner-centered. Individual instructors cannot use this developmental approach alone. However, when all of the instructors in an educational program plan their courses in an integrated way, as did the instructors in the Occupational Therapy program described in Box 9.2 and Table 9.6, they can achieve a very learner-centered curriculum.

Box 9.2. Planned Progression for Increasing the Balance of Power Across an Educational Program

The instructors in the Occupational Therapy program at the University of the Sciences in Philadelphia consciously planned the progression for increasing the Balance of Power dimension across their program (Kramer et al., 2007). This is a five-year program accepting students right out of high school and leading to a master's degree in occupational therapy.

During the first two years, called the preprofessional curriculum, the students satisfy the general education requirements of the university. The occupational therapy instructors do not teach these courses. They teach all of the courses in the last three years of the program, referred to as the professional curriculum (P1–P3 for the three professional years). Table 9.6 shows the learner-centered status of courses on the Balance of Power dimension according to the level within the curriculum. The expected level is marked with <P> in the cell. As the table shows, all of their professional courses are at least at the lower level of transitioning. For the first and fifth components there is a planned three-year transitioning to learner-centered teaching. When the first professional-year courses are at the higher level of transitioning—as in Components 2, 3, and 4—the transition to the learner-centered approach is quicker. This program requires attendance throughout all classes, because the instructors believe that students cannot negotiate attendance with employers. Therefore, all courses remain at the lower level of transitioning for the sixth component throughout the program.

TABLE 9.6

Development of the Balance of Power Dimension for an Occupational Therapy Program.

The Balance of Power

Component	Employs *instructor-centered* approaches →	→ Transitioning to learner-centered approaches →		Employs *learner-centered* approaches
		Lower level of transitioning	**Higher level of transitioning**	
1. Determination of course content	Instructor • Entirely determines course content *and* • Does not seek feedback on the content	Instructor • Determines course content *and* • Allows students to offer insights or feedback on content after course is over < **P1**>	Instructor • Determines course content *and* • Allows students to choose some assignment topics (with permission) <**P2**>	Instructor • Largely determines course content *and* • Encourages students to explore additional content independently or through projects <**P3**>

(Continued)

TABLE 9.6

Development of the Balance of Power Dimension for an Occupational Therapy Program. (*Continued*)

The Balance of Power

Component	Employs *instructor-centered* approaches →	→ Transitioning to learner-centered approaches →		Employs *learner-centered* approaches
		Lower level of transitioning	**Higher level of transitioning**	
2. Expression of alternative perspectives	Instructor expresses all of the perspectives.	Instructor infrequently allows students to express alternative perspectives, even when appropriate.	Instructor allows students to express alternative perspectives when appropriate. **< P1>**	Instructor encourages students to express alternative perspectives when appropriate. **<P2–3>**
3. Determination of how students earn grades	All performance and assignments count toward students' grades.	Instructor allows students to drop one assessment but provides no alternative opportunities for them to demonstrate mastery.	Instructor allows students to resubmit assignments or other assessments for regrading **<P1–P2>**	Instructor uses either mastery (students may retake exam until reaching acceptable performance standard) *or* contract grading (students contract for their grade based upon how much acceptable work they do) to determine what grade students will earn. **<P2 for electives, P3 required courses>**
4. Use of open-ended assignments	Even when appropriate, instructor does *not* use • Assignments that are open-ended or allow alternative paths *and* • Test questions that allow for more than one right answer	When appropriate, instructor uses *a few* • Assignments that are open-ended or allow alternative paths *and* • Test questions that allow for more than one right answer	When appropriate, instructor *sometimes* uses • Assignments that are open-ended or allow alternative paths *and* • Test questions that allow for more than one right answer **<P1–P2>**	If appropriate, instructor *routinely* uses • Assignments that are open-ended or allow alternative paths *and* • Test questions that allow for more than one right answer **<P3>**

(Continued)

TABLE 9.6 (*Continued*)

The Balance of Power

Component	Employs *instructor-centered* approaches →	→ Transitioning to learner-centered approaches →		Employs *learner-centered* approaches
		Lower level of transitioning	**Higher level of transitioning**	
5. Flexibility of course policies, assessment methods, learning methods, and deadlines	Instructor mandates all policies and deadlines *or* Instructor does not adhere to policies.	Instructor is flexible on *a few* • Course policies • Assessment methods • Learning methods • Deadlines *and* Instructor infrequently adheres to these flexible decisions. **<P1>**	Instructor is flexible on *some* • Course policies • Assessment methods • Learning methods • Deadlines *and* Instructor somewhat adheres to what they agreed upon. **<P2>**	Instructor is flexible on *most* • Course policies • Assessment methods • Learning methods • Deadlines *and* Instructor always adheres to what they agreed to. **<P3>**
6. Opportunities to learn	Instructor mandates that students attend all classes even when they are not expected to be active learners.	Instructor provides consequences for • Not attending classes *and/or* • Not participating in active learning experiences **<P1–3>**	Instructor provides • Attendance options for some classes so students may miss a few classes without penalty *and/or* • Participation options for some activities	Instructor • Helps students to take advantage of opportunities to learn *and* • Fosters understanding of consequences of not taking advantage of such learning opportunities, like missing class

P = year of the professional curriculum, from P1 (first professional year) to P3 (third professional year).

Chapter Summary

Can all courses be learner-centered? The short answer is, all courses can have *some* learner-centered components. Not all courses should be learner-centered on all components, but nearly every course can be learner-centered to some degree.

I compared course characteristics such as

- The type of students enrolled in the course
- The level of the course
- The number of students enrolled in the class
- The content of the course

with the learner-centered components of the five dimensions. These course characteristics may influence what instructors do in relation to some of these components. Many characteristics do not influence these learner-centered components.

Departments can use an integrated approach to making their courses more learner-centered. This approach uses a developmental progression to learner-centered, with all advanced courses being more learner-centered than earlier courses.

APPLICATION ACTIVITY

In this activity, you will analyze course characteristics to help you determine the potential learner-centered status of your course for each of the components of the five dimensions of learner-centered teaching. Table 9.7, for the Function of Content dimension, appears here as an example. To complete this activity for the other four dimensions, you can copy and complete Table 9.8. To do so, ask yourself which of these characteristics influence how learner-centered your course can be. If the characteristic is relevant, comment on how the characteristic influences your course. If the characteristic is not a relevant consideration for your course, leave the cell blank or mark it "NA."

TABLE 9.7

The Function of Content: Analysis of Your Course Characteristics.

Dimension: The Function of Content

Component	Type of students (less motivated, less mature, older, nontraditional)	Level of the course (beginning or advanced, professional or graduate)	Number of students enrolled in the class	Content of the course
1. Varied uses of content: Know why they need to learn content				
1. Varied uses of content: Acquire discipline-specific learning methodologies				
1. Varied uses of content: Use inquiry or ways of thinking in the discipline				
1. Varied uses of content: Learn to solve real-world problems				

(Continued)

TABLE 9.7 (*Continued*)

Dimension: The Function of Content

Component	Type of students (less motivated, less mature, older, nontraditional)	Level of the course (beginning or advanced, professional or graduate)	Number of students enrolled in the class	Content of the course
2. Level to which students engage in content				
3. Use of organizing schemes				
4. Use of content to facilitate future learning				

TABLE 9.8

Analyses of Your Course Characteristics by Dimension.

Dimension:

Component	Type of students (less motivated, less mature, older, nontraditional)	Level of the course	Number of students enrolled in the class	Content of the course

Chapter 10

Strategies for Overcoming Obstacles and Resistance

THE PREVIOUS CHAPTER discussed whether all courses can be learner-centered and mentioned that there are various sources of resistance to transforming your courses—including yourself and the culture of your institution. This chapter will discuss these obstacles to becoming a learner-centered instructor and offer some pragmatic suggestions for overcoming them.

Potential Obstacles to Becoming a Learner-Centered Teacher

Stakeholders—that is, people who have a significant investment in your course (Scriven, 1991)—can present a challenge as you begin or continue transforming your course. These include students, peers in your department, your department chair, other instructors and administrators at your institution, and, of course, yourself. Many of these stakeholders can also become part of your strategy for overcoming obstacles.

You May Be the Hardest Obstacle to Overcome

To overcome your own resistance, you need to reflect on your philosophy of teaching, your beliefs, and your practices. Reflect on these questions:

- Do you believe that learner-centered teaching is superior to instructor-centered approaches?

To make changes, you must believe that those changes will improve your teaching and student learning. I hope this book, as well as all of the cited literature, convince you that students will learn more with learner-centered teaching. Research shows that epistemological beliefs about teaching are an important predictor of the success and the long-term viability of changes in teaching (Polich, 2007; Brownlee, Purdie, & Boulton-Lewis, 2001).

- How much do you trust your ability to give up control or your ability to take risks to make your teaching more learner-centered?

- How much do you trust your students to take responsibility for their own learning and to share the balance of power?

If you do not trust yourself or your students, you will have a hard time making lasting changes. What can you do to establish more trust in yourself and your students? Seek support from other instructors who have become more learner-centered or from the Teaching Excellence Center, if your institution has one. Be courageous.

- What type of changes do you want to make?

Most instructors can use a few of the techniques described in this book without thoroughly changing how they teach. This is a good strategy when you begin your transition toward learner-centered teaching, especially if you lack the confidence or time to make larger changes.

If you trust yourself and your students and believe that learner-centered approaches result in more student learning, then you may be willing to make larger, more transformative changes. Instructors who want to improve student learning outcomes are more likely to make more transformative changes in their teaching than instructors who want to improve the quality and organization of how they deliver content (Akerlind, 2003). If you want to make more transformative changes, consider the following points.

Because this type of teaching is more labor intensive, especially in the beginning or in the planning stages, you need to consider your time commitments. Ask yourself the following questions as a way to determine whether you are ready and able to make big changes in your teaching:

- Do you have the time to make large-scale changes? How much time can you devote to changing your teaching now?

- What other competing forces in your life might take away from devoting more time to your teaching?

- How much time do you need to invest in your research?

- What else is going on in your life that might take time away from your teaching? (For example, you may have a major university commitment such as being chair of a search committee, or personal responsibilities such as having a baby or taking care of frail parents.)

- When are you going up for promotion and tenure?

- You may not want to make big changes that potentially could be unpopular with students or may not succeed the first time you try them in the year before you go up for promotion, tenure, or both.

- You may also need to devote more time to your research by trying to get grants or publications in the year before you submit your documents for promotion and tenure.

However, if the timing is right, this could be a good time to transform your course.

Students

Students often resist change. Learner-centered teaching is more labor intensive for them as well, and they may not want or be able to commit the extra time. They may also worry that they may not be able to succeed with a different educational style.

A common complaint about student presentations or small-group work is that the students are teaching each other and not hearing from a content expert. Students may resent the increased demands on their time or may feel uncomfortable learning in different ways. Therefore, students sometimes evaluate transformed courses lower than other students evaluated the same course before the change. It may also be a function of some rough edges the first time instructors implement innovations. Usually the evaluations rise again, but at the time it can be discouraging.

Instructors

Your peers and your chair in your department may appear resistant to your changes. They may not consider what you are doing to be *teaching*. About ten years ago, one young instructor I knew decided to implement a more learner-centered format in his course, using small-group discussions and problem-solving activities. When his chair came to observe one of his classes, he found that the students were talking to each other instead of listening to the instructor, who was sitting with one of the groups. The chair remarked to the instructor that he would come back to observe the class when the instructor was actually teaching. Again, this happened about ten years ago; I hope this would not be the case today.

Your Institution

The culture of your department, the educational program, and the institution at large can offer resistance. Although many campuses say they are student-centered, few people know what this means or what implementation looks like. The physical structure of your classroom—such as auditorium-style, bolted-down chairs each with a small writing pad support—may make it harder to encourage students to talk to one other or work with resources or technology. Marilla Svinicki (in a personal communication, 2003) said that the single most important change that got instructors at the University of Texas at Austin to use active learning techniques was when the university removed the bolted-down chairs from classrooms and replaced them with movable chairs.

The schedule for your course may also not support learner-centered teaching. It is harder to use complex active learning techniques in fifty-minute periods than in larger blocks.

Culture is institution- or program-specific. Some cultures are more accepting of learner-centered practices than others are, and some administrators encourage some learner-centered practices, but not others. Peer assessment may be more easily accepted in some departments than in others. Here are department-specific rationales from two types of programs, to help you see how the culture of a program fosters or inhibits adoption of specific learner-centered practices.

- Students in clinical programs often examine each other as they practice clinical skills. It may be easier to begin peer assessments when students are already sharing with each other. Further, if their instructors develop scoring rubrics to assess clinical skills, then students can receive training in how to use these rubrics for peer assessment. Thus, it may not be a big step to implementing peer assessments in these programs.

- However, where students do not share their work with their peers, it may be harder to use peer assessment. For example, some chairs of humanities departments may not support peer assessments of essays because they believe that only instructors or graduate students should assess these papers.

- In contrast, instructors in humanities departments usually encourage their students to express alternative perspectives and routinely use open-ended assignments, two components of the Balance of Power dimension. Clinical professors may not encourage the expression of alternative perspectives and the use of open-ended assignments as often.

Strategies for Overcoming Obstacles and Resistance

If you want to transform your teaching so that your courses are more learner-centered, use strategies for overcoming these obstacles. The following list summarizes some major strategies; six of them are described in more detail following the list.

Major Strategies for Overcoming Resistance to Becoming Learner-Centered

- Educate yourself on the benefits of learner-centered teaching.
- Start small.
- Plan incremental changes.
- Work with a partner.
- Talk to the chair of your department before you make changes.

- Get buy-in from your students.

- Consult print and web resources.

- Seek help from the Teaching and Learning Center or Center for Teaching Excellence at your institution, if one exists.

- Seek help from instructors who have implemented learner-centered approaches.

- Attend higher education conferences that focus on teaching, such as the Teaching Professor (www.teachingprofessor.com) or the regional or national Lilly Conferences (www.lillyconferences.org).

- Document your changes on your annual evaluation:

  - Show where you were on the rubrics prior to making changes and where you are now; note whether you have future plans.

  - Document your success on your annual evaluation by showing student documents or assessment evidence you have gathered.

- Share your changes and your successes with your peers on your campus and beyond through conferences and publications.

Educate yourself on the benefits of learner-centered teaching. You may want to reread the section in Chapter One that reviews the psychological and educational research supporting learner-centered approaches to help convince yourself that the students will have better learning experiences with learner-centered teaching. Read the other resources listed at the end of this chapter. Observe instructors who are using learner-centered techniques and ask them why it is working.

Start small. Begin by adopting a few easy-to-implement, low-risk techniques such as those described in this book. Choose techniques that your students will most likely accept easily. Look at the list of low-risk techniques that the Psych 101 instructor could easily implement, which appears at the end of Chapter Eight, The Balance of Power.

Plan incremental changes. You do not need to transform your course all at once—your changes can be incremental and iterative. See how you feel about the early changes before you make others. After you have made small changes that you feel are successful, you may be ready for larger, more transformative changes. Many of the Planning for Transformation exercises completed for the Psych 101 courses show examples of incremental changes.

Work with a partner. Choose a peer instructor to work with as you begin to transform your course. Your partner may be someone who teaches many of the same students or the same level of students. For example, two general education instructors, perhaps in different departments, could try out similar changes. Another good choice for a partner is another instructor in your department who teaches an upper-level course that students take at the same time they take your course. You and your partner can implement the same technique or transform the same component at once. Both of you can discuss ideas for change, troubleshoot together, observe each other implementing a change, and offer insights into why it is working or how to improve it. Most important, your partner will be a support for you as you begin to make changes.

Talk with your chair. By talking with your chair prior to beginning a major change in how you teach your course, you can determine how supportive he or she is of your becoming a more learner-centered instructor. Your chair may have good suggestions for implementation. If your chair is supportive, you might ask for the additional resources you need to make this change work well. You do not want your chair to hear student complaints about your course without your telling him or her about it in advance. Continue to talk to your chair as you implement your changes. Then document the changes and outcomes of your changes on your annual review of teaching.

Get your students to accept learner-centered approaches. Many of the resources listed at the end of this chapter discuss strategies for getting students to accept learner-centered teaching. I have found that it is very important to explain your expectations continually. On the first day of the course, explain what you will be doing and why you will be doing it. Tell the students what you expect them to do in class and outside of class. Do not give in to their complaints or become impatient with their early, inefficient attempts. It usually takes about a month for students to get used to a new level of responsibility or new type of learning. During that first month, you need to uphold your expectations consistently and to reinforce the attempts and progress that students make toward taking more responsibility for their learning and self-assessments or for coming prepared to class.

Share your changes and your successes with your peers through conferences and publications. Your transformation process can become an area of potential scholarship for you. People who do this type of scholarship call it *scholarship of teaching and learning.* Prior to doing actual research on your teaching, check with your chair to determine if this is an acceptable line of research for you. Most administrators feel it is legitimate scholarship as long it meets the standards of peer review (Shulman, 2004). Submit a proposal to present as either a paper or a poster to your discipline conference on how you teach using learner-centered approaches or to one of the higher education conferences devoted to teaching.

Resources

A good place to start overcoming obstacles to becoming more learner-centered is to read some of the excellent resources available. Here are a few of my favorite resources on this topic:

Specific Sources

Coffman, S. J. (2003). Ten strategies for getting students to take responsibility for their learning. *College Teaching, 51,* 2–4.

Felder, R., & Brent, R. (1996). Navigating the bumpy road to student-centered instruction. *College Teaching, 44*(2), 43–47.

Fink, L. D. (2003). *Creating significant learning experiences.* San Francisco: Jossey-Bass.

Oakley, B., Felder, R. M., Brent, R., & Elhajj, I. (2004). Turning student groups into effective teams. *Journal of Student Centered Learning, 2*(1), 9–23.

Weimer, M. (2002). *Learner-centered teaching.* San Francisco: Jossey-Bass.

Periodicals to Read Regularly

College Teaching published by Heldref Publications, www.heldref.org

The Journal of Faculty Development published by New Forums Press, Inc.

P.O. Box 876, Stillwater, OK 74076

The Teaching Professor newsletter published by Magna Publications, www.magnapubs.com

New Directions in Teaching and Learning published by Jossey-Bass, www.josseybass.com

Journal of Excellence in College Teaching published by the Center for the Enhancement of Learning and Teaching of Miami University of Ohio, http://ject.libmuohio.edu

Many disciplines have educational journals, such as *Cell Biology Education, Teaching and Learning in Medicine, Journal of Management Education,* or *PRIMUS* (Problems, Resources, and Issues in Mathematics Undergraduate Studies).

For a list of discipline-specific journals that publish articles on the Scholarship of Teaching and Learning, see http://www.libraries.iub.edu/index.php?pageId=3213.

Chapter Summary

This chapter discussed how the various stakeholders may offer resistance as you begin or continue transforming your course. I discussed strategies for overcoming resistance from each of them and identified resources for further information. Major strategies for overcoming resistance to becoming learner-centered include these three basics:

- Start small.

- Plan incremental changes.

- Consult resources and other people.

If you try, you will find overcoming any obstacles and resistance is well worth the effort. Although you are likely to encounter resistance, especially in the beginning, your efforts to become a more learner-centered instructor will have many benefits. Your students will learn more, have a more meaningful learning experience, be able to continue learning after the course is over, and be better prepared to succeed in their careers and as citizens in our global world. You will be more satisfied with your teaching, and you may even get recognition for your innovative teaching.

APPLICATION ACTIVITY

A. Identification of Sources of Resistance for You

How much will the following stakeholders be a challenge for you as you begin transforming your course?

Yourself:

❏ Not an obstacle, could be a help   ❏ A small obstacle

❏ Neutral   ❏ A large obstacle

Your students:

❏ Not an obstacle, could be a help   ❏ A small obstacle

❏ Neutral   ❏ A large obstacle

Your peers in your department:

❏ Not an obstacle, could be a help   ❏ A small obstacle

❏ Neutral   ❏ A large obstacle

Your chair:

❏ Not an obstacle, could be a help   ❏ A small obstacle

❏ Neutral   ❏ A large obstacle

Administrators in general at your institution:

❏ Not an obstacle, could be a help   ❏ A small obstacle

❏ Neutral   ❏ A large obstacle

(Continued)

B. Overcoming Resistance and Obstacles

1. What strategies can you use to overcome resistance from the stakeholders you have listed?

2. How can you overcome any reservations you have about the functions of content in your course?

3. How can you overcome any reservations about your roles as an instructor?

4. How can you overcome any reservations about giving your students more responsibility for their own learning?

5. How can you overcome any reservations you have about how and why you assess students?

6. How can you overcome any reservations about giving your students more control or power in the course?

7. What local resources can you consult? Where are they? List people who are doing learner-centered teaching.

8. Who can be your support? (For example, your dean, your chair, students, other instructors, the Teaching and Learning Center or Center for Teaching Excellence, instructional designers.)

9. Who can be your partner in the transformation process? (For example, who could be your sounding board or will be trying similar changes at the same time?)

10. What else can you do to overcome obstacles that you personally have identified?

Chapter 11

Conclusion

WE EDUCATORS RECOGNIZE the need to change the focus in our teaching from what we do as instructors to what our students are learning. Weimer (2002) describes an approach that includes five dimensions of learner-centered teaching. Although this model has appeal, it does not offer pragmatic suggestions. Therefore I refined the five broad dimensions into specific, concrete components. Further, I organized these components into rubrics that describe an incremental approach from instructor-centered to learner-centered teaching. Each of the components on these rubrics describes what an instructor can do. The rubrics suggest different ways you can implement a learner-centered approach.

The rubrics can serve two different purposes. First, this incremental approach helps you to begin to see where you can make changes to transform your teaching to make it more learner-centered. Second, you can use the rubrics as an assessment tool to determine the learner-centered status of educational programs or of your own teaching.

The goal, either in the transformation process or in assessment, should not be total learner-centeredness. Whether you use the rubrics as a self-assessment to begin the change process or as an assessment tool for educational programs, it is essential to understand that not all courses should be learner-centered on all components. Even the most learner-centered courses have some components that are not learner-centered. However, nearly every course can have some or even many learner-centered components.

Once you begin to implement some learner-centered approaches, you will see additional ways to change how you teach. You can start with the components that seem easy or natural to you. Successful implementation should increase your confidence and your trust that learner-centered teaching works and leads to the students learning more. With experience, you may be ready to try changes that are more comprehensive. Alternatively after making some changes, you may consider changing some components that challenge the way you teach or require a different philosophy of teaching. Thus you may begin an iterative process of transforming how you teach.

A Comprehensive System for Transformation

Throughout this book I have described a comprehensive, multistep system to transform a course to be more learner-centered. To recap:

1. *Understand why it is necessary for you to incorporate learner-centered teaching approaches.* Instructor-centered approaches often lead to passive students who cannot apply what they learned to new situations and do not have the skills to continue learning outside the formal educational structure. In contrast, learner-centered teaching leads to superior student learning and retention when compared with more traditional approaches. There are very strong research-driven rationales in the educational and psychological literature to support your use of learner-centered teaching. Once you know this robust literature, you can use this research evidence without being defensive or apologetic, because the efficacy data are on your side.

2. *Familiarize yourself with the various ways that other instructors implement learner-centered teaching.* The components of the rubrics show different facets of the five dimensions of learner-centered teaching. I have described numerous practical examples throughout this book. Implementing some of these learner-centered techniques may be a good beginning for becoming learner-centered. Most of these examples are easy to incorporate in your teaching without redesigning your entire course.

3. *Decide that becoming a learner-centered instructor is possible.* This step can be emotionally difficult because it requires a desire to change—and trust that the changes will improve your teaching. This decision also takes courage. You need the courage of your convictions that you are doing the right thing. You may face opposition from peers and from students. Prepare your rationale and explanations for those who resist your transformation. Cite the research literature and your own successful implementations. Planning and implementing learner-centered teaching also takes more time. Seek support from instructors who are already using learner-centered approaches or from a teaching support center.

4. *Plan your change process.* Pick one course to begin transforming. Then use all of the tools I describe in this book to systematically consider and plan how to transform your course. Do the application activities or reflection questions at the end of each chapter for the course, then complete the rubrics for the course. Once you identify the status of your course through the rubrics, you could aim for the next level of transitioning within a specific component as a way to transform your teaching.

5. *Select a few components that you want to change.* Choose components based on the type of course, the level of the students, personal insights,

feedback from students, faculty peers, political considerations, or climate for change. All of the components can come from one dimension or from different dimensions.

6. *Complete the Planning for Transformation exercise for your chosen components.* This exercise appears simple but actually requires much thought; you may need to review it a few times.

7. *Plan to make incremental changes in your teaching, because they are easier to implement.* You can make changes in your teaching gradually by changing only a few components within these dimensions at a time. Because each rubric describes four incremental levels, from an instructor-centered to a learner-centered course, you can make the transition gradually using every level. However, you can skip the transitioning level or levels on a component and change the course on that component to be learner-centered in one step. Even these small steps often have a large impact on the overall learner-centeredness of a course. Furthermore, small steps in one component often have spillover effects onto other dimensions.

8. *Review your proposed changes to plan the next steps.* You might consider these questions:

- Can you achieve all of your planned changes together as a group?

- How practical are they to do at once?

- Should you implement one before the others?

You may want to start with a few easy-to-implement changes as you plan for changes that are more comprehensive. Begin to secure the resources you will need. Plan how much time you will need to make these changes.

9. *Pace yourself and seek out support.* Transforming your overall approach to teaching a course may take several years, whereas moving from one level to the next on a component of one dimension is a realistic short-term goal. This transformation process to make courses more learner-centered is not an easy one, and you are likely to encounter a variety of obstacles along the way. You and your students need to trust that this new way to teach will lead to improved student learning. This can be a scary process, so seek as much support as you can from various sources to help you make these changes.

10. *Plan to track your progress.* As you begin planning for change, think about collecting assessment data on both the old way you teach and your transformed course. If possible, use the same assessment tools, such as assessments of student learning, both prior to transformation and after transformation to collect comparable data. This relates to the second purpose of the rubrics.

A Multipurpose Assessment Tool

It is common for educational programs or institutions to claim that they are learner-centered. We need to be accountable to show that we are doing what we claim we are doing. We often use assessment tools to support our claims. The rubrics for the five dimensions of learner-centered teaching can serve as an assessment tool to show the learner-centered status of specific courses, individual instructors, departments, educational programs, or an entire institution. The rubrics are easy to use, and many different types of courses or educational programs can use them effectively. We can use the rubrics to show a snapshot of our current implementation of learner-centered teaching. Alternatively, we can use these rubrics in a pre- and post-implementation of changes. For assessment purposes, in addition to completing the rubrics, you need to provide supporting evidence to justify your judgments. This evidence can be in the form of examples or rationales for selections. Use the Documentation to Support the Selected Status form to record this evidence. Further support can come from materials you develop for courses, such as assignments or student products they developed in these courses.

The various implementations of learner-centered teaching will show your own strengths as a teacher and reflect the unique aspects of your discipline. If you make several changes, a very different teaching-learning-assessment dynamic will emerge in your courses. The rubrics provide you with an assessment tool to document these changes and show others how learner-centered your course or your educational program is.

A Final Word

If I have achieved my purpose in this book, you will have a clear idea of how to transform your teaching to be more learner-centered. You will have a systematic plan for how to make changes, and you can be confident that you are making changes that will improve the quality of your students' learning.

I hope that this book has motivated you to become a learner-centered teacher and given you the skills to be able to do that. Trust yourself, be courageous, and enjoy teaching using learner-centered approaches.

Although time consuming and challenging, you will find using learner-centered approaches well worth the effort. Your students will learn more, be able to apply what they learn to new situations, and remember the material after the course is over. You will feel more satisfied with your teaching, and you should feel good that your teaching is consistent with the latest trends in higher education and meets regional and professional accreditation standards. If you share what you are doing with others, you may develop a working relationship with another instructor, and you can get recognition for your efforts. This can even become a new area of scholarship for you.

Now, with confidence, start or continue your own transformation process to become a learner-centered instructor.

References

Akerlind, G. (2003). Growing and developing as a university teacher: Variation in meaning. *Studies in Higher Education, 28*(4), 375–390.

Alexander, P., & Murphy, P. (2000). The research base for APA's learner-centered psychological principles. In N. Lambert & B. McCombs (Eds.), *How students learn* (pp. 25–60). Washington, DC: American Psychological Association.

Alsardary, S., & Blumberg, P. (2009). Interactive, learner-centered methods of teaching mathematics. *PRIMUS*, in press.

Ambrosius, L. (2006). *HIST202/202H: America after 1877.* Retrieved November 8, 2006, from http://www.courseportfolio.org/peer/potfolioFiles/anonF/1150296835303_ambrosius+2006–1.pdf

Angelo, T. A., & Cross, K. P. (1993). *Classroom assessment techniques* (2nd ed.). San Francisco: Jossey-Bass.

Association of American Colleges and Universities. (2002, July). *Greater expectations*: A New Vision for Learning as a Nation Goes to College *report on a national task force.* Retrieved October 15, 2002, from www.greaterexpectations.org/pdf/GEX.FINAL.pdf

Association of College and Research Libraries. (2004). *Information literacy competency standards for higher education.* Retrieved October 5, 2004, from http://www.ala.org/ala/acrl/acrlstandards/informationliteracycompetency.htm

Barr, R. B., & Tagg., J. (1995, November/December). From teaching to learning: A new paradigm for undergraduate education. *Change, 27,* 12–25.

Bean, J. (1996). *Engaging ideas.* San Francisco: Jossey-Bass.

Berg, T. H. (2006). *HIST 202 American History since 1877.* Retrieved November 13, 2006, from http:wwwcourseportfolio.org/peer/potfolioFiles/anonF/1150736784431_berg-t-2006–1.pdf

Biggs, J. (1999). *Teaching for quality learning at university.* Buckingham, UK: Open University Press.

Bloom, B. S. (Ed.). (1956). *Taxonomy of educational objectives. The classification of educational goals, Handbook I: Cognitive domain.* New York: McKay.

Blumberg, P. (2000). Evaluating the evidence that problem-based learners are self-directed learners: A review of the literature. In D. H. Evensen & C. E. Hmelo (Eds.), *Problem-based learning: A research perspective on learning interactions* (pp. 199–226). Mahwah, NJ: Lawrence Erlbaum Associates.

Blumberg, P. (2004). Beginning journey toward a culture of learning-centered teaching. *Journal of Student- Centered Learning, 2*(1) 68–80.

Blumberg, P. (2005). Assessing students during the problem-based learning (PBL) process. *Journal of the International Association of Medical Science Educators, 13*(1), 92–99.

Blumberg, P. (2006). A framework for assessing different types of student learning within problem-based learning. *Journal of the International Association of Medical Science Educators, 16*(2), 58–70.

Blumberg, P., & Everett, J. (2005). Achieving a campus consensus on learning-centered teaching: Process and outcomes. *To Improve the Academy, 23,* 191–210.

Bonwell, C., & Eison, J. (1991). *Active learning: Creating excitement in the classroom.* Washington, DC: The George Washington University, School of Education and Human Development.

Bowman, L. A. (2007). *The Who? What? Where? When? of Evaluating Information.* Retrieved June 17, 2007, from www.usip.edu/teaching/innovations/alpha_order_of_brightidea.pdf

Bransford, J., Brown, A., & Cocking, R. (2000). In J. Bransford, A. Brown, and R. Cocking (Eds.), *How people learn: Brain, mind, experiences and school.* Washington, DC: National Academies Press.

Brownlee, J., Purdie, N., & Boulton-Lewis, G. (2001). Changing epistemological beliefs in pre-service teacher education students. *Teaching in Higher Education, 6*(2), 247–268.

Bruner, J. (1966). *Toward a theory of instruction.* Cambridge, MA: Harvard University Press.

Brunner, B. (2006). *Use of groups, Just-in-Time teaching (JiTT), and response keypads in introductory physics.* Retrieved December 24, 2006, from http://www.usip.edu/teaching/innovations/innovation

Byrnes, D. (2001). Course contract encourages student responsibility and civility. *The Teaching Professor, 15*(9), 3–5.

Candy, P. (1991). *Self-direction for lifelong learning.* San Francisco: Jossey-Bass.

Coffman, S. J. (2003). Ten strategies for getting students to take responsibility for their learning. *College Teaching, 51*(1), 1–4.

Cudd, T. (2003). *VTTP 910 VTTP 912 physiology I & II.* Retrieved January 20, 2007, 2007, from http://www.courseportfolio.org/peer/potfolioFiles/authF/1127871308987_cudd-t=2003–1.pdf

Demers, P. (2006). *ANTH 498.898 Introduction to Historical Archaeology.* Retrieved February 3, 2007, from http://www.courseportfolio.org/peer/potfolioFiles/anonF/1150297324977__demers-p-2006–1.pdf

DeZure, D. (2000) *Learning from change.* Sterling, VA: Stylus.

Doherty, A., Riordan, T., & Roth, J. (2002). *Student learning: A central focus for institutions of higher education.* Milwaukee, WI: Alverno College Institute.

Epstein, M. L., Lazarus, A. D., Calvano, T. B., Matthews, K. A., Hendel, R. A., & Epstein, B. B. (2002). Immediate feedback assessment technique promotes learning and corrects inaccurate first responses. *The Psychological Record, 52*(2), 187–201.

Ewell, P. (2001). Editorial: Listening up. *Change, 33*(3), 4.

Felder, R., & Brent, R. (1996). Navigating the bumpy road to student-centered instruction. *College Teaching, 44*(2), 43–47.

Fink, L. D. (2003). *Creating significant learning experiences.* San Francisco: Jossey-Bass.

Flanagan, C. (2007). *Living Legacy Project.* Retrieved June 02, 2007, from http://www.usip.edu/teaching/innovations/alpha_order_of_brightidea.pdf

Gardiner, L. F. (1994) *Redesigning higher education: Producing dramatic gains in student learning.* Washington, DC: Graduate School of Education and Human Development, The George Washington University.

Gehrman, P. (2006). *Implementing service learning in a health psychology course.* Retrieved January 20, 2007, from http://www. usp.edu/teaching/innovations/innovation

Grasha, A. (1996). *Teaching with style.* Pittsburgh: Alliance Publishers.

Groccia, J. E., & Miller, J. E. (1996). Collegiality in the classroom: The use of peer learning assistants in cooperative learning in introductory biology. *Innovative Higher Education, 21*(2), 87–100.

Harris, R. L. (2003). Encouraging emergent moments: The personal, critical, and rhetorical in the writing classroom. *Pedagogy: Critical Approaches to Teaching Literature, Language, Composition, and Culture, 4*(3), 401–418.

Hertel, J., & Millis, B. (2002). *Using simulations to promote learning in higher education.* Sterling, VA: Stylus.

Hiller, T., & Hietapelto, A. (2001). Contract grading: Encouraging commitment to the learning process through voice in the evaluation process. *Journal of Management Education, 25*(6), 660–684.

Jensen, G., & DiTiberio, J. (1989). *Personality and the teaching of composition.* Norwood, NJ: Ablex.

Johnson, W. D. (1991). Student-student interaction: The neglected variable in education. *Educational Research, 10*(1), 5–10.

Kafai, Y., & Resnick, M. (1996). *Constructionism in practice.* Mahwah, NJ: Erlbaum.

Kearney, P., & Kramer, P. (2007). *Community based client fieldwork experience: The impact of the social, cultural, and physical environment on accommodations.* Retrieved June 07, 2007, from www.usip.edu/teaching/innovations/alpha_order_of_brightidea.pdf

Kramer, P. (2007). *Making students responsible for reading.* Retrieved June 07, 2007, from www.usip.edu/teaching/innovations/alpha_order_of_brightidea.pdf

Kramer, P., Ideishi, R., Kearney, P., Cohen, M., Ames, J., Shea, G., et al. (2007). Achieving curricular themes through learner-centered teaching. *Occupational Therapy in Health Care, New Directions in Occupational Therapy Education, 21*(1/2), 185–198.

Kramp, M., & Humphries, W. (1995). Narrative, self-assessment, and the habit of reflection. *Assessment Update, 7*(1), 10–13.

Kuh, G. D., Kinzie, J., Schuh, J. H., & Whitt, W. (2005). *Student success in college: Creating conditions that matter.* San Francisco: Jossey-Bass.

Lambert, N., & McCombs, B. (2000). Introduction: Learner-centered schools and classrooms as a direction for school reform. In N. Lambert & B. McCombs (Eds.), *How students learn* (pp. 1–15). Washington, DC: American Psychological Association.

Lee, K. M. (2003). *Astronomy 103 – fall semester, 2002.* Retrieved November 8, 2006, from http://www.courseportfolio.org/peer/pages/index.jsp?what=portfolio ObjectD&portfolioObjectId=110

Lipson, M. (1983). The influence of religious affiliation on children's memory for text information. *Reading Research Quarterly, 18,* 448–457.

Mahalingam, M., Schaefer, F., & Morlino, E. (2006). *Promoting student learning use of peer groups.* Retrieved July 2, 2008, from www.usp.edu/teaching/innovations/innovation

Maharaj, S., & Banta, L. (2000). Using log assignments to foster learning: Revisiting writing across the curriculum. *Journal of Engineering Education, 89*(1), 73–77.

Maritz, C., & Zappin, R. (2007). Creation of a model to promote the development of professional behaviors in students. *The Journal of Faculty Development , 21*(3): 193–200.

Matlin, M. W. (2002). Cognitive psychology and college-level pedagogy: Two siblings that rarely communicate. In D. F. Halpern & M. D. Hakel (Eds.), *Applying the science of learning to university teaching and beyond: New directions for teaching and learning* (pp. 97–103). San Francisco: Jossey-Bass.

Maxwell, W. E. (1998). Supplemental instruction, learning communities and students studying together. *Community College Review* (Fall). Retrieved December 20, 2005, from findarticles.com

McVeigh, J. (2006). *On-line instruction on how to read primary material within disciplines.* Retrieved July 2, 2008, from www.usp.edu/teaching/innovations/innovation

Michaelsen, L. K., Knight, A. B., & Fink, L. D. (2004). *Team-based learning.* Sterling, VA: Stylus.

Middle States Commission on Higher Education. (2003a). *Developing research and communication skills: Guidelines for information literacy in the curriculum.* Philadelphia: Middle States Commission on Higher Education.

Middle States Commission on Higher Education. (2003b). *Student learning assessment.* Retrieved October 2006 from http://www.msche.org/publications/characteristics

Miller, J., DiBiasio, D., Minasian, J., & Catterall, J. (Eds.). (2001). More student learning, less faculty work? The WPI Davis experiment in educational quality and productivity. In M. Miller, J. Groccia, & J. Miller (Eds.), *Student assisted teaching and learning: Strategies, model, and outcomes* (pp. 44–49). Bolton, MA: Anker.

Mostrom, A. (2007). *Using conceptual diagrams/maps to promote deep and meaningful learning.* Retrieved June 06, 2007, from //www.usip.edu/teaching/innovations/alpha_order_of_brightidea.pdf

Moulds, R. (2005). An interactive annotations assignment. In I. Shibley (Ed.), *The best of the teaching professor* (p. 77). Madison, WI: Magna.

National Survey of Student Engagement (NSSE). (2005). *Exploring different dimensions of student engagement.* Retrieved November 17, 2005, from NSSE2005_annual_report.pdf

Novak, G., Patterson, E., Gavrin, A., & Christian, W. (1999). *Just-in-time teaching: Blending active learning with web technology.* Upper Saddle River, NJ: Prentice Hall.

Novak, J. D. (1998). *Learning, creating, and using knowledge.* Mahwah, NJ: Erlbaum.

Oakley, B., Felder, R. M., Brent, R., & Elhajj, I. (2004). Turning student groups into effective teams. *Journal of Student Centered Learning, 2*(1), 9–23.

Patel, J. (2006). *Using game format in small group classes: Pharmacotherapeutics case studies.* Retrieved January 07, 2007, from http://www.usp.edu/teaching/innovations/innovation

Peck, L. (2007). *Major themes in biology.* Retrieved June 01, 2007, from http://www.usp.edu/teaching/innovations/alpha_order_of_brightidea.pdf

Perry, W. G. (1999). *Forms of intellectual and ethical development in college years: A scheme.* San Francisco: Jossey-Bass.

Peterson, A. (2006). *Learning centered teaching in a large classroom setting.* Retrieved June 03, 2007, from www.usp.edu/teaching/innovations/innovation

Piaget, J. (1963). *Origins of intelligence in children.* New York: Norton.

Pintrich, P. (2000). The role of goal orientation in self-regulated learning. In M. Boekarts, P. P. Pintrich, & M. Zeidner (Eds.), *Handbook of self-regulation* (pp. 451–502). San Diego, CA: Academic Press.

Pintrich, P. (2003). A motivational science perspective on the role of student motivation in learning and teaching contexts. *Journal of Educational Psychology, 95*(4), 667–686.

Polich, S. (2007). Assessment of a faculty learning community program: Do faculty members really change? *To Improve the Academy, 26,* 106–118.

Poon, C. (2006). *Online self-assessment activities.* Retrieved January 18, 2007, from www.usp.edu/teaching/innovations/innovation

Prince, M. (2004). Does active learning work? A review of the research. *Journal of Engineering Education, 93*(3), 223–231.

Ramsden, P. (2003). *Learning to teach in higher education* (2nd ed.). London: RoutledgeFalmer.

Resnick, L. B. (1991). Shared cognition. In L. Resnick, J. Levine, & S. Teasley (Eds.), *Perspectives on socially shared cognition* (pp. 1–20). Washington, DC: American Psychological Association.

Reynolds, H. (2004). *COAS E105 city as ecosystem.* Retrieved November 15, 2006, from http://www.courseportfolio.org/peer/potfolioFiles/anonF/1128043648847_reynolds-h- 2004–1.pdf

Sackett, D., Richardson, W., Rosenberg, W., & Haynes, R. (1997). *Evidence based medicine: How to practice and teach evidence-based medicine.* New York: Churchill Livingstone Publications.

Scriven, M. (1991). *Evaluation thesaurus.* Newbury Park, CA: Sage.

Shulman, L. S. (2004). *The wisdom of practice: Essays on teaching, learning, and learning to teach.* San Francisco: Jossey-Bass.

Slavin, R. E. (1990). *Cooperative learning theory, research, and practice.* Needham Heights, MA: Allyn and Bacon.

Sorcinelli, M. D., Austin, A. E., Eddy, P. L., & Beach, A. L. (2006). *Creating the future of faculty development.* Bolton, MA: Anker.

Springer, L., Stanne, M., & Donovan, S. (1999). Effects of small-group learning on undergraduates in science, mathematics, engineering, and technology (health sciences): A meta-analysis. *Review of Educational Research, 69*(1), 21–51.

Sternberg, R. J., & Grigorenko, E. L. (2002). The theory of successful intelligence as a basis for instruction and assessment in higher education. In D. F. Halpern & M. D. Hakel (Eds.), *Applying the science of learning to university teaching and beyond: New directions for teaching and learning* (pp. 45–54). San Francisco: Jossey-Bass.

Suskie, L. (2004). *Assessing student learning.* Bolton, MA: Anker.

Svinicki, M. (2004). *Learning and motivation in the postsecondary classroom.* Bolton, MA: Anker.

Tagg, J. (2003). *The learning paradigm college.* Bolton, MA: Anker.

Tietze, K. (2007). A bingo game motivates students to interact with course material. *American Journal of Pharmaceutical Education, 71*(4): 1–6.

Vas, L. (2005). *Bridging mathematics and chemistry.* Retrieved December 27, 2005, from http://mpcs.usip.edu/faculty/vas/Special_Topics/Topics_Syllabus.html

Vygotsky, L. S. (1978). *Mind in society: The development of higher mental process.* Cambridge, MA: Harvard University Press.

Walvoord, B. E. (2004). *Assessment clear and simple: A practical guide for institutions, departments, and general education.* San Francisco: Jossey-Bass.

Weimer, M. (2002). *Learner-centered teaching: Five key changes to practice.* San Francisco: Jossey-Bass.

Wright, R. (2006). Walking the walk: Review of: *Learner-centered teaching,* by Maryellen Weimer. *Life Sciences Education, 5*(311), 312.

Appendix A

Glossary

Active learning: The use of teaching or learning methods or instructional strategies in which the students are not passive. Active learning methods allow students to construct their own meaning of the content.

Aligned curriculum: Curriculum in which all major aspects of a course—including the goals of the course, teaching or learning methods, and the assessment of student learning—are integrated and consistent.

Assessment: Use of evidence to guide decisions. An essential purpose of assessment is to give students constructive feedback to assist them to improve. Assessment is concerned with improvement.

Audience response system: System in which the students use individual keypads (sometimes referred to as clickers) to choose their answers to multiple-choice questions and the instructor receives this feedback. This enables instructors to quickly determine how many students choose each alternative.

Authentic assessment: Method that aims to assess what students learned based on actual situations such as used by practitioners or similar to what practitioners and professionals do.

Balance of Power: One of the five learner-centered dimensions. Learning-centered teaching achieves an appropriate balance of power between the teacher and the students by giving students some control over the policies; the schedule, including deadlines; methods of learning; and methods of assessment, but not the content of the course. Teachers control less, but students are more involved in their own learning.

Bloom's taxonomy of objectives: A classification system for cognitive, affective, and psychomotor objectives. The cognitive domain taxonomy moves from the simple, using rote knowledge, to the complex, involving evaluations.

Classroom assessment techniques: Easy-to-use methods that integrate assessment for the purposes of feedback (formative assessment) into regular class learning opportunities. The instructor determines how much the students understand a topic but usually does not assign a grade to individual students.

Concept map: Graphic representation of content, particularly showing the relationship among the concepts, such as cause and effect, consequences, or a series of events; also called *knowledge map* or *graphic organizer*. Commonly used concept maps include flowcharts, tables, and figures with arrows.

Content: The material or knowledge base covered in a course that instructors want students to learn.

Contract grading: Grading system whereby students select the amount of assignments they will do in a course, often in advance, to determine what final grade they are aiming for. Students contract for the grade they are seeking based on how many assignments they do and how much the assignments count. However, they do not receive the grade they are seeking if they do not complete assignments well.

Discipline-specific learning methodologies: The learning skills that are necessary to learn more of this discipline in the future. Some of these learning skills are reading, writing, and speaking appropriately in this discipline. The specific learning skills vary depending on the level and type of the course.

Documentation to Support the Selected Status form: A vehicle that can be used to show why you made your decisions on the rubrics. You should include this form for formal assessments of your teaching.

Evaluation: The process of gathering data on the adequacy of learning or mastery of skills to make judgments about a person, such as to give a final grade. Providing feedback to the learner is optional.

Formative assessment: Assessment used for the purposes of giving feedback and to foster improvement.

Function of Content: One of the five dimensions of learner-centered teaching. Approaches that do not separate learning strategies from content are learner-centered. The functions of the content in learning-centered teaching are (1) to develop a knowledge base, (2) to practice using the inquiry or ways of thinking skills of that discipline, (3) to apply these knowledge and skills to solving problems, and (4) to learn the skills of how to learn the discipline.

Immediate Feedback Assessment Technique (IF-AT): Answer sheets that provide immediate feedback on the accuracy of selected answers.

Information literacy: As defined by the Association of College & Research Libraries (ACRL), information literacy skills include the following:

Framing the research question

Accessing sources

Evaluating sources

Evaluating content (the learner reads the material with understanding and incorporates selected information in his or her knowledge base and value system)

Using information for a specific purpose

Understanding issues affecting the use of information; observing laws, regulations, and institutional policies inquiry

Instructor-centered teaching: Approach that focuses on what the instructor does, usually emphasizing content coverage.

Just-in-Time Teaching (JiTT): Teaching method in which instructors electronically ask students questions on the material before class. The instructor then teaches only the material that the majority of the students did not answer correctly on the preclass questions.

Learner-centered teaching: Approach that shifts the role of the instructor from one of giver of information to one of facilitating student learning or creating an environment for learning.

Learning environment: Environment created by the instructor to facilitate student learning through the organization and use of material and what the students do to learn.

Learning-to-learn skills: Skills that foster further learning, which good students can use to make their learning time more efficient. These skills include the following:

Time management

Metacognition (thinking about one's learning while learning, or monitoring the process of learning)

Self-monitoring

Ability to define what to learn

Ability to plan and implement learning

Techniques for independent reading

Techniques for conducting original research

Learning style: An individual's preferred ways for processing and organizing information and for responding to stimuli, such as visual or auditory learning, or learning by doing. Instructors can accommodate these individual learning style preferences by giving open-ended assignments.

Lifelong learning: Pursuit motivated by the desire and ability to learn outside of formal education. Lifelong learning skills include determining a personal need to know more, knowing who to ask or where to look for information, and self-determination of when one has fulfilled the information need.

Mastery grading: Grading system whereby the instructor determines a minimum acceptable level (usually a high standard) that the students need to reach to pass. Students either receive full credit for attaining the acceptable level of performance or do not receive any credit for their attempt because it was below the acceptable level.

Open-ended assignments: Assignments that are open to a variety of completion methods; they can be open-ended in terms of the content, the methods of achievement, alternative paths to completion, or consideration of more than one right answer.

Organizing scheme: A discipline-specific conceptual framework or overriding theme that helps integrate much of the material.

Planning for Transformation exercise: Exercise that provides an organized way to think about how to begin transforming your course, including describing planned changes, answering tactical questions, and considering outcomes.

Problem-based learning: A learner-centered teaching approach using iterative discussions of real problems or cases. These discussions, within small groups, intrinsically stimulate learning because the students raise questions that they then research to solve the problem.

Purposes and Processes of Assessment: One of the five dimensions of learner-centered teaching. It includes assigning grades and providing opportunities for improvement to further learning. Learner-centered teaching uses assessment as a part of the learning process through formative assessment and self- and peer assessment.

Readiness Assessment Test: Test administered at the beginning of a unit, when students come to class prepared to take a short activity assessing their understanding of the key concepts covered in their assigned reading. This activity assesses their readiness to apply the information contained in the readings. The students first answer the questions individually, then discuss their answers in small groups.

Reflection: Activity whereby learners think about what they are reading, learning, or doing to make their own meaning out of it or put it into their own context or experiences. Reflection is not just summarizing in someone else's words, but includes the student's own perspectives.

Responsibility for Learning: One of the five dimensions of learner-centered teaching. Students take responsibility for their own learning and engage with the content. Instructors create opportunities for students to take this responsibility and help students develop skills such as self-assessment and learning skills.

Role of the Instructor: One of the five dimensions of learner-centered teaching. With learning-centered approaches, the instructor creates an environment that fosters student learning by the way the course is structured and motivates students to accept responsibility for their own learning.

Rubric: A written matrix used to evaluate work, which identifies important traits and states the standards and criteria applied.

Self-assessment of learning: Students' ability to assess their own learning and how much mastery they have. Self-assessment of learning should focus on a combination of the learner, what was learned, and how it was learned.

Self-assessment of strengths and weaknesses: Assessment that covers many different types of strengths and weaknesses, including, but not limited to, interpersonal skills, organization, ability to meet deadlines, mastery of skills and knowledge.

Self-directed learning: Similar to *lifelong learning.* The dimensions include the process of learning itself, learning strategies, and performance outcomes.

Self-regulated learning model: Self-efficacy model, developed by Pintrich, that entails learning on one's own; it is composed of will, resource management, and learning skills.

Service-learning: Course-embedded work done to benefit the community that uses the content from the course. It differs from volunteering because students must reflect on their community work and connect it to their course learning.

SMART objectives: A mnemonic device used for writing measurable objectives:

Specific (what change will result)

Measurable (how much change is expected)

Attainable (who or what will change)

Relevant (where the change will occur)

Time oriented (when the change will occur)

Stakeholder: Anyone who has a significant investment in an effort and outcome; in the case of teaching, a significant investment in the course. The instructor and the students are the main stakeholders in courses.

Student learning goals: The outcomes of a course specified in terms of what the students will learn, become able to do, or value.

Summative assessment: Assessment used for the purpose of making a decision, such as assigning a grade, without providing constructive feedback for improvement.

Teaching or learning methods: Methods instructors use that should ensure that students learn the material. Some methods allow students to be passive; others require the students to be actively engaged in their learning process.

Team-based learning: An instructional activity sequence for each instructional unit, consisting of preclass preparation, readiness assessment using the Readiness Assessment Test, and increasingly complex team application of course concepts.

Triangulation of data: The practice of collecting assessment data from different sources or over time, thereby avoiding dependence on the validity of only one source of information.

Ways of thinking in the discipline. For example, using proofs is a fundamental inquiry method in mathematics.

Appendix B

Rubrics, Planning for Transformation Exercise, and Documentation to Support the Selected Status Form

FOR YOUR CONVENIENCE, this appendix presents each of the rubrics for the five dimensions of learner-centered teaching, the Planning for Transformation exercise, and the Documentation to Support the Selected Status form.

Using the Rubrics as a Tool to Begin the Transformation Process

If you are doing a self-assessment to begin to transform your course, complete the rubrics for all five dimensions of learner-centered teaching and the Planning for Transformation exercise for the components you want to change. You will complete the Planning for Transformation exercise for each component you plan to change.

Using the Rubrics to Assess an Educational Program or to Place in a Teaching Dossier

If you are determining the status of your course or documenting how you teach as a part of an assessment of an educational program or of how you teach, complete the rubrics for all five dimensions and the Documentation to Support the Selected Status Form.

You may copy these forms as many times as you need them, provided the following reference appears on each page: Blumberg, P. (2009). *Developing Learner-Centered Teaching: A Practical Guide for Faculty.* San Francisco: Jossey-Bass.

TABLE B.1

The Rubric for the Function of Content Dimension of Learner-Centered Teaching.

The Function of Content

| Component | Employs *instructor-centered* approaches → | → Transitioning to learner-centered approaches → | | Employs *learner-centered* approaches |
		Lower level of transitioning	Higher level of transitioning	
1. Varied uses of content In addition to building a knowledge base, instructor uses content to help students:	Instructor uses content that helps students build a knowledge base.	In addition to building a knowledge base, instructor uses content to help students:	In addition to building a knowledge base, instructor uses content to help students:	In addition to building a knowledge base, instructor uses all four subcriteria to help students in the following ways:
• Know why they need to learn content		• Recognize why they need to learn the content	• Identify why they need to learn content	• Evaluate why they need to learn content
• Acquire discipline-specific learning methodologies (such as how to read primary source material)			• Use discipline-specific learning methodologies with instructor's assistance	• Acquire discipline-specific learning methodologies
• Use inquiry or ways of thinking in the discipline			• Use inquiry or ways of thinking in the discipline with the instructor's assistance	• Practice using inquiry or ways of thinking in the discipline

(Continued)

TABLE B.1 (*Continued*)

The Function of Content

Component	Employs *instructor-centered* approaches →	Transitioning to learner-centered approaches →		Employs *learner-centered* approaches
		Lower level of transitioning	Higher level of transitioning	
• Learn to solve real-world problems	Instructor and content help students solve problems or Instructor uses any one or none of the four subcriteria for uses of content	• Apply content to solve problems with instructor's assistance or Instructor uses any two of the four subcriteria for uses of content	• Learn to apply content to solve real-world problems with instructor's assistance or Instructor uses any three of the four subcriteria for uses of content	• Learn to solve real-world problems
2. Level to which students engage in content	Instructor allows students to memorize content.	Instructor provides content so students can learn material as it is given to them without transforming or reflecting on it.	Instructor assists students to transform and reflect on *some* of content to make their own meaning out of *some* of it.	Instructor encourages students to transform and reflect on *most* of the content to make their own meaning out of it.
3. Use of organizing schemes	Students learn content without a clearly defined organizing scheme provided by instructor.	Instructor provides *limited* organizing assistance.	Instructor provides *some* organizing schemes to help students learn content.	Instructor provides and uses organizing schemes to help students learn content.
4. Use of content to facilitate future learning	Instructor provides content so students can learn it in isolation, without providing opportunities for them to apply knowledge to new content.	Instructor provides students with limited opportunities to apply knowledge to new content.	Instructor frames content so students can see how it can be applied in the future.	Instructor frames and organizes content so students can learn additional content that is not taught.

TABLE B.2

The Rubric for the Role of the Instructor Dimension of Learner-Centered Teaching.

The Role of the Instructor

Component	Employs *instructor-centered* approaches →	→ Transitioning to learner-centered approaches →		Employs *learner-centered* approaches
		Lower level of transitioning	**Higher level of transitioning**	
1. Creation of an environment for learning through (1) organization and (2) use of material that accommodates different learning styles	Instructor uses the same approach or approaches throughout the course even if the students are not learning.	Instructor does not focus on creating a learning environment, but students do learn.	Instructor creates a learning environment through use of one out of the two subcriteria.	Instructor creates a learning environment by using both subcriteria: through organization and use of material that accommodates different learning styles.
2. Alignment of the course components—objectives, teaching or learning methods, and assessment methods—for consistency	Instructor does *not* align objectives, teaching or learning methods, and assessment methods	Instructor • *Minimally* aligns objectives, teaching or learning methods, and assessment methods *or* • Aligns two out of the three course components	Instructor *somewhat* aligns objectives, teaching or learning methods, and assessment methods.	Instructor explicitly, coherently, and consistently aligns objectives, teaching or learning methods, and assessment methods.
3. Teaching or learning methods appropriate for student learning goals	Instructor • Does *not* have specified learning goals *or* • Uses teaching and learning methods that conflict with learning goals	Instructor • Uses teaching and learning methods without regard for student learning goals *and/or* • Does not use active learning activities	Instructor uses *some* teaching or learning methods that are appropriate for student learning goals.	Instructor intentionally uses *various* teaching or learning methods that are appropriate for student learning goals.

(Continued)

TABLE B.2 (*Continued*)

The Role of the Instructor

Component	Employs *instructor-centered* approaches →	Transitioning to learner-centered approaches →		Employs *learner-centered* approaches
		Lower level of transitioning	**Higher level of transitioning**	
4. Activities involving student, instructor, content interactions	Instructor uses no activities in which students actively interact with material, or instructor, or each other.	Instructor uses a *few* activities in which students actively interact with material, or instructor, or each other.	Instructor uses *some* activities in which • Students actively interact with material, or instructor, or each other *or* • There are some three-way interactions	Instructor *routinely* uses activities in which students actively interact with material, and instructor, and each other.
5. Articulation of SMART objectives: • **S**pecific • **M**easurable • **A**ttainable • **R**elevant • **T**ime oriented	Instructor • Articulates vague course objectives *and/or* • Does not articulate objectives in syllabus	Instructor articulates in syllabus course objectives that do not have all five attributes of SMART objectives.	Instructor articulates SMART objectives in syllabus but does not refer to them throughout the course.	Instructor articulates SMART objectives in syllabus and regularly refers to them throughout the course.
6. Motivation of students to learn (intrinsic drive to learn versus extrinsic reasons to earn grades)	Instructor extensively uses extrinsic motivators to get students to earn grades.	Instructor • Provides *limited* opportunities for students to become intrinsically motivated to learn • Uses extrinsic motivators to get students to earn grades	Instructor provides *some* opportunities for students to become intrinsically motivated to learn.	Instructor inspires and encourages students to become intrinsically motivated to learn.

TABLE B.3

The Rubric for the Responsibility for Learning Dimension of Learner-Centered Teaching.

The Responsibility for Learning

Component	Employs *instructor-centered* approaches →	→ Transitioning to learner-centered approaches →		Employs *learner-centered* approaches
		Lower level of transitioning	**Higher level of transitioning**	
1. Responsibility for learning	Instructor assumes *all* responsibility for student learning:	Instructor assumes *most* responsibility for student learning:	Instructor provides *some* opportunities for students to assume responsibility for their own learning.	Instructor provides *increasing* opportunities for students to assume responsibility for their own learning, leading to achievement of stated learning objectives.
	• Provides content to memorize	• Provides detailed notes of content to be learned		
	• Does not require students to create their own meaning of content			
	• Tells students exactly what will be on examinations	• Reviews content to be examined while helping students learn the material and meet objectives		

(Continued)

TABLE B.3 (*Continued*)

The Responsibility for Learning

Component	Employs *instructor-centered* approaches →	→ Transitioning to learner-centered approaches →		Employs *learner-centered* approaches
		Lower level of transitioning	**Higher level of transitioning**	
2. Learning to learn skills for the present and the future—including, for example: • Time management • Self-monitoring • Goal setting • How to do independent reading • How to conduct original research	Instructor allows students to meet course objectives without developing further learning skills.	Instructor directs students to develop a *few* skills for further learning.	Instructor directs students to develop *some* skills for further learning.	Instructor facilitates students to develop *various and appropriate* skills for further learning.
3. Self-directed, lifelong learning skills—including, for example: • Determining a personal need to know more • Knowing who to ask or where to seek information • Determining when need is met *and* • Development of self-awareness of students' own learning abilities	Instructor does *not* consider: • Self-directed learning skills relevant *or* • Self-awareness of students' learning abilities relevant	The instructor does *not* assist students to become • Self-directed, lifelong learners *or* • Aware of their own learning and abilities to learn	Instructor assists students to become: • Self-directed, lifelong learners in a few areas *and* • Somewhat aware of their own learning, and abilities to learn	Instructor facilitates students to become: • Proficient, self-directed, lifelong learners *and* • Fully aware of their own learning and abilities to learn

(Continued)

TABLE B.3

The Rubric for the Responsibility for Learning Dimension of Learner-Centered Teaching. (*Continued*)

The Responsibility for Learning

Component	Employs *instructor-centered* approaches →	→ Transitioning to learner-centered approaches →		Employs *learner-centered* approaches
		Lower level of transitioning	**Higher level of transitioning**	
4. Students' self-assessment of their learning	Instructor • Believes that instructors alone assess student learning *or* • Does not consider self-assessment of learning relevant	Instructor does not direct students to assess their own learning.	Instructor sometimes provides direction to help students assess their own learning.	Instructor motivates students to routinely and appropriately assess their own learning.
5. Students' self-assessment of their strengths and weaknesses	Instructor believes that only instructors should assess students' strengths and weaknesses.	Instructor does not direct students to practice self-assessments.	Instructor helps students practice some self-assessment skills.	Instructor encourages students to become proficient at self-assessment.
6. Information literacy skills: (a) framing questions, (b) accessing sources, (c) evaluating sources, (d) evaluating content, (e) using information legally (as defined by the Association of College and Research Libraries)	Instructor does not help students acquire any information literacy skills.	Instructor helps students acquire two of the five information literacy skills.	Instructor helps students acquire four of the five information literacy skills.	Instructor facilitates students to become proficient in all five information literacy skills.

TABLE B.4

The Rubric for the Purposes and Processes of Assessment Dimension of Learner-Centered Teaching.

The Purposes and Processes of Assessment

Component	Employs *instructor-centered* approaches →	→ Transitioning to learner-centered approaches →		Employs *learner-centered* approaches
		Lower level of transitioning	**Higher level of transitioning**	
1. Assessment within the learning process	Instructor • Sees assessment as less important than teaching *and* • Does not integrate assessment within the learning process	Instructor *minimally* integrates assessment within the learning process.	Instructor *somewhat* integrates assessment within the learning process.	Instructor *mostly* integrates assessment within the learning process.
2. Formative assessment (giving feedback to foster improvement)	Instructor • Uses only summative assessment (to make decisions to assign grades) *and* • Provides students with no constructive feedback	Instructor • Uses *a little* formative assessment *and/or* • Provides students with limited constructive feedback	Instructor gives students *some* • Formative assessment *and* • Constructive feedback following assessments	*Consistently* throughout the learning process, instructor integrates • Formative assessment *and* • Constructive feedback
3. Peer and self-assessment	Instructor does not • Consider peer and self-assessments relevant *and/or* • Factor these assessments into final grade	Instructor *rarely* requires students to use peer and self-assessments.	Instructor requires students to use *some* peer and self-assessments.	Instructor *routinely* encourages students to use peer and self-assessments.

(Continued)

TABLE B.4

The Rubric for the Purposes and Processes of Assessment Dimension of Learner-Centered Teaching. (*Continued*)

The Purposes and Processes of Assessment

Component	Employs *instructor-centered* approaches →	→ Transitioning to learner-centered approaches →		Employs *learner-centered* approaches
		Lower level of transitioning	**Higher level of transitioning**	
4. Demonstration of mastery and ability to learn from mistakes	Instructor does *not* provide any opportunities for students to demonstrate that they have learned from mistakes and then show mastery.	Instructor provides a *few* opportunities for students to demonstrate that they have learned from mistakes.	Instructor provides *some* opportunities for students to demonstrate mastery after making mistakes.	Instructor offers students *many* opportunities to learn from their mistakes and then demonstrate mastery.
5. Justification of the accuracy of answers	Instructor • Determines accuracy of answers *and* • Does not allow students to ask why they got answers wrong	Instructor allows students to ask why they got answers wrong.	Instructor allows students to justify their answers when they do not agree with those of instructor.	Instructor encourages students to justify their answers when they do not agree with those of instructor.
6. Timeframe for feedback	Instructor • Not provide a timeframe for feedback. *or* • Not return tests or does not grade assignments.	Instructor • Provides a timeframe for feedback, without seeking students' input *and* • Usually follows the timeframe for providing feedback.	Instructor • Provides a timeframe for feedback, with students' input *and* • Usually follows the timeframe for providing feedback.	Instructor and students: • Mutually agree on a timeframe for feedback *and* • Always follows the timeframe for providing feedback.
7. Authentic assessment (what practitioners and professionals do)	Instructor *rarely or never* uses authentic assessment.	Instructor uses a few assessments that have authentic elements.	Instructor uses some authentic assessments or assessments that have authentic elements.	Instructor uses authentic assessment throughout the course.

TABLE B.5

The Rubric for the Balance of Power Dimension of Learner-Centered Teaching.

The Balance of Power

Component	Employs *instructor-centered* approaches →	→ Transitioning to learner-centered approaches →		Employs *learner-centered* approaches
		Lower level of transitioning	**Higher level of transitioning**	
1. Determination of course content	• Instructor entirely determines course content *and* • Does not seek feedback on the content	• Instructor determines course content *and* • Allows students to offer insights or feedback on content after course is over	• Instructor determines course content *and* • Allows students to choose some assignment topics (with permission)	• Instructor largely determines course content *and* • Encourages students to explore additional content independently or through projects
2. Expression of alternative perspectives	Instructor expresses all of the perspectives.	Instructor infrequently allows students to express alternative perspectives, even when appropriate.	Instructor allows students to express alternative perspectives when appropriate.	Instructor encourages students to express alternative perspectives when appropriate.
3. Determination of how students earn grades	All performance and assignments count toward students' grades.	Instructor allows students to drop one assessment but provides no alternative opportunities for them to demonstrate mastery.	Instructor allows students to resubmit assignments or other assessments for regrading.	Instructor uses either mastery (students may retake exam until reaching acceptable performance standard) *or* contract grading (students contract for their grade based upon how much acceptable work they do) to determine what grade students will earn.

(Continued)

TABLE B.5

The Rubric for the Balance of Power Dimension of Learner-Centered Teaching. (*Continued*)

The Balance of Power

Component	Employs *instructor-centered* approaches →	→ Transitioning to learner-centered approaches →		Employs *learner-centered* approaches
		Lower level of transitioning	**Higher level of transitioning**	
4. Use of open-ended assignments	Even when appropriate, instructor does *not* use • Assignments that are open-ended or allow alternative paths *and/or* • Test questions that allow for more than one right answer	When appropriate, instructor uses *a few* • Assignments that are open-ended or allow alternative paths *and/or* • Test questions that allow for more than one right answer	When appropriate, instructor *sometimes* uses • Assignments that are open-ended or allow alternative paths *and/or* • Test questions that allow for more than one right answer	If appropriate, instructor *routinely* uses • Assignments that are open-ended or allow alternative paths *and/or* • Test questions that allow for more than one right answer
5. Flexibility of course policies, assessment methods, learning methods, and deadlines	Instructor mandates all policies and deadlines *or* Instructor does not adhere to policies.	Instructor is flexible on *a few* • Course policies • Assessment methods • Learning methods • Deadlines *and* Infrequently adheres to these flexible decisions.	Instructor is flexible on *some* • Course policies • Assessment methods • Learning methods • Deadlines *and* Somewhat adheres to what they agreed upon.	Instructor is flexible on *most* • Course policies • Assessment methods • Learning methods • Deadlines *and* Always adheres to what instructor has agreed to with the students.
6. Opportunities to learn	Instructor mandates that students attend all classes even when they are not expected to be active learners.	Instructor provides consequences for • Not attending classes *and/or* • Not participating in active learning experiences	Instructor provides • Attendance options for some classes so students may miss a few classes without penalty *and/or* • Participation options for some activities	• Instructor helps students to take advantage of opportunities to learn *and* • Fosters understanding of consequences of not taking advantage of such learning opportunities, like missing class

The Planning for Transformation Exercise

Use this form to begin to transform a course to be more learner-centered. Complete the Planning for Transformation exercise for each component you plan to change. If you are completing the rubrics for the purposes of a formal assessment of an educational program or of teaching, you can skip this form.

A. Status of your course now   Date:

    1. Dimension of learner-centered teaching:

    2. Component:

    3. Current level:

       ❏ Instructor-centered

       ❏ Lower level of transitioning

       ❏ Higher level of transitioning

       ❏ Learner-centered

    4. Briefly describe your current implementation (to document your baseline prior to transformation).

B. Desired changes:

    1. Describe the desired changes you wish to make for this component in the near future.

    2. What is the level you want to achieve with this/these changes?

       ❏ Instructor-centered

       ❏ Lower level of transitioning

       ❏ Higher level of transitioning

       ❏ Learner-centered

C. Tactical planning questions:

    1. What do you need to do, decide, or learn about prior to making changes?

(Continued)

2. What obstacles or challenges do you need to overcome to implement this change successfully? (Resistance may come from your philosophy of teaching, your chair, your peers, your students, or the culture of your institution.)

3. Identify specific strategies (such as learning about successful implementations, trying a small pilot implementation, explaining to your students and other instructors why you are making these changes) for overcoming each obstacle or challenge.

4. What resources (such as time, money, student assistants, or computer software) would help you implement your change?

5. What do you need to do to get your students to accept this change? (Possibilities include repeated explanations for why you are doing what you are doing or having the activity count in the final grade.)

D. Outcomes of the change:

1. In what ways will implementing this change influence other aspects of your course to be more learner-centered? (For example, when you incorporate various teaching or learning methods that are consistent with your student learning goals [Component 3 of the Role of the Instructor dimension], most likely the students will more actively engage in the content [Component 2 of the Function of Content dimension].)

(Continued)

2. In what ways (such as increased learning) will your students benefit from this change? How will the students behave differently (such as increased participation in class or greater engagement with the content)?

3. In what ways will you benefit from this change? (For example, more enjoyment of teaching, satisfaction that your students are learning more, anticipation of fewer student complaints.)

E. Possible future changes:

1. What is the optimal level for this component for this course?

❑ Instructor-centered

❑ Lower level of transitioning

❑ Higher level of transitioning

❑ Learner-centered

2. In the long term, what additional changes, if any, might you make to further transform this component to reach this optimal level of the learner-centered approach?

The Documentation to Support the Selected Status Form

Complete this form if you are doing an assessment for the purposes of educational program evaluation, or as part of a teaching dossier. If you are completing the rubrics for the purposes of beginning to transform your teaching, you can skip this form.

Refer to the rubrics as you complete this form.

Name: _____   Date: _____

What are you assessing?

    Course Name(s) _____

    Educational Program Name _____

    Other _____

    Purpose of this assessment:

The Function of Content

Component 1. *Varied uses of content*

In addition to building a knowledge base, instructor uses content to help students: know why they need to learn content, acquire discipline-specific learning methodologies such as how to read primary source material, use inquiry or ways of thinking in the discipline, learn to solve real-world problems.

    Current level:

    ❏ Instructor-centered

    ❏ Lower level of transitioning

    ❏ Higher level of transitioning

    ❏ Learner-centered

Rationale for or example to support level chosen:

(Continued)

Component 2. *Level to which students engage in content*

  Current level:

  ❏ Instructor-centered

  ❏ Lower level of transitioning

  ❏ Higher level of transitioning

  ❏ Learner-centered

Rationale for or example to support level chosen:

Component 3. *Use of organizing schemes*

  Current level:

  ❏ Instructor-centered

  ❏ Lower level of transitioning

  ❏ Higher level of transitioning

  ❏ Learner-centered

Rationale for or example to support level chosen:

Component 4. *Use of content to facilitate future learning*

  Current level:

  ❏ Instructor-centered

  ❏ Lower level of transitioning

  ❏ Higher level of transitioning

  ❏ Learner-centered

Rationale for or example to support level chosen:

(Continued)

The Role of the Instructor

Component 1. Creation of an environment for learning through organization and use of material that accommodates different learning styles

Current level:

❑ Instructor-centered

❑ Lower level of transitioning

❑ Higher level of transitioning

❑ Learner-centered

Rationale for or example to support level chosen:

Component 2. Alignment of the course components: objectives, teaching or learning methods, and assessment methods for consistency

Current level:

❑ Instructor-centered

❑ Lower level of transitioning

❑ Higher level of transitioning

❑ Learner-centered

Rationale for or example to support level chosen:

(Continued)

Component 3. Teaching or learning methods appropriate for student learning goals

    Current level:

    ❏ Instructor-centered

    ❏ Lower level of transitioning

    ❏ Higher level of transitioning

    ❏ Learner-centered

Rationale for or example to support level chosen:

Component 4. Activities involving student, instructor, content interactions

    Current level:

    ❏ Instructor-centered

    ❏ Lower level of transitioning

    ❏ Higher level of transitioning

    ❏ Learner-centered

Rationale for or example to support level chosen:

Component 5. Articulation of SMART objectives (SMART = Specific, Measurable, Attainable, Relevant, Time oriented)

    Current level:

    ❏ Instructor-centered

    ❏ Lower level of transitioning

    ❏ Higher level of transitioning

    ❏ Learner-centered

Rationale for or example to support level chosen:

(Continued)

Component 6. Motivation of students to learn (intrinsic drive to learn versus extrinsic reasons to earn grades)

Current level:

❑ Instructor-centered

❑ Lower level of transitioning

❑ Higher level of transitioning

❑ Learner-centered

Rationale for or example to support level chosen:

The Responsibility for Learning

Component 1. Responsibility for learning

Current level:

❑ Instructor-centered

❑ Lower level of transitioning

❑ Higher level of transitioning

❑ Learner-centered

Rationale for or example to support level chosen:

Component 2. Learning-to-learn skills or skills for future learning

Current level:

❑ Instructor-centered

❑ Lower level of transitioning

❑ Higher level of transitioning

❑ Learner-centered

Rationale for or example to support level chosen:

(Continued)

Component 3. *Self-directed, lifelong learning skills*

Current level:

❏ Instructor-centered

❏ Lower level of transitioning

❏ Higher level of transitioning

❏ Learner-centered

Rationale for or example to support level chosen:

Component 4. *Students' self-assessment of their learning*

Current level:

❏ Instructor-centered

❏ Lower level of transitioning

❏ Higher level of transitioning

❏ Learner-centered

Rationale for or example to support level chosen:

Component 5. *Students' self-assessment of their strengths and weaknesses*

Current level:

❏ Instructor-centered

❏ Lower level of transitioning

❏ Higher level of transitioning

❏ Learner-centered

Rationale for or example to support level chosen:

(Continued)

Component 6. Information literacy skills of (a) framing questions, (b) accessing and (c) evaluating sources, (d) evaluating content, (e) using information legally

    Current level:

    ❑ Instructor-centered

    ❑ Lower level of transitioning

    ❑ Higher level of transitioning

    ❑ Learner-centered

Rationale for or example to support level chosen:

The Purposes and Processes of Assessment

Component 1. Assessment within the learning process

    Current level:

    ❑ Instructor-centered

    ❑ Lower level of transitioning

    ❑ Higher level of transitioning

    ❑ Learner-centered

Rationale for or example to support level chosen:

Component 2. Formative assessment

    Current level:

    ❑ Instructor-centered

    ❑ Lower level of transitioning

    ❑ Higher level of transitioning

    ❑ Learner-centered

Rationale for or example to support level chosen:

(Continued)

Component 3. Peer and self-assessment

    Current level:

    ❏ Instructor-centered

    ❏ Lower level of transitioning

    ❏ Higher level of transitioning

    ❏ Learner-centered

Rationale for or example to support level chosen:

Component 4. Demonstration of mastery and ability to learn from mistakes

    Current level:

    ❏ Instructor-centered

    ❏ Lower level of transitioning

    ❏ Higher level of transitioning

    ❏ Learner-centered

Rationale for or example to support level chosen:

Component 5. Justification of the accuracy of answers

    Current level:

    ❏ Instructor-centered

    ❏ Lower level of transitioning

    ❏ Higher level of transitioning

    ❏ Learner-centered

Rationale for or example to support level chosen:

(Continued)

Component 6. Timeframe for feedback

Current level:

❏ Instructor-centered

❏ Lower level of transitioning

❏ Higher level of transitioning

❏ Learner-centered

Rationale for or example to support level chosen:

Component 7. Authentic assessment

Current level:

❏ Instructor-centered

❏ Lower level of transitioning

❏ Higher level of transitioning

❏ Learner-centered

Rationale for or example to support level chosen:

The Balance of Power

Component 1. Determination of course content

Current level:

❏ Instructor-centered

❏ Lower level of transitioning

❏ Higher level of transitioning

❏ Learner-centered

Rationale for or example to support level chosen:

(*Continued*)

Component 2. *Expression of alternative perspectives*

Current level:

❑ Instructor-centered

❑ Lower level of transitioning

❑ Higher level of transitioning

❑ Learner-centered

Rationale for or example to support level chosen:

Component 3. *Determination of how students earn grades*

Current level:

❑ Instructor-centered

❑ Lower level of transitioning

❑ Higher level of transitioning

❑ Learner-centered

Rationale for or example to support level chosen:

Component 4. *Use of open-ended assignments*

Current level:

❑ Instructor-centered

❑ Lower level of transitioning

❑ Higher level of transitioning

❑ Learner-centered

Rationale for or example to support level chosen:

(Continued)

Component 5. *Flexibility of course policies, assessment methods, learning methods, and deadlines*

Current level:

❏ Instructor-centered

❏ Lower level of transitioning

❏ Higher level of transitioning

❏ Learner-centered

Rationale for or example to support level chosen:

Component 6. *Opportunities to learn*

Current level:

❏ Instructor-centered

❏ Lower level of transitioning

❏ Higher level of transitioning

❏ Learner-centered

Rationale for or example to support level chosen:

Appendix C

Development of the Rubrics

How did I come to choose to use rubrics to help instructors transform their courses? When I first started to educate instructors at my university about learner-centered teaching, I drew a comparison between instructor-centered and learner-centered approaches, like that given in my article "Beginning Journey Toward a Culture of Learning-Centered Teaching" (Blumberg, 2004). I found that instructors were unable to accept this stark contrast, so I began to talk about instructor-centered and learner-centered teaching as a continuum, explaining that courses can be placed at different points along the instructor-to learner-centered continuum. Instructors more readily accepted this concept of a continuum because it meant that they did not have to reject all their current teaching methods. However, I have found that the most convincing argument for using a continuum is that it illustrates incremental small steps that can be transformative, yet are easy and practical to achieve.

I found that it was helpful to faculty to organize specific dimensions according to Weimer's (2002) five separate large practices that need to change. Because instructors appreciate Weimer's concepts of learner-centered teaching, I chose to develop a rubric for each of her five practices. I found that rubrics offered a very effective way for instructors to see how to make incremental changes. Instructors are often familiar with rubrics as an objective and effective way to grade student assignments, and they know that rubrics provide concrete, incremental steps. Thus using rubrics helps instructors see incremental steps in the process of transformation toward learner-centered teaching.

Development Cycle

I began by developing components for each of the five learner-centered dimensions and identifying the teacher-centered contrasts for each of these learner-centered components. I chose components and the levels within the rubrics based on the literature on learner-centered teaching. Over a three-year period, I used drafts of these rubrics in workshops and discussions with faculty and faculty developers.

More than seventy faculty developers at the 2004 and 2005 annual meetings of the Professional and Organizational Developers Network

(POD) and a majority of the instructors at the University of Sciences in Philadelphia contributed to the draft versions of the rubrics. During 2006 and 2007, I used completed versions of the rubrics at additional conferences intended for faculty, faculty developers, and administrators. To date, more than 250 people have used and reviewed the rubrics. This cycle of feedback and corrections has validated the components and the rubrics.

Because instructors representing many different disciplines and all levels of higher education have offered feedback and validation, I am confident that the specific items transcend disciplines and different types of courses. I am indebted to the many people who offered their ideas and constructive criticism.

Selection of Order of Dimensions

Although you can read the rubrics in any order, I selected the order of the dimensions to fit a logical sequence of how instructors think about their teaching and their courses. I started with the Function of Content because most instructors think the content is the most important part of a course, and most teachers begin planning a course by deciding what content to cover.

After instructors make decisions about the course content, they begin to realize that if they change how they and the students use the content, the role of the instructor will need to change as well. Thus the Role of the Instructor came next.

If the instructor creates an environment for learning, the responsibility for learning shifts from the instructor to the student. Therefore, I placed the Responsibility for Learning dimension discussion after the Function of Content and the Role of the Instructor.

After instructors plan the content, what they will do, and what the student will do, then they often plan how and why to assess students. Thus the next dimension is the Purposes and Processes of Assessment.

I have found that some instructors have the most resistance to the Balance of Power dimension—giving it a logical placement as the last dimension. Many instructors will work on the Balance of Power only after working on at least one other dimension.

Thus this order of organization is logical in that it reflects the way many instructors think about and develop courses. Just keep in mind that all of the dimensions are interrelated, because once an instructor changes one aspect of one dimension, he or she often sees ways or reasons to change other dimensions.

Index

Vas, L., 77
Vygotsky, L. S., 16

W

Walvoord, B. E., xxi, 24
Weimer, M., xxi, 3, 4, 5, 18, 25, 29, 111, 127, 157, 187, 192, 193, 194, 253, 303
Whitt, W., 132

Wright, R., xxi
Writing: learning logs, 135; letters and portfolios of student, 135; "muddiest point" of teaching, 161; reviewing student drafts, 158

Z

Zappin, R., 163